Austin, San Antonio & the Texas Hill Country

EXPLORER'S GUIDES

Austin, San Antonio & the Texas Hill Country

A Great Destination

Amy K. Brown

The Countryman Press   Woodstock, Vermont

SECOND EDITION

3 1984 00317 1830

Interior photographs by the author unless otherwise specified
Maps by Erin Greb Cartography, © The Countryman Press
Book design by Bodenweber Design
Composition by Eugenie S. Delaney

Published by The Countryman Press, P.O. Box 748, Woodstock, VT 05091
Distributed by W. W. Norton & Company, Inc., 500 Fifth Avenue, New York, NY 10110
Printed in the United States of America

10 9 8 7 6 5 4 3 2 1

Austin, San Antonio & the Texas Hill Country
978-1-58157-153-0

This book is dedicated to my family.

Austin, San Antonio & Hill Country

Contents

Acknowledgments and Introduction

EVERYTHING REALLY IS BIGGER IN TEXAS.

The people in Central Texas have huge hearts, plenty of patience, and a friendliness that seems supersized.

As I traveled the region researching this book, Texans graciously answered numerous questions, refilled countless cups of coffee, and served up some of the biggest slices of pie I've ever seen. They shared generously the names of their favorites—from burgers to honky-tonks, enchiladas to swimming holes.

While the list was long, a guidebook can only be so big. This book is big enough to include all the basics and many of the extras, but as you make your way between the featured establishments, feel free to stray from the path I've laid out. Change your plans, pull into a farm stand, stop at a bakery, have a beer, and by all means ask a Texan for directions, suggestions, and recommendations. Let 'em lay some hospitality on you.

Extra-large thanks to all the good folks living in Austin, San Antonio, the surrounding communities, and the towns of the Hill Country. I gratefully appreciate your courtesy, knowledge, and kindness. Since most of you did not know I was writing a guidebook, the sincerity of your gestures was truly heartwarming.

Enormous thanks to the folks at Countryman—Kim Grant, Kermit Hummel, Jennifer Thompson, and Lisa Sacks—for the opportunity to write about a region I love.

Deepest gratitude to my fantastic family.

> Thank you.
> Amy K. Brown
> www.amykbrown.com

The Way This Book Works

THIS BOOK IS DIVIDED into two introductory chapters followed by four main chapters—on Austin, San Antonio, the Hill Country, and Nearby and In Between—each with suggestions of lodging, dining, and things to do and see, arranged by neighborhood. The first, introductory chapter describes the region's shared landscape and common history, and it is followed by a short chapter on regional transportation. The unique histories of Austin and San Antonio and the towns of the Hill Country are addressed in the introductions to their respective chapters. Considering the scale of Texas, the cities, towns, and parks covered in this book are relatively close to one another, so as you read bear in mind that many destinations make easy stopovers or day trips.

All the information in this book was verified at the time of its writing. However, things change, and it is always prudent to call ahead. Web site addresses have been provided for the establishments that have them, and I would strongly encourage their use, as you will find details, menus, updates, photos, and sometimes discounts online. Please assume that all establishments accept cash or credit cards, unless otherwise noted. Most of the establishments in this book will not accept personal checks.

Austin, San Antonio, and the Hill Country

DEEP IN THE HEART OF TEXAS

THE SUBJECT OF LEGENDS AND LORE, Texas has a reputation that has always preceded it. And as an icon of strength and swagger, Texas plays an essential part in the story of America. Filled with opportunistic cattle rustlers and hunky cowboys thundering off into the endless crimson sunset, the Texas of myth and movies is larger than life, hotter than hell, and rougher than a ride at the rodeo.

Deep in the heart of Central Texas is a region that will challenge all your assumptions with its distinct mix of friendly casualness, edgy creativity, discerning taste, and a strong inclination toward celebration. Each city and town offers its own incomparable mix of culture, food, music, and heritage, and plenty of festivals—from cultural to culinary, kites to *kolaches*—which give visitors numerous opportunities to experience life in Central Texas as an honorary Texan-for-a-day.

With roots stretching back to the 17th century, San Antonio (see chapter 2) is now home to over a million people. Its pedestrian-friendly downtown, the celebrated Alamo, historic Mission Trail, and bustling Riverwalk cluster together to give the city an intimate feeling that belies its size. A strong sense of cultural history pervades all, with San Antonio's Native American origins, Spanish influences, and Mexican overtones zealously expressed in art, food, architecture, and festivals.

While San Antonio embodies something quintessentially Texan, people are fond of observing that Austin (see chapter 1) inhabits a category all its own. Austinites are an educated, energetic, and decidedly unconventional bunch, and while they tend to be less conservative than the rest of the state, their live-and-let-live attitude very much mirrors the overall spirit of Texas. Nightlife in Austin abounds, thanks to its internationally recognized live music scene, though acres of parks, bike trails, and gardens make recreational activities almost as popular.

LEFT: Dining along the River Walk in San Antonio

The Hill Country (see chapter 3), easily accessible from either Austin or San Antonio, is the place to be if you really want to slow down and smell the bluebonnets. To drive the lazy, winding, rural roads past wineries and lavender fields, around limestone outcroppings, and through shady state parks is to experience carefree wanderlust at its most enjoyable. The region's rustic towns are brimming with gourmet restaurants, antiques and knickknack shops, and bed and breakfasts and make pleasant stopovers or destinations unto themselves. Nearby and In Between (see chapter 4), several towns along I-35 make wonderful day trips for the thrill of area amusement parks or tubing along cool spring-fed Texas rivers.

The folks in Central Texas are passionate about living here, and their infectious enthusiasm begins with the land that they love, a land rich in both resources and beauty that has been fought over for centuries.

NATURAL WONDERS

Though now divided into two major cities, many towns, and numerous communities, Central Texas shares a common natural history that has been ages in the making.

Based on fossils of fish and aquatic plants, and other clues dating from the Cretaceous period (65–144 million years ago), we know that the Central Texas region was once submerged under a shallow lake. At some point, possibly 10–20 million years ago, movement along the Balcones Fault uplifted a massive hunk of limestone now known as the Edwards Plateau. The southeastern edge of this uplift was exposed to the elements, and its newer, softer rock eroded to form the dramatic cliffs and rocky outcroppings characterizing the present-day Balcones Escarpment, the ridge separating the undulating Hill Country to the west from the level Texas Coastal Plain to the southeast.

The movement in the earth's crust also created the Edwards Aquifer. A karst aquifer, the Edwards was formed over time as limestone and bedrock dissolved, creating holes through which water enters from the surface and an underground honeycomb network of pockets and caverns through which it percolates. The sinkholes, disappearing streams, and cave entrances of the Hill Country are all telltale signs of karst regions. When it rains, water rushes over the Cretaceous limestone streambeds of this "contributing zone" and into the aquifer, topping off its massive holdings. As the Edwards is also an artesian aquifer, the water within is held under hydrostatic pressure, producing the region's many springs, such as Barton Springs in Austin, Comal Springs in New Braunfels, and Aquarena Springs in San Marcos. While the aquifer contains enough water for use well into the future, if its levels drop, so too does the flow of its springs, threatening the vegetation and many endangered species that rely upon them. Central Texans are aware of their own complete dependency on the Edwards Aquifer, a circumstance made increasingly complicated by rapid growth and growing demands for water.

For the nature enthusiast, the biodiversity of flora and fauna living in or migrating through Austin, San Antonio, and the Hill Country can be fascinating. For instance, millions upon millions of Mexican free-tailed bats roost in the nooks, crannies, and caves of Central Texas; the region is home to one of the largest maternity roosts for bats in the world. The bats give birth in area caves, take turns feeding and minding their young, and scour the countryside for insects, devouring

Hill Country backroad

tens of thousands of pounds' worth each night between May and October. While their presence has not always been met with much enthusiasm or tolerance, in time and with education folks around here grew to enjoy them, and public sentiment has morphed from fear to appreciation. With half a million bats, the Congress Avenue Bridge in Austin is home to the largest urban bat population in the world, and watching them take flight each night is a popular entertainment.

Sharing the great Texas sky with the bats is the state's huge variety of birds. An astonishing three-fourths of all American birds are represented throughout the diverse avian habitats of Texas. Some birds are residents and others migratory, passing through Central Texas on the 300-mile-wide "Central Flyway," one of the great routes for migration between Canada and Central and South America. Of the thousands of birds to make the trip, the golden-cheeked warbler is the only one to nest exclusively in Texas and, due to loss of habitat, is the most critically endangered of all warblers.

Also traveling the Central Flyway is the monarch butterfly, Texas's state insect. Monarchs are unusual among butterflies in that they migrate instead of hibernate; those that make the trip through Texas tend to originate in the upper Midwest, funneling through the Central Flyway on their way to Mexico. During this migration, in October, Central Texas enjoys the spectacle of millions of orange and black monarchs gliding along on favorable winds or resting and refueling at area gardens.

Central Texas has a wealth of parks and trails, making the region a natural spot for ecotourism. One of the best ways to commune with nature is to visit a state park, and there are many to choose from. From the bald pink dome of Enchanted Rock to the limestone canyons of Lost Maples, the state parks showcase the

Texas History Online

The history of Texas is fascinating in its depth and breadth. A cultural crossroads for centuries, the state is crisscrossed by the footprints of many. Some have just passed through, while others hung their hat for a while. Texas's roots are deep and spread wide. In addition to the recommended readings at the end of this book ("Suggested References" in the Information chapter), a wealth of information exists online for anyone wanting to learn more.

Center for American History (www.cah.utexas.edu): a useful site for locating sources of information regarding the various ethnic groups in Texas

Texas Almanac (www.texasalmanac.com): timelines, photos, and historical essays clearly presented

Texas Archeological Research Lab at the University of Texas at Austin (www.texas beyondhistory.net): interactive Web site offering archaeological facts and information

The Texas State Historical Association (www.tshaonline.org): exhaustive online handbook of Texas history

Texas Historical Commission (www.thc.state.tx.us): comprehensive site including information on historic courthouses, cemeteries, and archaeological sites

Texas Parks and Wildlife (www.tpwd.state.tx.us): information and photographs regarding the natural and cultural history of Texas

diversity of the regional landscape and the variety of wildlife it supports. Gray fox, armadillo, coyote, opossum, raccoon, bobcat, rock squirrel, roadrunner, white-tailed deer, and javelina are all common, and the patient observer can sometimes catch a glimpse of rarer species, such the Cagle's map turtle, the San Marcos salamander, or the Guadalupe bass.

THE PEOPLES OF TEXAS

The unique terrain of Central Texas, with its clear springs, sheltering caves, and abundant wildlife, has made the region naturally attractive to humans for well over 11,000 years. Looking to the relatively recent past, Tonkawa and Lipan Apache Indians are thought to have lived here from the 14th century, with the Comanche and Kiowa arriving in the 18th century. While many of the other peoples living concurrently in neighboring regions had already begun to live in villages, the groups living in this region were fairly nomadic, following food sources throughout the seasons and varying weather conditions. Although there is still much to learn, the archaeological record of the region is extraordinary, certainly one of the longest continuous records of hunters and gatherers in North America. Prior to the arrival of Europeans, approximately 45,000 Native Americans lived in the region, organized in groups, each with its own language, identity, and customs. However, the elements that attracted the first peoples would, of course, attract others, and people kept coming.

TEJANOS

From the 1600s through the 1800s, pioneers from Mexico journeyed north and began settling into the Texas frontier, creating towns, building roads and ranches, and governing themselves. Throughout the 1700s they put down roots, establishing the settlements that would become El Paso, Galveston, Laredo, San Antonio, Victoria, and the large ranches of Central and South Texas. Those industrious pioneer ranchers, in particular, were so successful that they were able to contribute 2,000 head of longhorn cattle to the Revolutionary War effort, driving a herd from Texas to New Orleans in 1776.

As the land under them shifted from Spanish, French, Mexican, Texan, then American governance (see sidebar, "Six Flags over Texas"), these people of Mexican, Spanish, or indigenous descent continued to live independently. Generations passed, citizenship changed, and cultural influences came and went; these early settlers created their own unique culture, calling themselves *Tejanos* as early as the 1830s. Distinguished Tejanos Gregorio Esparza and Toribio Losoya both died in 1836 defending the Alamo, the mission that had been their birthplace, and José Antonio Navarro and José Francisco Ruiz were the only native Texans to sign the Texas Declaration of Independence that same year.

Migrating Monarch butterfly

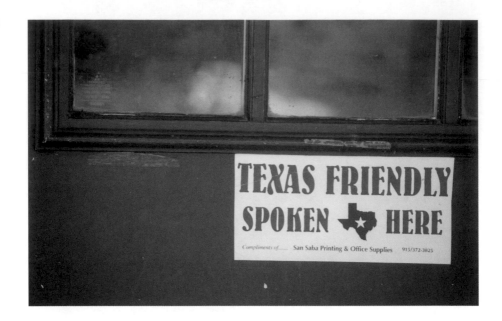

SPANISH

Though the Spanish explorer Alonso Álvarez de Pineda mapped the Texas coast-
line in 1519, the first Europeans to really get their boots dirty with Texas soil were
Álvar Núñez Cabeza de Vaca and several companions, who found themselves ship-
wrecked on the Gulf Coast in 1528. Once ashore, Cabeza de Vaca and his men
spent years living with Native Americans before heading to Mexico City and, eventually, back to Spain. The journey of these men, while extraordinary, might have
been entirely forgotten had Cabeza de Vaca not prepared a report of his adventures and delivered it to the Spanish court in the late 1530s, thus providing the
first written record of the land and peoples of Texas.

After colonizing Mexico the Spanish made inroads north, bringing with them
the horse, which the Apache quickly mastered and rode to regional domination.
The Comanche followed suit, and together the mounted Native Americans proved
such a threat that the Spanish were hard-pressed to set foot in the region for
another two hundred years. In the 1700s Franciscans passed through on their way
to East Texas to convert Native Americans into Roman Catholics and Spanish
citizens. There the threat of the French and French-allied Native Americans near
the Louisiana border forced them to backtrack to Central Texas, where they established the mission San Antonio de Valero, later known as the Alamo.

NATIVE AMERICANS

The arrival of Europeans was clearly the pivotal historic moment for Native Americans in Texas, as elsewhere. When the Franciscans arrived in the 1700s proposing
mission life, the reaction of the Native Americans varied immensely. Some wanted
nothing to do with the newcomers, while some smaller groups saw the missions as
a refuge from harassment and hostilities at the hands of larger groups. In the

Six Flags over Texas

The flags of six countries have flown over Texas, making it one of the most sought-after and fought-over pieces of land in North America. Spain was the first, claiming Texas as its own from 1519 to 1685 as an extension of its holdings in Mexico, but it never created much of an actual presence in its far-flung acquisition.

In 1685 the French, emboldened by their success in Louisiana, planted their flag on Texas soil just across the eastern border, but mishaps and misfortune caused them to abandon their claim in 1690, at which time the Spanish regained control, which they kept until 1821.

During their rule the Spanish focused on expanding their empire and establishing a solid foothold in North America. In Texas, *presidios* (forts) were built to protect and defend, and *misiones* (missions) were established in the hopes that self-sustaining communities of Spanish Catholic citizens might arise.

When Mexico won independence from Spain in 1821, Texas became the land of opportunity for both Hispanic pioneers from the south and Anglos from the north, all considering themselves citizens of Mexico. Out on the frontier people were used to being their own masters, however, and when General Santa Anna dismissed the Mexican Constitution, effectively declaring himself king, they revolted.

Battles at Gonzales and the Alamo in San Antonio tested the resolve of the revolutionaries, but the definitive battle at San Jacinto on April 21, 1836, secured their independence, giving rise to the fourth flag, that of the Republic of Texas.

The republic had its ups and downs during its almost 10 years of existence from 1836 to 1845, but its rugged individualism, gritty determination, and boundless energy, not to mention lots and lots of land, made it a very attractive addition to the United States, which it joined on December 29, 1845.

Sixteen years later, the Civil War tore the fledging nation apart, and Texas, though advised by Governor Sam Houston to remain neutral or reestablish a republic, sided with the Southerners, and the flag of the Confederacy flew over Texas from 1861 to 1865. While Texans valiantly fought, and won, the last battle of the Civil War, it was, unfortunately, after the Confederacy had already surrendered, and Texas suffered the rebels' fate. The flag of the United States of America has hung over Texas, the 28th state, since 1865.

Still, for many Texans, the flag that suits Texas best is its state flag, that of the tumultuous but short-lived former republic—the simple, straightforward, iconic Lone Star Flag, a proud reminder that though Texas may have been ruled by many, it has been controlled by none.

1800s settlers came to Texas by the wagonload, bringing with them the notion of land claiming. Native Americans asked for, and were promised, ownership of the land they considered theirs, yet years of fighting, alliances, treaties, surprise attacks, and broken promises failed to yield documentation. While land ownership remained elusive, tensions boiled.

Lucky, TX

Always self-reliant, Texans have also been blessed with tremendous good luck. Rebounding from defeats suffered in the Civil War, Texans returned to find a population explosion of wild longhorn cattle. Rounded up by cowboys and taken to market along the Chisholm Trail in legendary cattle drives between 1867 and 1884, they provided a steady source of income for a state in dire need. Agriculture too flourished. Then, in 1901, one of the state's greatest natural resources was

Longhorn Cattle

tapped at Spindletop, near Beaumont. After drilling for hours, amid much skepticism, exhausted workers struck "black gold," and a 150-foot geyser of the oil that would finance much of Texas's future came rocketing out of the ground.

President Sam Houston of the Republic of Texas brokered treaties with the Tonkawas, the Lipan Apaches, the Comanches, Kichais, Tawakonis, Wacos, and Taovayas throughout 1837 and 1838, creating a tenuous peace. In the 1850s, after Texas joined the United States of America, these many treaties and agreements were broken, and many Native Americans were forced to leave Texas or relocate to reservations. The disastrous Red River War in 1874 was the final straw, and in June 1875 the mighty Comanche surrendered at Fort Sill. In short, the 1800s were catastrophic for Native Americans in Texas, leaving their populations decimated by disease, violence, starvation, or genocide. These days, their descendants host the Austin Powwow and American Indian Heritage Festival, the largest annual Native American gathering in Texas, a huge celebration of Native American heritage and a commemoration of their shared history.

ANGLOS

Anglos, a convenient term for people of various European backgrounds arriving primarily from the United States, came to Texas following the promise of plentiful, inexpensive land at precisely the time that Spain was having difficulty convincing its own citizens that this isolated, unknown, and generally hostile environment was a good investment. As long as these incoming Anglos agreed to become both Catholic and Spanish, they were guaranteed large land grants, and many, sincere or not in their desire to convert, took the bait. When Mexico gained independence from Spain in 1821, it extended the deal, giving *empresarios*, those willing to help organize and oversee large groups of immigrants, land grants to begin their settlements. During this time, immigrants came for many reasons. Some, Stephen F. Austin for one, made the trip with the promise of land ownership, while others came on the lam, taking advantage of the fact that the United States and Mexico had not yet established an extradition agreement. Slave-owners brought slaves, incensing the Mexican government, which not only had forbidden the African slave trade, but whose president, Vicente Ramón Guerrero, had emancipated all slaves on September 15, 1829, in commemoration of Mexican independence. Nevertheless, slaves were bought and sold in Texas until 1840, with Mexico turning a blind eye in the hopes that the cotton production so dependent on slave labor might prove profitable.

Being so far removed from the long reach of government, over time the new Texans started to organize, think, and act for themselves. In 1830, after much tension and fearing rebellion, the Mexican government passed the Law of April 6th, effectively making unorganized immigration from the United States to Texas illegal. Europeans, however, kept coming, and in 1831 Johann Friedrich Ernst, his wife, and their children were the first German family to arrive in Texas, settling near present-day Austin. Ernst was so impressed with his new surroundings that he wrote glowing letters back to Germany detailing his new home. Word spread, and by 1850 people of German descent totaled 5 percent of the state's total population, settling mostly in New Braunfels or fanning out into the Hill Country.

Lone Star State

Texans soon began to chafe under Mexican leadership, growing restless for self-determination. In 1833 Antonio López de Santa Anna Pérez de Lebrón, the legendary Santa Anna, was installed as the president of Mexico. A lifelong military man, Santa Anna, though elected as a liberal, once in power established himself as a dictator. After crushing opponents in Mexico, he headed north to San Antonio to confront the growing rebellion in Texas, attacking the Alamo in the early morning hours of March 6, 1836. His victory there—a dramatic example of winning the battle but losing the war—only galvanized Texans' support for independence. Months later, Mexico was defeated at the battle of San Jacinto, and the Republic of Texas was born. When Texas passed from a republic to a state, tiny Austin was thrust into the limelight—a brand-new city for a brand-new Texas.

HAUPTSTRASSE
S. MAIN STREET

E. SAN ANTONIO AVE.
MAIN STREET DISTRICT

ONE WAY

Transportation

TO AND FROM THE REGION

INTERSTATE 35 LINKS AUSTIN AND SAN ANTONIO. Sometimes called the NAFTA Highway, I-35 originates at the Mexican border and bisects the United States on its way to Duluth, Minnesota, on Lake Superior. Consequently, the six-lane route is constantly jammed with 18-wheelers, livestock trailers, delivery trucks, and overloaded pickups headed north and south. When traffic is flowing, I-35 is perfectly functional, but when it's not, be prepared to sit and wait . . . and wait and wait. In and around both Austin and San Antonio, it is always wise to budget some extra time into your itinerary for inevitable congestion. Conversely, traffic in the Hill Country flows at a leisurely pace; generally speaking, you can breeze undeterred over the windy, rural roads between towns.

Inside Austin and San Antonio the paths of interstate highways, U.S. highways, and state highways often merge. In San Antonio, for example, I-10 is also US 87 or US 90 at various points; US 281 north of town suddenly becomes I-37 south of town. Some state highways have names in addition to their numbers. Loop 360 in Austin is known as Capital of Texas Highway. Loop 1, also in Austin, is commonly referred to by its nickname, "MoPac." The Hill Country is traversed by plenty of small highways known as farm–to-market (FM) or ranch-to-market (RM) roads, which were built to be reliable trade routes between agricultural Texas and nearby cities or market centers. Constructed in the 1940s, these secondary roads are well maintained by the Texas Department of Transportation. County roads (CR), maintained by individual counties, are also secondary roads, though their size and conditions vary.

LEFT: Hauptstrasse, or Main Street, in Boerne

Got Wheels?

Most visitors to the region rent a car, and most major rental companies have kiosks in each airport. While it is possible to get around most of Austin or San Antonio using public transportation, a car is essential for touring the Hill Country. The percentage of uninsured motorists in Texas is high, and while lawmakers are attempting to curb the problem, a fender bender, regardless of fault, may end up costing you a pretty penny. Be sure to check your insurance policy before you drive.

Reservations are strongly recommended.

Advantage (800-777-5500; www.arac.com)

Alamo/National (800-462-5266; www.alamo.com)

Avis (800-331-1212; www.avis.com)

Budget (800-527-0700; www.budget.com)

Dollar (800-800-3665; www.dollar.com)

Enterprise (800-261-7331; www.enterprise.com)

Hertz (800-654-3131; www.hertz.com)

Thrifty (800-847-4389; www.thrifty.com)

GETTING TO CENTRAL TEXAS

By Air

Air travelers coming to the region might consider flying into either Austin or San Antonio. Depending on your destination and time of travel, prices can vary widely; being flexible in your travel plans can sometimes yield big savings.

Austin-Bergstrom International Airport (512-530-2242; www.ci.austin.tx.us/austin airport) 3600 Presidential Blvd., Austin, TX 78719. The airport is located in southeast Austin, just east of the intersection of TX 71 and US 183, approximately 8 miles from downtown.

Taxi

American Yellow Checker Cab (512-452-9999; www.yellowcabaustin.com) Price: approximately $25.

Airport Shuttle

Super Shuttle (512-258-3826 or 800-258-3826; www.supershuttle.com) Price: $12.

Bus

Capital Metro Bus (512-474-1200; www.capmetro.org) The *Airport Flyer* travels between the airport and two centrally located downtown stops, Sixth St. & Brazos and 18th St. & Congress Ave. It connects downtown and UT to the airport. Price: $1.

San Antonio International Airport (210-207-3433; www.sanantonio.gov/aviation)
9800 Airport Blvd., San Antonio, TX 78216. The airport is located near the
intersection of Loop 410 and US 281, approximately 8 miles from downtown
San Antonio.

Taxi
San Antonio Taxis (210-444-2222; www.sataxis.com) or **Yellow Checker Cab**
(210-222-2222; www.yellowcabsa.com) Price: approximately $20–25.

Airport Shuttle
SATRANS (210-492-4144; www.saairportshuttle.com) Price: One-way $18,
round-trip $32.

Bus
VIA Metropolitan Transit (210-362-2020; www.viainfo.net) Price: $1.
While train or bus travel to the region and between its cities and towns is possible,
it is not very efficient.

By Train
Amtrak (800-872-7245; www.amtrak.com)
Austin: 250 N. Lamar Blvd., Austin, TX 78703
San Marcos: 338 S. Guadalupe St., San Marcos, TX 78666
San Antonio: 350 Hoefgen St., San Antonio, TX 78205

By Bus
Greyhound (www.greyhound.com)
Austin: 512-458-4463; 916 E. Koenig Lane, Austin, TX 78751
San Antonio: 210-270-5824; 500 N. St. Mary's St., San Antonio, TX 78205

Austin

RISING STAR

THE SEAT AND CENTER OF TRAVIS COUNTY, Austin is smaller than San Antonio and just a fraction of the size of Dallas or Houston but nevertheless the capital of Texas. The city is, and has always been, quick with opinions, purposeful in action, and unlikely to follow anyone else's lead. An intellectual powerhouse, Austin has a nationwide reputation for brains and creativity, encouraged and supported by the University of Texas, whose campus occupies a large swath of the city. Sunshine, hike-and-bike trails, parks, and rooftop bars satisfy the city's penchant for all things outdoors. At open-air concerts or just lounging under the shady oaks, Austin is a city that likes to hang out, having perfected the art of doing so. And here in the "Live Music Capital of the World," you can see performances every day and dozens of music festivals throughout the year.

EARLY DAYS

Situated at the eastern edge of the Edwards Plateau, where the land of prairies and lakes is thrust suddenly into the dips and curves of the Hill Country, Austin is blessed with natural resources and beauty. In 1839 the then thinly settled area anchored by the tiny village of Waterloo was chosen for the capital of the Republic of Texas and was promptly named after its most famous Anglo-American, Stephen F. Austin, who was revered long before being immortalized along with the other fallen heroes of the Alamo. Standing on the edge of the western frontier, in full view of Mexicans and Native Americans, both of whom had their eye on the property, Austin seemed unsafe, its future uncertain. Some, including Sam Houston, were skeptical of the choice. But the republic's president, Mirabeau B. Lamar, who had become smitten with the location on a buffalo hunt, gave the go-ahead for the purchase of 7,735 acres along the Colorado River. Surveyors, planners, and

LEFT: Street musician on South Congress Avenue

Austin Area

0   1   2
Miles

N

WALNUT CREEK
METROPOLITAN
PARK

CITY PARK RD

EMMA LONG
METROPOLITAN
PARK

Colorado River

BRIGHT LEAF
STATE NATURAL
AREA

W ANDERSON LN

Northcross
Mall

Lake
Austin

Mt. Bonnell

Mayfield
Park

Austin Museum of Art-
Laguna Gloria

Highland
Mall

Elisabet Ney
Museum

W 35TH ST

MARTIN
LUTHER
KING BLVD

W 45TH ST

38TH
ST

Hyde
Park

UT

MANOR RD

BEE CREEK
NATURE
PRESERVE

West End/
Clarksville

Deep Eddy
Pool

Univ of
Texas at
Austin

Town
Lake

ZILKER
METROPOLITAN
PARK & PRESERVE

15TH
ST

12TH
ST

George Washington
Carver Museum &
Cultural Center

CESAR

Texas State
Cemetery

East
Austin

Barton Creek
Square Mall

Umlauf Sculpture
Gardens

CHAVEZ ST

E 7TH ST

LOOP
343

Downtown

BARTON CREEK
GREENBELT

South
Austin

South of
Congress
(SoCo)

ROY G. GUERRERO
COLORADO RIVER
PARK

To Austin Zoo

RIVERSIDE DR

To Lady Bird Johnson
Wildflower Center

Austin-Bergstrom
International
Airport

MC KINNEY FALLS
STATE PARK

LOOP
275

SPICEWOOD SPRINGS RD

MANOR RD

N LAMAR BLVD

N LAMAR BLVD

GUADALUPE ST

LAVACA

PLEASANT VALLEY RD

Colorado River

S CONGRESS AVE

S 1ST ST

S 1ST ST

MANCHACA RD

© The Countryman Press

Mural in South Austin

workers immediately set about building a city, with the hope of having it finished by the next scheduled meeting of the Texas Congress, just months away in November 1839. A grid of 14 blocks was laid out on a 640-acre plot starting at the river, bounded on two sides by Shoal and Waller Creeks; Congress Avenue bisected the grid on its way northward to the hill on which a temporary one-story wooden capitol was built. Austin was incorporated on December 27, 1839, Congress successfully convened as planned, and the city welcomed diplomats from England, France, and its neighbor to the north, the United States.

Austin's status as capital didn't sit well with everyone. In 1842 Sam Houston, who had succeeded President Lamar, demanded that the national archives and state-related records be brought to Houston. Folks in Austin took the news personally, feeling that moving the papers would mean moving the fledgling capital, and staunchly refused. Houston acquiesced, allowing Austin to keep the documents, but moved the government all the same, first to Houston and later to Washington-on-the Brazos. Houston quickly grew to regret his hasty compromise; he wanted the papers, and he sent armed men to Austin to get them. In what would become known as the Archive War, the men were met by enraged citizens, and in the end the papers remained in Austin, while the government remained in Houston. It wasn't until the 1845 annexation of Texas by the United States that Austin was established, officially, as capital of Texas—with one caveat. The designation was temporary; a vote would be held in 20 years to let the people decide once and for all.

Taking its role as capital to heart, by 1853 Austin had completed a permanent capitol building and, by 1856, a Governor's Mansion. The city was growing, but it was still essentially an outpost on the edge of the frontier, with only unreliable roads for trading. Austin lobbied hard for railroads, but the Civil War halted all new construction as resources were diverted to the war effort. While the city was initially against secession, skyrocketing food shortages, inflation, and casualties shifted its sentiments. At end of the war in 1865, Union troops occupied a bedraggled Austin.

On December 25, 1871, Austin, still suffering the effects of the war and Reconstruction, was gratefully connected to the greater and newly unified country as the Houston and Texas Central Railway passed through the city. The city's economy took this shot in the arm, and Austin almost immediately became a bustling hub of materials, products, and, most important, immigrants. By 1870, five years after the end of the Civil War and the Emancipation Proclamation, 36 percent of Austin's population was African American. These newcomers quickly went to work settling various Austin neighborhoods, opening churches and businesses, and sending their children to local schools. By 1875 there were 757 residents from Germany, 215 from Ireland, 138 from Sweden, and 297 from Mexico—the first from that nation—with each group contributing to the economy of the young and growing city. Public life was getting crowded and chaotic; gas street lamps were installed in 1874, a streetcar line was established in 1875, and a bridge spanned the Colorado River the following year.

In 1872 Austin triumphed at the polls and was declared, once and for all, the Texas capital. In 1881 Austin prevailed again in a statewide ballot, this time for the site of the University of Texas, which started educating students two years later. Also in 1881, the city organized a public school system, and the Tillotson Collegiate and Normal Institute began offering instruction to African American students. Four years later St. Edward's Academy was chartered as St. Edward's College. In 1888 the city finished construction of the huge granite capitol, still so prevalent in its skyline, anchoring Austin at the symbolic center of Texas.

In 1905 despite its statewide importance, Austin had only one paved street, deplorable sanitary conditions, and very few public services. All this changed with the 1928 city plan, the first plan drawn up since the town's beginnings in 1839, and the passage of a $4.25 million bond issue. The money was used to finance a library, a hospital, an airport, roads, and sewers and to further the city's primary goal of boosting its image as the go-to city for education and culture in Texas. A recreation department was put into place; soon after, the city had made huge strides in beautification, giving itself parks, pools, and recreation programs. These public improvements asserted the ideals that define Austin today, a city with progressive ideas and proactive planning.

THE 20TH CENTURY

The Great Depression of the 1930s did not spare Austin, but by all accounts it was the skills of Mayor Robert Thomas Miller and Congressman Lyndon Baines Johnson that kept the city afloat. The population exploded, increasing 66 percent in the 1930s, and with this growth came increasing demands on services. The University of Texas saw enrollment practically double and quickly began construction to expand the campus. The devastating flood of 1935 prompted plans to dam the Colorado River; the Tom Miller Dam, finished in 1940, gave the city Lake Austin,

Downtown Austin

while the Mansfield Dam, completed the following year, created Lake Travis. Dams farther north created the Highland Lakes, used for recreation, water supply, and power. The dawn of World War II brought Del Valle Air Base, later called Bergstrom Air Force Base, and later still retrofitted to become the Austin-Bergstrom Airport.

The 20th century brought radical social changes to Austin. Mirroring other cities throughout the country, Austin was mired in the politics and interpersonal dynamics of segregation. While African Americans had previously lived throughout the city, the city plan of 1928 recommended a "Negro district" be established in the city's East Side. By the 1940s this ghettoizing allowed the city to systematically restrict African Americans' access to schools, parks, transportation, and other municipal services, despite the fact that blacks had established numerous businesses, dozens of churches, and two colleges in the city and had participated in civic life since the city's inception. As the city grew, the African American population remained relatively stable in numbers but dropped dramatically in percentage.

At the same time, the number of Hispanic residents jumped from 1.5 percent of the population to 11 percent. Though laws permitted discrimination against African Americans, the discrimination experienced by Mexican Americans, while pervasive, was not as systematic or organized. Over the years, local African American leaders and their supporters worked tirelessly to desegregate schools and other institutions, and in 1956 the University of Texas admitted black students, the first large southern university to do so. The nationwide demonstrations and sit-ins of the 1960s brought about the Civil Rights Act of 1964, which provided some measure of legal protection from discrimination. Ironically, while two African Americans sat on Austin's city council in 1880, African Americans did not serve again until 1968, an advance soon repeated by Hispanic citizens.

Austin is still a young city. Coming of age in the mid-20th century, it has seen its growth hastened by wars, railroads, and social movements. In the 1950s Austin began positioning itself for a future in technology, as several research laboratories and think tanks sprang up and prospered, benefiting from their proximity to the university. By the 1970s rapid growth in the city was met by a politically active population who formed civic groups to preserve the city's history, neighborhoods, and environment and to protect the rights of its citizens. Austin remains the state's undisputed educational and cultural center, with enough parks, lakes, recreation, and cultural events to keep everyone happy. As the popularity of the loosely organized movement "Keep Austin Weird" (www.keepaustin weird.com) demonstrates, the city loves its free-thinkers, artists, and musicians. If, as John Steinbeck wrote, "Texas is a state of mind," then Austin, an unencumbered free spirit of a city, is surely its perfect capital.

The Frost Bank Building in downtown Austin

NEIGHBORHOODS

Downtown

Overseen by the Capitol, downtown is organized around Congress Avenue, which divides cross streets into east and west. Much of the city's nightlife is located either on Sixth Street, bounded by Congress to the west and Red River Street to the east, or the Warehouse District, on Fourth and Fifth Streets between Congress and Guadalupe.

South Austin and South of Congress (SoCo)

While crossing over the Congress Avenue Bridge used to feel like crossing into a different world, a recent rejuvenation of the area has tempered its edge. Large-scale commercial and residential developments are now springing up in this artsy enclave. Filled with inexpensive eateries, music venues, and funky art and resale shops, South Austin embodies some of the best of Austin.

West End/Clarksville
The area west of Lamar Boulevard between Enfield Road to the north and West Fifth Street to the south, West End and Clarksville is a deceptively modest-looking neighborhood conveniently located beside downtown. The area is atmospheric, with large trees, art galleries, several upscale restaurants, and sidewalks for strolling.

UT and Hyde Park
To the north of the Capitol, the sprawling 350-acre University of Texas campus is bounded by Guadalupe Street (also known as "The Drag") to the west, I-35 to the east, and Martin Luther King Jr. Boulevard to the south. Located just a mile north of the University of Texas, Hyde Park is bounded by Guadalupe Street to the west, Duval Street to the east, 45th Street to the north, and 38th Street to the south. Developed as Austin's first suburb, the neighborhood features homes from the 1930s and '40s interspersed with commercial centers, folksy restaurants, and coffee shops. Students, professors, and young families call Hyde Park home, and the area feels lived in, with bikes in the yards and swings on the porches.

East Austin
Comprising the neighborhoods east of I-35, East Austin retains its historic roots. A diverse neighborhood, it is also home to significant cultural institutions such as the George Washington Carver Museum and Cultural Center and the Texas State Cemetery. Recent economic development has changed the face of East Austin, but its infectious community spirit is still thriving.

TRANSPORTATION

Getting Around Austin
Austin is not a large city, so driving into, out of, or around it is not a particularly difficult task. However, the major routes that approximate the boundaries of the city are known by several names, making navigation a challenge.

I-35 runs along the eastern part of Austin, dividing East Austin from the rest of the city. Following the western border is Loop 1, also known as the MoPac Expressway, or MoPac, for the Missouri-Pacific Railroad, which runs parallel to it in many places. Farther west is Loop 360, often referred to as Capital of Texas Highway.

US 183 originates in East Austin as Ed Bluestein Boulevard, becoming Anderson Lane, Research Boulevard, and finally Bell Boulevard as it snakes it way along the northern edge of the city. At the southern reaches of the city, TX 71 is also known as US 290 and Ben White Boulevard.

Downtown Austin is more straightforward for both drivers and pedestrians. Spread out in a grid, with generously sized blocks, downtown is easily taken in on foot, but to get to sights in South Austin and beyond, consider riding one of the city's buses.

See Austin's Capital Metro's Web site for details; www.capmetro.org.

Pick Your Spot

Best places to stay in and
around Austin

DOWNTOWN

Hotel chains dominate the lodging
choices in Austin, and many of them
cater primarily to business travelers
and politicians, charging additional
hefty fees for parking, use of fitness
facilities, and Internet service; be sure
to inquire about such details when
making your reservation, and keep in
mind that parking on the streets in
Austin is free on the weekends. Austin
has several historic hotels, boutique
hotels, and Bed & Breakfasts located
throughout the city that offer character
and individuality, not to mention free
WiFi and parking. They are also quick
to hand out snacks, drinks, business
discounts, DVDs, flowers, and restaurant advice without batting an eyelash
or charging you an extra penny. If you
appreciate this sort of personal attention, consider patronizing one of these
very worthy alternatives.

When choosing an area of town,
keep in mind that the neighborhoods
surrounding Sixth Street tend to stay
up late for the nightlife on which the
city has grown its reputation. If you
are staying downtown, consider asking
for a room as high up as possible.
They don't call Austin the Live Music
Capital of the World for nothing; if you
are used to city sounds, the noise level
may not bother you, but if you require
silence to sleep, you might consider a
hotel in a quieter neighborhood several
blocks removed or one of the B&Bs,
which have strictly enforced quiet
hours. Keep in mind that rates tend
to rise during holidays, festivals, and
special events. B&Bs often require a
two-day minimum stay, possibly three
days during holidays, festivals, and
special events.

You really can't get more Austin than
the **Driskill Hotel** (512-474-5911;
www.driskillhotel.com). Constructed by
cattle baron Jesse Lincoln Driskill in
1886, a time when the rest of the city
was built low to the ground, the hotel
was the largest, grandest, and most
elaborate structure in Austin. Financial
problems came to plague the hotel and
eventually the Heritage Society of
Austin stepped in, drumming up support, investment, and interest in the
building and making it what it is
today—the elegant centerpiece of
downtown. Dine at the Driskill Grill
(see "Local Flavors," below), have a
drink at the bar, or a muffin at the
1886 Bakery, while enjoying the stylish
atmosphere of the hotel. Remember
that the hotel is old through and
through, so modestly sized rooms and
quirky layouts are the norm. All amenities have been modernized; the bathrooms have granite countertops, and
the decor is refined with soft linens,
sumptuous drapes, and rich accents.
While this sort of luxury isn't cheap,
experiencing this grand piece of Austin
history is worth it.

Another downtown charmer, the
InterContinental Stephen F. Austin
(512-457-8800; www.austin.inter
continental.com) was built in 1924 and
consequently does not have the cookie-
cutter consistency associated with
many of Austin's newer downtown
hotels. In general, the standard rooms
tend to be small, though tasteful décor
keeps them from feeling cramped. The
hotel's age also means different floor
plans and different levels of service
and amenities, so spending the extra
$40–60 to upgrade to deluxe rooms
may very well be worth the money; be
sure to inquire about specifics. While
the Stephen F. Austin may not have

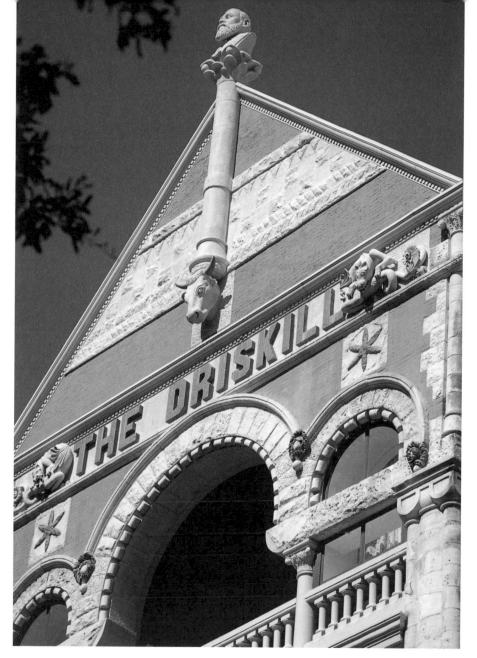

The Driskill Hotel in downtown Austin

the historic provenance of the Driskill, it is lighter, brighter, and just as well situated.

Though a national chain, the **Four Seasons** (512-478-4500; www.four seasons.com/austin) has enough of a Texas twang to warrant a mention. Perched on a bluff overlooking Lady Bird Lake just south of César Chávez Street near the Congress Avenue Bridge, the Four Seasons is wonder- fully located, within easy driving

Bridge over the Colorado River at dusk

distance and, in many cases, walking distance of all major points of interest. Directly outside the hotel is a hike-and-bike path where you can join locals for a run. The lovely pool, with lake views, is a great spot for a dip. Inside, rooms are average size; though the ceilings are somewhat low, the generous windows help compensate. Rooms have either a city view or a lake view (extra charge), and each is enjoyable in its own way. Downstairs, the Café at the Four Seasons (see "Local Flavors," below) is one of the best places to eat in town, and the bar is a favorite spot for locals to unwind over after-work drinks.

SOUTH AUSTIN

New boutique hotels are springing up in South Austin, but one of the originals is the eclectic **Austin Motel** (512-441-1157; www.austinmotel.com), known for its telling tagline "so close in, yet so far out." The oldest part of

this independently owned motel dates to 1938; the kidney-shaped pool was constructed in the 1950s, and the two-story addition in 1968. There are spacious suites, cozy singles, and poolside rooms, all with various bed configurations, making this a popular choice for small groups in town for festivals. Rooms are individually decorated, and the décor includes everything from wall-sized photo murals of sunsets to

The funky Austin Motel on South Congress Avenue

vintage kitsch and fluffy floral coverlets covered with pandas. The Austin Motel is an older establishment and very reasonably priced—just bear in mind that one person's worn-in might be another's worn-out.

Originally opened in 1939, the **Hotel San José** (512-444-7322; www.sanjosehotel.com) has since been remodeled in a style that harks back to its roots as an "ultramodern motor court" but might now be best described as hacienda-meets-bento box. It's compact and efficient, with an understated simplicity that is utterly serene. The European-style hotel has only 40 rooms, ranging from the small and spartan shared bathrooms to the generously sized Courtyard Suite with a balcony view. The minuscule pool, lovely gardens, laid-back bar, and adjacent coffee shop amplify the air of yesteryear and create a sophisticated oasis of calm on South Congress.

Liz Lambert, the hotelier behind Hotel San José, is also responsible for the nearby **Hotel St. Cecilia** (512-852-2400; www.hotelsaintcecilia.com). Tucked into an old home located in a shady neighborhood just a few blocks off South Congress, the St. Cecilia embodies rock-meets-Texas-meets-beat-poet, with an overarching feeling of free-spirited romance. There are five quirky suites, six peaceful poolside bungalows, and three spacious studios on its expansive grounds. Each room is unique and the details make the difference—worn wood floors, tons of art, velvet couches, record players, pressed tin ceilings, and whimsical wallpapers. It's pricey, but one-of-a-kind.

Several blocks away, the **Kimber Modern Hotel** (512-912-104; www.austin-kimbermodernhotel.info) is modern, yet cozy. The hotel has just a few rooms, two suites, a common area, and an enormous shared deck under the sprawling shade of a grove of live oak trees. Dramatic design shines—plenty of crisp white walls, linens, and furniture, a pops of color here and there—but floor-to-ceiling windows and whimsical touches keep the hotel from feeling too cool. Though located in the heart of the SoCo bustle, the Kimber Modern feels private and intimate, with a folksiness you might expect of a hipster hostel for well-behaved grownups.

Deeper into Travis Heights, you'll find **Casa Kenwood** (310-936-1122; www.casakenwoodguesthouses.com). The casa is actually two guest houses—a studio and a free-standing casita—set amid lush greenery, native landscaping, and tweeting birds. Both options are spacious, with kitchenettes, comfy chairs for lounging, and plenty of room for family and friends. Clean, comfortable, folksy, and free-spirited, guests love Casa Kenwood for its cheery individuality. The low prices, peacefulness, and proximity to downtown are hard to beat.

UT/HYDE PARK

The Adams House Inn (512-453-7696; www.theadamshouse.com) is right at home deep in Hyde Park. The inn's four rooms and free-standing bungalow are light, bright, and airy, with wood floors, plantation shutters on the windows, and a few well-chosen antiques. Spotlessly clean and refreshingly uncluttered, the inn has all the character you'd expect of an older home paired with a freshly updated modern feel. Sit down with a book in the sunroom of the Adams Suite, and you just might stay all afternoon. Warm and welcoming innkeepers Liz and Eric are the icing on the cake.

The Austin Folk House Bed and Breakfast (512-472-6700; www.austin folkhouse.com), which has a wonderfully eclectic collection of folk art, happens also to be very folksy. Each room is different, but all have warm color schemes and are simply decorated with personal touches such as handmade comforters, canopy beds, and rustic armoires. Breakfast includes raspberry pancakes, *migas* or quiche, and coffee served in a mug from its mismatched collection.

Friendly, comfortable, and relaxed, the Folk House is located beside UT, making it a good choice for university visitors who would like stay close to campus. Its sister property, the **Star of Texas Inn** (512-472-6700; www.starof texasinn.com) is located just one block away and comparable in look, feel, and price.

The considerate owners of the **1110 Carriage House Inn** (512-472-2333; www.carriagehouseinn.org) have truly thought of everything. Each room of the inn, which is located near the University of Texas, has gleaming hardwood floors, large wood beds, and pretty lace curtains to catch the sunlight. The bathroom sizes and configurations vary according to room; some have tubs and some have showers, so be sure to inquire if you need one or the other. Breakfast is always homemade, using organic ingredients when available and taking into concern the dietary restrictions of its guests. The lovely organic gardens, featuring a koi pond and seating under a gazebo, are a great place to unwind.

WEST END/CLARKSVILLE

Lofty ceilings, hardwood floors, and dark wood moldings are all hallmarks of **Brava House** (512-478-5034; www .bravahouse.com), a Victorian beauty

built in the 1880s. The two rooms and three suites in Brava House are well decorated with antiques that feel casual and comfortable, not formal or fussy. The small and sweet Van Gogh Room is wheelchair accessible, the generously sized and dapper Garbo Suite and Art Deco Fitzgerald Suite have foldout couches for extra guests, and the large Monroe Suite is really more of a miniapartment with a full kitchen. A buffet-style breakfast is served each morning, and the cozy backyard deck is a nice place to sit and enjoy it. Brava House is remarkably well located in a quiet West Austin neighborhood near the intersection of North Lamar Avenue and 12th Street, just four blocks north of the Whole Foods Market on Lamar.

EAST AUSTIN

The **Heywood Hotel** (512- 271-5522; www.heywoodhotel.com) sits calmly on busy stretch of East Cesar Chavez in the heart of East Austin. The hotel is composed of a renovated bungalow and its attached addition, which together capture all the design of a modern hotel and the charm and warmth of a B&B. The rooms have clean lines, stylish décor, sumptuous sheets, and clean-as-a-whistle bathrooms. Other pluses include a lovely outdoor patio, proximity to funky East Austin eateries, and the owner, Kathy, who is as friendly and helpful as can be. The Heywood is the perfect boutique hotel for guests who prefer personal touches and a just-off-the-beaten-path location.

OUTER AUSTIN

If you enjoy spas and resorts, consider the **Lake Austin Spa and Resort** (512-372-7300; www.lakeaustinspa.com). While *Travel and Leisure* and *Condé*

Heywood Boutique Hotel in East Austin

Nast Traveler have given it high praise, Lake Austin Spa's biggest compliments have come from its guests, who leave relaxed and rejuvenated. With views of the lake at every turn and expansive use of native Austin limestone and huge cedar beams, this midsize resort with 40 guest cottages has that earthy, laid-back, rustic feel that typifies the area; the overall effect is both cozy and chic. A popular place for couples, the Lake Austin Spa has a more feminine, weekend-of-pampering vibe, easily enjoyed by some men, though the lack of testosterone may be noticeable to others. Prices include three gourmet meals a day and access to all fitness classes, including yoga, pilates, hiking, and fun salsa aerobics. A bevy of activities and classes, from cooking to stargazing to watercolor, is also on offer. All spa services are à la carte. Of course, the price of this level of luxury is steep, but the Lake Austin Spa is a good value when compared to similar facilities nationwide.

For those who like to relax by doing, **Travaasa** (855-868-7282; www.travaasa.com) is a full-service, campus-style spa resort with a twist. Challenge yourself to a ropes course, walk the Hill Country Trails, horseback ride, or learn to play harmonica. You can take a yoga class, practice your mechanical bull riding skills, and finish off with a wine tasting. Nature takes center stage at Travaasa. Each of the 70 rooms features rustic headboards, clean lines, big windows, and wide views of the surrounding countryside. There are leather couches, stone fireplaces, soaring ceilings, shady patios, and an infinity pool overlooking Lake Travis and the hills beyond. From sunrise to stunning sunset, Travaasa is well matched with its surroundings, in both atmosphere and spirit.

Local Flavors

Taste of the town—local
restaurants, cafés, bistros, etc.

In general, Austinites are an adventurous and easygoing bunch, and the restaurants that serve them tend to reflect this sensibility. Austin is a relatively small city, and its roots as an overgrown college town are most apparent in its food scene, which is largely dominated by modestly priced menus served in a relaxed atmosphere. Not surprisingly, the most represented cuisines in Austin are American, BBQ, Continental, Mexican, southern, and Tex-Mex, and the variations and combinations of these themes seem endless. While those who live here would warmly welcome more selection— new restaurants are quickly mobbed— visitors still have plenty to choose from.

The secret to dining in Austin is to focus on the well-done. Whether you're in an upscale restaurant or a neighborhood coffee shop, the charm of eating out in Austin is in the details, with an emphasis on quality and personality. At any price level, many menus feature creative seasonal fare accompanied by plenty of vegetables, meal-sized salads, and hearty soups, frequently made with organic ingredients. Vegetarians and the health-conscious will find themselves in unusually good company in Austin, where restaurant menus tend to be diverse. Austin chefs love using locally grown or produced items, and regional wines, cheeses, game, fruits, and vegetables are often highlighted. The many, many individually owned and operated restaurants in Austin are very much rooted in their neighborhoods and their city, with a large number of them supporting local causes, partici-

pating in community events, and providing venues for local musicians and visual artists.

Now for the details. As you will undoubtedly notice, casual attire— some people wear shorts and flip-flops throughout the better part of the year—is commonplace. Wearing "business casual" is appropriate for most of the pricier establishments, though you won't feel out of place should you decide to dress up for a fancy, formal meal. Families seem especially welcome in Austin's eating establishments, most of which offer booster seats, kids' menus, and a friendly atmosphere. Generally, credit cards are accepted, and I have noted the occasional place where they are not. Reservations should be considered essential at the more expensive and popular spots, and I have recommended making them if necessary. You are not allowed to smoke in any public building or within 15 feet from the entrance to one. There are several establishments exempt from this regulation, at least through 2012, and they are listed under "Nightlife," above. As with everything, details change, so please call ahead to ensure your visit to one of Austin's restaurants goes smoothly.

The restaurants below are local favorites and include those that are frequently and enthusiastically voted onto citywide "best of" lists. Many have been around for years, changing with tastes or remaining exactly the same. Some are uniquely Austin, and others have a more universal appeal. Some are exquisitely appointed, with lovely stemware and thick napkins, while others are earthy, with sticky beer-stained barstools and self-serve plastic cutlery, but all are filled with the locals who love them. This list is by no means exhaustive, and if your taste buds have you salivating for something specific, check out www.austin360.com, the *Austin American-Statesman's* online listing of food, entertainment, and events, for all restaurant reviews ever written, organized by cuisine.

DOWNTOWN

In downtown Austin you are as likely to find a $100 meal as you are a $2 breakfast taco, not to mention plenty of places to stop in for drinks and noshes (see page 59). This variety is what makes it a great place to eat for politicians, professionals, visitors, and students alike. See "Drinks," below, for suggestions of eateries to stop by for noshes, nibbles, or late-night desserts.

TRIO Restaurant (512-685-8300; www.fourseasons.com/austin) at the Four Seasons Hotel is one of the most elegant and sophisticated dining experiences in Austin. Featuring prime steaks, fresh seafood, and fine wine, the menu highlights Texas ingredients with local quail, chicken, goat cheese, heirloom tomatoes, and olive oil. The Sunday brunch is particularly outstanding. From the sweet pancakes and chicken and waffles to smoked meats and made-to order omelets, sushi, and seafood, brunch is a decadent way to sample, or stuff yourself with, all the dishes the Four Seasons has to offer. The dining room is roomy, warm, and inviting, but if the weather is right, the terrace can't be beat, with cozy cushions, white umbrellas, gentle breezes, and views of Lady Bird Lake.

The **Driskill Grill** (512-391-7162; www.driskillhotel.com), in the Driskill Hotel at the corner of Brazos and Sixth Streets, has become one of Austin's favorite fancy dining restaurants. The thrill of the Driskill is the marriage of its lovely, old-time surroundings, a level of opulence not usually witnessed in Central Texas, and its innovative offer-

ings. The menu is market-driven, as in the farmer's market. Items such as heirloom tomatoes served with mozzarella and a black pepper brioche, hot smoked Bandera quail with a coriander orange curd, and the local Jameson Farms rack of lamb accompanied by a mushroom risotto are the sorts of dishes that make the Driskill Grill so very representative of Austin and the surrounding region. The dessert menu includes Orange Marshmallow with Earl Grey Caramel, Kumquat Preserve, Malted Milk Chocolate Fredo, and Vanilla Vodka Ice—all good examples of the sort of inspired creativity you can expect to the very last bite. The attached Driskill Bar (see page 34) is a good place for drinks.

Also located in the Driskill Hotel, the **1886 Café and Bakery** (512-391-7066: www.1886cafeandbakery.com), or as the hotel likes to call it, "Austin's Original Socializing Parlor," serves wonderful soups, sandwiches, baked goods, and desserts amid lavish surroundings. The all-day menu is more modestly priced than the Driskill Grill and is served until 10 PM. The Hippy Hollow, a breakfast scramble of eggs, spinach, and goat cheese, the waffles with Texas pecans, bananas, and blackberry jam, and the eggs Benedict with grilled beef tenderloin, jack cheese, and salsa on a toasted muffin are several items that make this café a great place to stop in for a taste of Texas.

Congress (512-827-2760; www.congressaustin.com), at Congress and Second, is classy, but still slightly casual, with great food and a top-flight wine list that earned it a spot on *Wine Enthusiast's* list of 100 Best Wine Restaurants. Try the seared sea scallops with jicama salad, coconut cream, cocoa and chocolate nibs, and ask for a pairing suggestion. Its companion eatery, **Second Bar and Kitchen**

Texas for Foodies

Central Texas makes some fantastic food, much of it easily found in the upscale food emporiums of Austin-based Whole Foods (512-476-1206; www.wholefoods market.com) and San Antonio-based Central Market (512-206-1000; www.central market.com).

With an emphasis on quality produce and products, both Whole Foods and Central Market have tapped into the market of conscious consumers. While doing all your grocery shopping at these stores can get pricey, the elaborate deli services, self-serve soup and salad bars, a variety of prepared foods, and wonderful coffees and baked goods make them the perfect spots to grab a bite. The wide range of regional specialties, including Texas wines, makes for fun browsing. Both establishments have become destinations in their own right, places locals love to bring out-of-towners.

(512-827-2750; www.congressaustin .com), is less pricey, though still posh. Try the small plates, including the avocado fundido with super fresh chunks of avocado and spicy chorizo, black truffle pommes frites with aioli, garlic and chive potato gnocchi, and fried pickles with gorgonzola. Bar Congress (see page 59) is a good choice for drinks and noshes.

Stop in at Frank (512-494-6916; www.hotdogscoldbeer.com), the gourmet hot dog spot on Colorado just south of Fifth Street, for a taste of the popular "Jackalope"—an antelope, rabbit, and pork sausage hot dog served with huckleberry compote, sriracha aioli, and cheddar. Make any frank a veggie dog for 50 cents, or, for a buck twenty-five, they'll take the Daily Dog, stuff it with white American cheese, wrap it in bacon, and plunge it into the deep fryer for ya. Round out your meal with waffle fry nachos, and finish with a bacon chocolate chip cookie. Or go out on a limb and try one of its super creative and intensely flavorful mixed drinks (see "Drinks," page 59).

Moonshine (512-236-9599; www .moonshinegrill.com) is just the place

for an early-morning brunch buffet that includes comfort food favorites like sweet potato casserole with mini marshmallows, ham smothered in pineapple chipotle glaze, and savory green chile cheese grits. Try the "corn dog" shrimp with honey mustard and blueberry sauce, the beer-battered fried asparagus, and the green chile macaroni with grilled chicken, corn relish, and a smooth green chile cheese sauce, and you'll know why there's a line out the door. Moonshine is in a sweet little two-story stone building with a patio on Red River, between Third and Fourth Streets.

Vibrant, colorful, and energetic, La Condesa (512- 499-0300; www.la condesaaustin.com), on West Second Street in the Warehouse District, has made a name for itself with ambitious, upscale Mexican and Latin dishes. The must-order item here is the piping-hot, creamy, and slightly spicy Mexican-style street corn, known as *elotes*. Folks also love the margaritas and guacamole sampler appetizer, which includes a mix of chipotle and almonds, watermelon with pomegranate molasses, and crab, apple, and coconut vinegar. The simple, citrus-rubbed half rotisserie chicken with three-day *mole* and grilled cebollitas is fantastic, and *chile rellenos* stuffed with quinoa, butternut squash, and manchego is a tasty twist on a classic. Desserts are exceptional.

"Fancy BBQ" isn't an oxymoron at nearby **Lambert's Downtown BBQ** (512-494-1500; www.lambertsaustin .com), where the food is served on plates, not butcher paper. The dining room blends cosmopolitan and country, as does the menu, where updated comfort foods such as daikon slaw, fried okra with remoulade, and sautéed lemon spinach are served alongside classics such as baked mac and cheese and jalapeño cornbread muffins. The Crispy Wild Boar ribs with honey, Sambal, and blue cheese; Black Angus brisket with a crusty, caramelized brown sugar and coffee rub; pork ribs with maple and coriander; and the rib eye with brown sugar and mustard served with a whole roast garlic bulb; are standouts.

Head west on Sixth Street to **Hut's Hamburgers** (512-472-0693; www.huts frankandangies.com) is one of those crowded, chock-full-of-memorabilia places that everybody loves. Diners happily overlook sticky soda spills and elbow-to-elbow seating because the great burgers always come out hot, smothered with creative toppings, and accompanied by mounds of fries or onion rings. Blue-plate specials change constantly, and the two-for-one deal offered Monday, Wednesday, and Friday at lunchtime is a hard bargain to resist. Vegetarians are surprisingly well served.

24 Diner (512-472-5400; www.24 diner.com), on North Lamar, is as delicious for midmorning brunch as it is for the midnight munchies. Some say the chicken and waffles, covered in maple syrup and brown sugar butter,

are worth the trip alone. There are burgers, milkshakes, fancy deviled eggs, and light-as-air goat cheese frittatas all week long and chicken and dumplings every Tuesday until midnight. Sure, it's a little pricey, but it's really more of a bistro than a diner, so it's hard to complain. After all, the food is super fresh (local and often organic), the atmosphere is bright and pleasant, and the doors are open 24/7.

Nearby, the tiny **Counter Café** (512-708-8800; www.thecountercafe .com) grills up pimento cheese sandwiches, massive bacon-n-blackberry pancakes, and some of the best burgers in the city. Though the café is casual, it's not your average greasy spoon, and while the high quality ingredients command slightly higher prices, one bite of a Counter Burger and you'll be rest assured you got just what you paid for.

SOUTH CONGRESS

Directly across Lady Bird Lake from downtown, South Austin is home to a disproportionate number of fun and funky local favorites, which are usually filled for breakfast, lunch, and dinner.

The first thing you'll notice about **Perla's** (512-291-7300; www.perlas austin.com), on South Congress, is the spacious front deck spread out under the oak trees and dotted with colorful umbrellas. The restaurant's casual upscale atmosphere is a great match for its menu, which features an oyster bar, scallops, and Texas Gulf snapper served with spicy garlic, tomato *sofrito*, and wood-grilled vegetable sides. The weekend brunch offerings are a mix of seafood—crab Florentine on an English muffin, for instance—and breakfast treats like brioche French toast served with coconut sorbet, maple syrup, and fresh berries.

Next door, **HopDoddy Burger Bar**

Food Trucks

Food trucks are a great fit for Austin, and many have a devoted following of adventurous diners. Some are seasonal, some are mobile, and hours vary; check Web sites before making a special trip. Not all food trucks accept credit cards, so keep cash on hand just in case. The following have a particularly Texas twang.

A cultural crossover, the kimchi fries at **ChiLantro** (512-568-0256; www.chilantrobbq.com) are a tasty Korean/Mexican

Food Truck

mix of caramelized kimchi, Korean BBQ, chopped grilled onions, cheddar and Monterey Jack cheese, cilantro, "magic sauce," sriracha, and sesame seeds atop a pile of French fries. Central Texas's German roots resonate at the **Best Wurst** (512-912-9545; www.thebestwurst.com), where juicy brats are served piping hot in a bolos roll and smothered in your choice of grilled onions, sauerkraut, curry ketchup, or spicy mustard. **Torchy's** (512-366-0537; www.torchystacos.com) and **Holy Cacao** (512-851-2253; www.theholycacao.com) have moved in together at the South Austin Trailer Park on South First Street, which means you can start with a fantastic Trailer Park taco—fried chicken with green chiles and drizzled with a poblano sauce—and finish with a frozen Mexican drinking chocolate infused with ancho chile, cayenne, and cinnamon. The **Peached Tortilla** (512-761-3241; www.thepeachedtortilla.com) moves around town, bringing delicious chicken satay and Pad Thai tacos with it. Check Web site for locations.

(512-243-7505; www.hopdoddy.com) makes ultra-juicy, freshly ground Angus beef burgers served with a multitude of tasty toppings on warm homemade buns. Diners love the Texas goat cheese with pesto and roasted poblano chiles paired with apple-smoked bacon, and the Primetime justifies its high price ($12) with plenty of brie and truffle aioli. Vegetarians will enjoy the Janis Joplin—a hemp seed veggie patty with avocado, sprouts, Tillamook Cheddar, and a tab of horseradish honey mustard.

A few doors down, in the 100-year-old Central Feed and Seed building, the cavernous dining rooms at **Güero's Taco Bar** (512-447-7688; www.gueros tacobar.com) are always filled with the sound of diners munching chips and the clatter of its bustling wait staff. Güero's enormous menu is centered on classic favorites such as enchiladas, tacos, and fajitas, reshuffled into endless combinations; nightly specials keep things interesting. Handmade tortillas, a self-serve salsa bar, and a great number of margaritas made with fresh-squeezed limes add to the cantina-like appeal. The adjacent oak grove, festooned with tiny white lights, is Güero's music venue; check the Web site for the lineup.

Cross the street for a slice. Stop in at **Home Slice Pizza** (512-444-7437; www.homeslicepizza.com) for NY-style pies made with zesty sauce, gooey cheese, and a crisp, yeasty crust. Eat in the bustling sit-down restaurant or order by the slice at the take-out outpost nearby. Huge, crisp salads, hot garlic twist rolls, and smooth, dense, and creamy cheesecakes make Home Slice a home run.

A block south, folks come to the **South Congress Café** (512-447-3905;

www.southcongresscafe.com) for the piping hot *migas*, carrot cake French toast (that's right, carrot cake!), and the tuna tartare teaser, served with marinated avocado and a spicy mango sauce. The brunch menu is available every day until 4 PM, when dinner picks up the slack. The smoked duck breast finished with a port cherry chipotle glaze is outstanding. While the menu can feel fancy, the open, airy dining room—with its big windows, fresh flowers, and friendly servers—is chic, yet casual.

At the other end of the block, **Vespaio** (512-441-6100; www.austinvespaio.com), Italian for "hornets' nest," is constantly buzzing; diners swarm to this wonderful Italian trattoria and are willing to wait for over an hour for the chance to sit at one of the 15 tables and dig in. While the standard menu of pasta, pizza, and antipasto is superb, regular diners enjoy ordering from the specials menu, featuring offerings like a recent version

Desserts at Enoteca on South Congress Avenue

Cup o' Joe

While the middle of a parking lot may not sound like a great spot for a café, it works at **Jo's** (512-444-3800; www.joscoffee.com). Located beside the Hotel San José (see page 37) on South Congress Avenue, Jo's has a walk-up window where you place and retrieve your order before searching for a vacant chair on the dog-friendly outdoor patio. You'll find friendly staff, great caffeinated drinks, and super sandwiches. The downtown location on Second between Lavaca and Colorado has a similar menu, the same great coffee, and actual indoor seating.

of an eggplant parmesan dish that had disks of lightly fried fresh eggplant layered with cheese, covered with a ladleful of homemade tomato sauce, and served with a side of rustic, garlicky pasta. A well-thought-out wine list provides the final touch. The wonderful food aside, the sophistication without pretension, fairly reasonable prices for such fare, and that feeling of enjoying a glass of wine surrounded by the casual and comforting din of other diners, make Vespaio a destination unto itself.

Though run by the same folks as Vespaio and located right next door, **Enoteca** (512-441-7672; www.austin vespaio.com) has a much more casual look and feel, with small, informal, cloth-covered bistro tables dotting the room, as well as seating under umbrellas for alfresco dining. The front of the restaurant features a deli case with cheeses, meats, and plenty of antipasto dishes, and shelves stocked with olive oils, capers, and other Italian essentials. As befits a relaxed, European-style café, the simple all-day menu, served from 11 AM onward, features panini, pasta, pizza, salads, and daily specials. An extensive wine list leaves many opportunities for pairings. Dessert here is hard to resist after you've caught sight of the lovely *panna cotta* in the dessert case near the entrance. Enoteca is a wonderfully atmospheric

place for a simple cup of morning coffee, pastry, or Sunday brunch. Squint your eyes and you could be in Europe.

Three blocks farther south, **Magnolia Café** (512-445-0000; www .cafemagnolia.com) is the place to go for gingerbread, whole wheat, buttermilk, or cornmeal pancakes 24 hours a day, seven days a week. Omelets, breakfast tacos, *huevos rancheros,* and a tantalizing version of *migas* made with what Magnolia calls "LOVE butter" (butter with fresh garlic and serrano peppers) are also available all day long. Entrées include enchiladas, quesadillas, fajitas, and tacos, and are made with endless combinations of tomatoes, grilled chicken breast, spinach, spicy ground beef, avocado, catfish, and the like. There are huge salads with homemade dressings, burgers, including the Jalapeño Cheese Burger and the Voodoo Bleu Cheese Burger with blackened spices, and plenty of pastas. Vegetarians and the health conscious will enjoy ample choice.

An Austin landmark, **Threadgill's World Headquarters** (512-472-9304; www.threadgills.com), on West Riverside Drive, is built on the former site of the Armadillo World Headquarters, the legendary dance hall whose 10-year run figures prominently in local lore. Loaded with memorabilia, Threadgill's pays tribute to the history of the Austin music scene. The menu is classic stick-to-your-ribs southern cooking, with items like fried green tomatoes, chicken-fried steak, and fried okra. While the food is fine, many come for the ambience, the live music lineup, and to experience a little bit of nostalgia. The Sunday Gospel Brunch is a great time to visit, especially for families.

The big meals at **Freddie's Place** (512-445-9197; www.freddiesplace austin.com) on First Street are steak-heavy—there are chicken-fried steaks, tuna steaks, Salisbury steaks, and even a battered-and-fried portabella mushroom "steak" smothered in cream gravy that won't fool a carnivore but will have vegetarians shouting hallelujah—and accompanied by such vintage side dishes as green bean casserole. Freddie's Heart Attack, an open-face sandwich with Texas toast, tomatoes, and ten slices of bacon slathered with *queso,* may have you throwing a couple extra rounds of washers (a game akin to horseshoes) in the backyard just to stabilize your cholesterol. Combine live music, movies, sports, happy-hour specials, an outdoor pool table, pets, and free-ranging children streaked with ketchup and ice cream, and Freddie's ends up being the fun-loving backyard you wish you had.

Over on South Lamar, James Beard Award winner Chef Tyson Cole has captivated Austin with **Uchi** (512-916-4808; www.uchiaustin.com). The restaurant is completely at home in an old South Austin house painted a deep red, whose interior has been carved out to reveal vaulted ceilings, views into the kitchen, and a combination of tables and minimalist booths for diners. Appetizers are categorized as either Cool (for example, maguro sashimi and goat cheese with cracked pepper,

apples, and pumpkin seed oil) or Hot (panko-fried green tomatoes). The sushi and sashimi menu includes delicate, melt-in-your-mouth tuna, baby yellowtail, snow crab, striped bass, octopus, salmon roe, and sea urchins, some raw and some cooked. If you like surprises, consider the *Omakase,* or tasting menu, which is designed for two and decided entirely by the chef. The desserts at Uchi are a must, if only for a chance to actually taste the items so temptingly described in words. Examples include the Valrhona chocolate and wasabi fondant with five-spice *tuile* and chocolate curry cookie, and the hydroponic basil-Prosecco sorbet. Uchiko (see page 50), Cole's second restaurant, is on North Lamar.

The restaurants on Barton Springs Road are a great place to stop before or after a trip to Zilker Park (see page 62), the Umlauf Sculpture Garden (see page 64), or Barton Springs (see page 62) itself. Enjoy an archetypal burger with all the fixings at **Shady Grove** (512-474-9991; www.theshady grove.com), whose style is best described as 1940s burger joint meets state park lodge. While some may consider it heresy, Shady Grove also makes a nice veggie burger. Take in live music or classic movies in the pecan grove under the stars. Check the Web site for the lineup. Owned by the same folks, Chuy's (512-474-4452; www.chuys .com) is a local chain of Tex-Mex restaurants known for its wacky décor, super-casual atmosphere, and huge portions of fresh, hot homemade food. An overgrown college town café, **Austin Java Company** (512-476-1829; www.austinjava.com) has imaginative coffee-based drinks and a substantial menu of healthy sandwiches, salads, pastas, and breakfast items all day. Stumble into **Flipnotics** (512-480-8646; www.flipnotics.com) for your morning coffee, or mellow out with a beer on the shady back deck in the evening. Flipnotics serves up live music and local favorites, including breakfast tacos, bagels, and vegetarian empanadas.

EAST AUSTIN

East Austin has a lot of homegrown favorites, each serving up comfort food and a warm welcome. Recently, trendy coffeehouses, restaurants, and eateries have also been staking their claim. All give diners good reason to cross the I-35 divide to the east side.

The fact that **Franklin BBQ** (512-653-1187; www.franklinbarbecue.com) has sold out of meat every single day since it opened in 2009 should impress you. If that doesn't, the line outside the door and snaking around the block just might. Aaron Franklin started serving his piping hot brisket from a food truck and quickly expanded it into a restaurant; demand hasn't slowed one bit. Meats are served with purple cabbage slaw and mustard-based potato salad. There are even some wonderful pies and Dublin Dr. Pepper. The sign out front says they're open from "11 AM

Pulled pork sandwich at Franklin's in East Austin

until out of food," and food this good goes fast!

Juan in a Million (512-472-3872; www.juaninamillion.com), on East Cesar Chavez, makes a breakfast burrito to be reckoned with. An enormous mound of eggs, onions, and potatoes, barely contained in a flour tortilla and priced to sell, the "Don Juan" is the sort of dining experience some walk away from and others run toward. Either way, it's hard not to appreciate the warm welcome and hearty handshake from the owner.

On East 11th Street, the **Blue Dahlia** (512-542-9542; www.bluedahlia bistro.com) is a sweet French bistro that's both simple and special. The cozy backyard terrace is a big draw, and folks like to dine al fresco on fancy *tartines*. The brie with walnuts and apricot preserves or the *chevre*, with olive tapenade, roasted red pepper, and

Franklin Barbecue in Austin

parmesan are lovely appetizers. Diners also enjoy the fresh pastas, unfussy fish dishes, and refreshing soups.

Casa Columbia (512-495-9425; www.casa-columbia.com) serves wonderful fresh ceviche, beef *arepas*—little corn flour patties topped with shredded beef—and *pechuga rellena*, chicken breast stuffed with cheese, mushrooms, and spinach and served with black beans, perfectly cooked fried plantains, and slices of ripe avocado on the side. The restaurant is tucked into a retro-fitted East Austin house on East Seventh Street, and the tasty, homemade food and casual, cozy dining room make it feel a bit like grandma's house.

Also on East Seventh, but farther west, **Joe's Bakery & Mexican Food** (512-472-0017; www.joesbakery.com) has no-frills, family-style Mexican food, including hot and spicy *migas* in the morning and all sorts of Mexican pastries. Open only for breakfast and lunch, Joe's has been feeding Austinites for over 50 years.

When the folks at the **Eastside Café** (512-476-5858; www.eastside cafeaustin.com), on Manor Road, say "fresh," they mean, quite literally, "We are on our way out the back kitchen door to dig around in our on-site organic garden and pick the ingredients just for you!" Now that's fresh. The menu leans toward the free-spirited and health-conscious, with the grilled ruby trout with a shitake mushroom ginger cream sauce, wild mushroom crepes with walnuts, ricotta, and jack cheese, and salmon dumplings with a spicy yellow coconut curry sauce being several examples. The chef's specials chalked on the blackboard change daily.

Also on Manor Road, **Hoover's** (512-479-5006; www.hooverscooking .com) is honest-to-goodness cooking inspired by owner/chef Hoover Alexander's mother, Dorothy, and his Texas roots, which run five generations deep. For diners this translates into great chicken-fried steak, meat loaf, char-broiled catfish, and Elgin sausage from down the road a piece, served with mashed potatoes made from scratch and jalapeño creamed spinach and washed down with homemade lemonade. Whether it's BBQ smothered with pickles, onions, and sauce, chicken-fried chicken breast smothered in a homemade cream gravy, or fresh fruit pie smothered in Blue Bell ice cream, Hoover's is just aching to smother you with their comfort food the same way your grandmother might smother you with love—in a good way! Austin loves Hoover's for its fantastic no-nonsense food served in a no-frills dining room and no-holds-barred use of the good stuff.

WEST END
CLARKSVILLE
NORTH LAMAR

Residential in feel and dotted with commercial centers that are home to restaurants, art galleries, and antiques shops, the West End, Clarksville, and the nearby stretch of North Lamar are wonderful, less urban options for diners who might like to eat and take a stroll through leafy, local neighborhoods. Austin is a small enough city that "North Austin" really means only several miles north of center, a 10- to 15-minute drive, for which you will be richly rewarded with great local fare well off the beaten tourist path. The restaurants in this section stretch up North Lamar to 45th Street.

Finding themselves in cattle country, many visitors to Austin set out in search of a steak. **Austin Land and Cattle** aims to please (512-472-1813;

www.austinlandandcattlecompany
.com). Ribeye, filet mignon, top sirloin, New York strip, and the extraordinary 2-pound T-bone, served with the chef's choice of vegetables and your choice of potato or rice, are sure to satisfy any craving while setting you back close to $40. On the menu for non-red-meat eaters are chicken, seafood, and pasta dishes, and vegetarian diners will be relieved to discover that Austin Land and Cattle also serves a plump and juicy giant portobello mushroom steak. And for dessert, the tart, fresh raspberry pie served with homemade whipped cream is a sweet ending. On North Lamar near 12th Street.

Farther north on Lamar, aptly named **Wink** (512-482-8868; www.wink restaurant.com) is personal, intimate, and flirty, with food so deceptively simple and earnestly pure you feel as if you are experiencing taste for the first time. Samples from a recent menu include roasted quail with ginger quinoa, shiitakes, baby leeks and golden raisin sauce, and a sauté of monkfish with cauliflower, alba mushrooms, amaranth, and pistachio oil emulsion. Simple yet complex, unfussy yet anything but ordinary. The extensive and carefully chosen wine list only heightens the experience, and, for dessert, Wink's lemon meringue pot is a revelation. The dining room, with crisp white tablecloths offset by a sweet-potato-colored wall and mobiles of semi-translucent "eyes" hanging from the ceiling, is both stylish and comfortable. Wink is simple done perfectly. Or, perfection simply done.

Uchiko (512.916.4808; www.uchi austin.com) sits on North Lamar between 42nd and 43rd Streets. Chef Tyson Cole's second restaurant roughly translates as "offspring of Uchi" and is every bit as inspired as its namesake. The theme here is "Japanese farm-

house" and everything from the décor to the dishes embodies a down-to-earth simplicity. The cuisine is vibrant, honest, intense, absolutely delicious, and worth every penny. The menu is perfectly balanced. While every item is a taste revelation, be sure to wrangle at least a sample of the wagyu beef seared over Japanese river rock, the Brussels sprouts with lemon chile, and the fried milk dessert. Don't be shy about asking for recommendations from the sushi menu. After all, you wouldn't come to a place like Uchicko to hold back.

Fortunately for the rest of us, some people have vision enough to create the things we all grow to love,

Wink on North Lamar

and such is the case with **Fonda San Miguel** (512-459-4121; www.fondasan miguel.com), located on North Loop Boulevard just off Burnet Road. Started in 1975 by Tom Gilliland and Miguel Ravago, who were undaunted by the scarcity of ingredients north of the border at the time or the public's skepticism, Fonda San Miguel won over diners one homemade tortilla and fresh lime margarita at a time. Starters include a hot corn soup with cheese and roasted poblano peppers, a nopal cactus salad with chopped tomatoes and onions with *queso fresco,* and a *chile con queso* that has never, ever been violated by the addition of Velveeta. Main courses offer a choice of rotisserie broiled meats, filet of fish broiled with *achiote*, a bright and earthy spice, variations of the *chile relleno*—including one with spinach, goat cheese, raisins, and pine nuts— and *Pollo Pibil,* chicken baked in a banana leaf, a Yucatan specialty. Its legendary Sunday brunches are sublime— the perfect chance to sample a huge array of dishes and delicacies to your heart's content. To celebrate its 30th anniversary, Fonda San Miguel wrote a cookbook as functional, beautiful, and enjoyable as the restaurant.

UT/HYDE PARK

Bright, light, funky, and friendly, the **Kerbey Lane Café** (512-451-1436; www.kerbeylanecafe.com) started in 1980 in the minds of two UT grads looking for a healthy, affordable, and casual spot to eat in Austin. Over 25 years later, the idea has proved to be such a good one that there are now four area locations, each with its own distinct identity, but all serving Kerbey Lane's exhaustive menu 24/7. The food here is healthy, creative, and affordable. The huge buttermilk, ginger-

bread, blueberry, or apple whole wheat pancakes are very popular, as are the French toast and its signature sticky muffin, a gooey sticky bun/muffin hybrid. On the entrée menu, the pecan crusted trout with peach vinaigrette, served with braised spinach brightened with lemon and a side of sweet potato fries, is a standout. Additionally, there are inventive sandwiches, hearty soups, meal-sized salads, and the usual Tex-Mex roster of enchiladas, quesadillas, and tacos, each with its own health-food spin. In an effort to serve super-fresh produce, Kerbey Lane has partnered with an independently owned area farm and now grows some of its own. The owners' energetic philanthropy has benefited many communities within their beloved Austin.

The closer you get to UT, the more likely you'll find sandwich shops. One local favorite is **Fricano's** (512-482-9980; www.fricanosdeli.com). The Will da' Beast, a house specialty, involves mountains of pastrami, a liberal amount of garlic herb spread, and grilling. The pesto and curry chicken salads are two specials to watch for, and the Reubens are probably the best in Austin (they have the trophy to back that up).

Foodheads (512-420-8400; www .foodheads.com), in a cute little house-turned-café, is a fantastic place to stop for lunch. Try the pork tenderloin baguette with smoked Gouda cheese and a sweet-n-spicy apple relish or the vegetarian grilled squash and fresh mozzarella sandwich with cilantro pesto and a spritz of blackberry balsamic vinaigrette.

Dirty Martin's Place (512-477-3173; www.dirtymartins.com), known simply as Dirty's, is a venerable Austin institution near campus that has cooked up countless burgers to feed the scores of UT students who every day buzz by the white frame drive-in looking for that perfect lunch, dinner, or late-night snack. Counter seating gives you a great view of the griddle. Russet fries and thickly breaded onion rings round out an experience that some would say is a must. Speaking of burgers, head over to **Burger Tex II** (512-477-8433) on Guadalupe for one of its outstanding bulgogi burgers—strips of thinly sliced beef marinated in a soy sauce, ginger, and garlic marinade that are served on a homemade bun. The saucy twang keeps diners coming back for more.

Also located on Guadalupe, but south of UT, the **Clay Pit** (512-322-5131; www.claypit.com) features contemporary Indian curries, grill items, seafood, and a range of vegetarian dishes spiced with fresh ginger, cumin, garlic, and tangy tamarind chutney of varying degrees of heat that are sure to please any palate. The house specialty, *Khuroos-E-Tursh,* is a moist chicken breast stuffed with seasoned spinach, mushrooms, onion, and cheese, and simmered in a rich cashew-almond cream sauce that is both sweet and savory. Vegetarian options are plentiful. Prompt, friendly service and the restaurant's sophisticated interior design, complete with thick cloth napkins and pleasantly low lighting, give it an upscale feel, while large portions, modest prices, and a plentiful daily lunch buffet make the Clay Pit a great value.

Meandering into Hyde Park, the **Hyde Park Bar and Grill** (512-458-3168; www.hpbng.com) serves burgers, sandwiches, pastas, and any number of southern comfort foods in a slightly upscale business-casual atmosphere. But what sets this place apart are its French fries—strings of Idaho potatoes, dipped in buttermilk, dredged in seasoned flour, and fried in peanut oil

just before arriving, hot and crisp, at your table. The Hyde Park Bar and Grill stays open late, making it both a neighborhood hangout and a citywide favorite for nocturnal noshing. The enormous fork marks the spot.

Farther Afield
Farther out of town, overlooking Lake Travis, is **Hudson's on the Bend** (512-266-1369; www.hudsonsonthebend .com). While the diamondback rattlesnake cakes crusted with pistachios and the espresso-chocolate-chile-rubbed elk sound exciting, it is really the ingredients of the Five Species Creature Feature Antipasto appetizer for two that pushes the limits of adventurous eating. They are pheasant pâté, pastrami kangaroo, candied smoked

Hyde Park Bar and Grill

Ice Cream Dream

Amy's Ice Cream (512-458-6895; www.amysicecream.com). An Austin original, Amy's makes tons of super-premium ice cream so thick and creamy you can barely lick it, much less scoop it out of a dish with a little plastic spoon. A changing roster of flavors includes everything from the subtle mainstay Sweet Cream to Blueberry Muffin and boozy Shiner Bock. You'll see shops on Sixth Street, South Congress, and even in the airport. Check Web site for other locations.

salmon, venison sausage, and pecan-grilled alligator. The menu always reflects the season, as illustrated by the summertime specials of watermelon wild boar and antelope served with cantaloupe, which tastes as spunky as it sounds. Needless to say, folks who love to eat fearlessly will fall in love with Hudson's on the Bend, but those who steer more toward the straight and narrow should not be deterred; Hudson's does most everything well and has a special way of making more mundane dishes seem just a tiny bit daring. The options on what they call the Way Too Many Wines List are endless, as is the view.

Nightlife

Best places to go after hours

Austin is well known for the scene on Sixth Street, roughly bounded by Red River Street to the east and Congress Avenue to the west and taking in a several-block strip of bars, restaurants, and clubs on Fifth Street. The adjacent Warehouse District, on Fourth and Fifth Streets between Congress Avenue and Guadalupe Street, is also hopping at night, and together these areas have an irresistible nighttime allure for students and twentysomethings who pack the streets with boisterous revelry. Radiating out from Sixth Street, things mellow out considerably. Slightly east, on Red River Street, a more local scene prevails, and farther south, the South Congress neighborhood offers individual music venues and late-night eateries.

Practically speaking, clubs and bars card people religiously; so whether you consider it a hassle or a compliment, have your ID at the ready. Those under 21 will not be allowed to drink but are sometimes allowed in for the entertainment; call in advance for the official policy. While credit cards are accepted for sit-down drinks and meals, cash is generally used for tips, cover charges, and the $2 beer specials. Since ATM machines in these areas see a lot of use, they are frequently out of cash, so consider bringing with you what you plan to spend.

For up-to-the-minute information on Austin's very active nightlife, pick up one of the free copies of the *Austin Chronicle* available around town at bookstores, breakfast and lunch spots, and sidewalk kiosks, or visit its Web site at www.austin chronicle.com. Additionally, Austin 360 at www.austin360.com is a comprehensive online guide to nightlife, movies, entertainment, and dining, and the Calendar section of the *Austin American-Statesman,* Austin's local newspaper, is accessible online at www.statesman.com and lists more of the same.

The scene comes alive at night on Sixth Street

The line between music venues, bars, and restaurants is blurred in Austin, with many offering a variety of everything. Austinites love to debate the triumphs and shortcomings of the city's best-loved nightlife, but one thing is certain—the classics are classics, and the rest aspire to be.

MUSIC

The "Live Music Capital of the World" doesn't disappoint. Venues are listed alphabetically below.

Antone's (512-800-4628; www.antones.net) has been around the block a few times. Opened by Clifford Antone in 1975, the club has relocated several times before landing in its current home just blocks from where it started. Throughout the years, Antone's has earned a reputation for serving up the finest blues around, and the club, not to mention the music store (see "Shopping," above) and recording label, is still a hands-down favorite among aficionados. Sadly, Antone himself passed away in May 2006, breaking the city's heart, but the music he dedicated his life to nurturing stills envelopes the club he built, and for that Austin will always be grateful. A few blocks away, the large and loud **Austin Music Hall** (512-289-1777; www.musichallaustin.com) is a good place to catch big concerts with 2,999 other music lovers.

A huge open-air venue nestled into the Hill Country, shaded by hundreds of live oak trees, **The Backyard** (512-651-5033; www.thebackyard.net) hosts music events filled with pure magic. With multilevel decks, patios, and a grassy knoll, the Backyard is so relaxed that it feels like, well, your own backyard—except, of course, Willie Nelson, Norah Jones, the Neville Brothers, and Lyle Lovett probably wouldn't play at your house.

Austin City Limits

In 1975 local PBS affiliate KLRU, riding the wave of the city's burgeoning music scene, began taping live performances of singers, songwriters, and musicians to broadcast, calling its show *Austin City Limits.* Simple production and an intimate stage allowed the music to stand on its own, and the combination was an immediate hit. Since its inception, the show has hosted more than five hundred artists, some well known and others less so, but all immensely talented. *Austin City Limits* has brought a tremendous range of music to its viewers, from country and bluegrass to blues, folk, and zydeco. Watching the show is both a pleasure and an education.

It is possible to watch a live taping of *Austin City Limits,* but only a precious few have the privilege each year. Visit www.acltv.com for details of the recording schedule and complicated ticket distribution process. The show used to be taped in a small studio on the sixth floor of the University of Texas College of Communication; it is now on display at the Rock and Roll Hall of Fame and Museum in Cleveland, Ohio. The music lives on at *Austin City Limits'* new digs inside the impressive, state-of-the-art Moody Theater. While chances of seeing a taping of the show might be slim, visitors are able to tour the studio (512-475 9077; www .klru.org) and purchase tickets to see extraordinary musicians perform year-round at the Moody Theater; visit www.acl-live.com for a schedule of performances. Don't miss the fantastic Austin City Limits Music Festival (see "Festivals," above) in September.

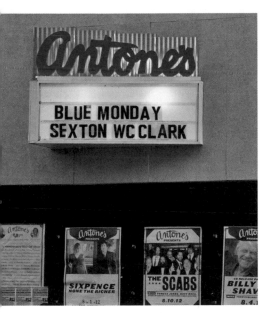

Antone's Nightclub, legendary live music venue

Pull up to the nondescript, low-slung building on South Lamar that houses the **Broken Spoke** (512-442-6189; www.brokenspokeaustintx.com) and you won't guess that you are sidling up to a venerable Austin legend. The Broken Spoke has been hosting honky-tonk a good long time, and they've booked everyone from Tex Ritter to Willie Nelson, George Strait to Jerry Jeff Walker, and they have the pictures on the wall to prove it. The Broken Spoke sells chicken-fried steaks, burgers, and the like, which you can wash down with a Lone Star longneck before hitting the dance floor.

Not many university campuses have a music venue with a national reputation for superb acoustics and a list of past performers that reads like a Who's Who of the country, folk, and

Outlaws

Some of the best portraits of Texas are sung by its family of musicians, many of whom have earned national recognition for the genius of their technique, the depth of their songwriting, and the sheer amount of heart in their songs. "Outlaw" country music, which took roots in the bars and honky-tonks of Austin and bloomed prolifically throughout the 1970s, offers up some great examples.

In the 1960s a disillusioned Willie Nelson decided he'd had his fill of predictable drinking and cheating songs shined to a high gloss in Nashville studios, and quit Tennessee for Texas. In Austin he met renegades Waylon Jennings, Billy Joe Shaver, Kris Kristofferson, and Townes Van Zandt, among others, and they put their guitars and songs together and invented the genre of outlaw country.

While the name came from Jennings's 1972 song "Ladies Love Outlaws," the spirit came directly from the musicians themselves. Intent on bucking the system, they wrote raw country music influenced by the revolutionary rock and folk music of their era, and their intensely personal lyrics struck a chord with listeners. Powered by fierce individuality and abundant talent, this antiestablishment music broke into the mainstream, influencing countless musicians along the way.

Statue of Willie Nelson outside the Moody Theater

Besides the pioneers listed above, Johnny Cash, Guy Clark, David Allan Coe, Jessi Colter, Joe Ely, Jimmy Dale Gilmore, Butch Hancock, Johnny Rodriguez, Kimmie Rhodes, and Jerry Jeff Walker, though they are not all from Texas, are classic outlaws. Stop in at any local record store and have a listen.

singer-songwriter circuit. Then again, when that university is UT-Austin, it all makes sense. The **Cactus Café** (512-475-6515; www.utexas.edu/student/txunion/ae /cactus) opened in 1979 in the Student Union and has since hosted such musicians as Lyle Lovett, Lucinda Williams, Alison Kraus, the Dixie Chicks, Nanci Griffith, and Loudon Wainwright III, to name a few. A café by day with pizza, baked goods, and light lunch fare, the Cactus transforms into an intimate coffeehouse by night, serving coffee and beer. Tickets are first come, first served unless otherwise noted on its Web site. Advance tickets are available for special attractions, booked at the larger Texas Union Theatre and the much larger Texas Union Ballroom. Call the Texas Box Office (512-477-6060) for more information.

The only place in Austin where you get to pick the music, the **Casino el Camino** (512-469-9330; www.casinoelcamino.net) on Sixth Street has ruled the realm of self-serve sounds for years. Order up a table full of burgers, hot dogs, buffalo wings—or a grilled eggplant sandwich with olive tapenade for vegetarians—and french fries, pop quarter after quarter into the legendary jukebox, and sit back and enjoy your customized evening soundtrack. That is, until someone else's intervenes.

The **Cedar Street Courtyard** (512-495-9669; www.cedarstreetaustin.com) on Fourth Street mixes martinis with live music in its outdoor courtyard. Consider kick-starting your night with the Koffee Kerouac—a Fris vodka, Kahlua, and Bailey's creation with a shot of coffee. Or, mellow out with a Zilker—Stoli vodka shaken with Midori melon liqueur. Smoking is permitted. If the party gets rained on, things tend to move next door to Málaga Tapas and Bar (see "Local Flavors," below), which is owned by the same folks.

The **Continental** (512-441-2444; www.continentalclub.com) has been a heavy hitter in the live-music scene since it opened in 1957, but its current owner is responsible for giving it the retro look and feel that have become such a part of its identity today. While it is still known for booking great music almost every night of the week, what makes this place really popular are its rockin' happy hours, most notably on Tuesday, when the fun starts at 4 PM. The Continental is smack in the middle of SoCo, so it's always a good time.

Even though it is in a basement, the **Elephant Room** (512-473-2279; www.elephantroom.com) is the high-water mark for jazz in Austin. Identifiable by the small neon sign that glows from a window at sidewalk level, the club is intimate, dim, and alluring in the way that these sorts of venues should be. Twenty different draft beers and plenty of high-quality acts make this Congress Avenue venue a great alternative to the Sixth Street scene.

While **Elysium** (512-474-2285; www.elysiumonline.net) "encourages fabulousness always," you can wear anything you'd like to this good-natured industrial Goth dance lair on Red River Street. Weekends (Thursday through Saturday) are reserved for live music, and Wednesday and Sunday are earmarked for popular throwback '80s theme nights.

Emo's (512-800-4628; www.emosaustin.com) has two venues in Austin. The Emo's on Red River Street has two music stages, one inside and one out, a beer garden, and a bar, which makes it well equipped for its admitted specialty: drunken debauchery. The bands here tend to be loud, the energy high, and the patrons young. Emo's is known for top-notch, almost-nightly bookings and is certainly one venue to keep your eye on for local talent or rising stars. By comparison, Emo's East on East Riverside, south of Lady Bird Lake, is bigger and more spacious, with better views of the stage, a new sound system, usable bathrooms, and air conditioning. Either is a trade-off; take your pick.

For 25 years, **Maggie Mae's** (512-478-8541; www.maggiemaesaustin.com) has been keeping Sixth Street rocking with that archetypal college town combination of

Stevie Ray Vaughan Memorial

A tribute to the Austin blues-man whose life was cut short tragically when he died in a heli-copter crash in 1990 at the age of 35, the statue of Stevie Ray Vaughan was placed on the south shore of Lady Bird Lake by the city of Austin in 1993. At the time of his death, Vaughan had released five albums and won three Grammy Awards, and an additional two were awarded posthumously. He was a revered musician, and tracks from the solo albums *Family Style* and *The Sky Is Crying*, along with those recorded with his band Double Trouble, *Couldn't Stand the Weather, Soul to Soul, Texas Flood,* and *Live at Carnegie Hall,* are radio main-stays. Vaughan left a legacy of heartfelt music to his fans; for Austin his statue is an expres-sion of love and respect for all its musicians.

beer and cover bands. The maze of rooms and outdoor areas, each with its own music and scene, makes this bar an endless party.

Free-flowing draft beer and nightly music, mostly singer-songwriters and Texas talent, make the **Saxon Pub** (512-448-2552; www.thesaxonpub.com) on South Lamar a terrific spot to kick back with the locals. The free happy-hour con-certs Tuesday through Friday start at 6. Darts, pool, sports on the big screen, and free WiFi keep patrons busy in between sets. Great music and down-to-earth affability put the Saxon Pub on the short list of classic Austin hangouts.

Scholz Garten (512-474-1958; www.scholzgarten.net) has been in business since 1866, and this German *Biergarten* is the place to stop in, whet your whistle, and listen to some oompah music courtesy of the house Wurst Band. Or maybe you'll just want to join the pandemonium of the crowds on game night. Located on San Jacinto, just south of campus.

The story of **Stubb's Bar-B-Q's** (512-480-8341; www.stubbsbbq.com) begin-nings is a tale unto itself. With personality, talent, and sheer will, Christopher

"Stubb" Stubblefied managed to cook his way from Lubbock, through the Korean War with the 96th Field Artillery (the last all-black army infantry), to the center of the burgeoning music scene in Austin in the 1970s. Combining two loves, BBQ and music, Stubb's restaurant was soon booking musicians like Muddy Waters, John Lee Hooker, Willie Nelson, Johnny Cash, and many others who loved playing the outdoor venue to the sweet smell of slow-cookin' 'cue. These days, a more commercial and streamlined Stubb's on Red River Street is a major music venue and sells sauce in a bottle, but the old Austin favorite remains 100 percent pure Texas.

A former Mexican restaurant located at a bend on West Fourth Street, La Zona Rosa (512-478-7211; www.lazonarosa.com) now serves as a major music venue with two stages—the smaller in a club atmosphere and the larger just wide-open space—both filled nightly with big sound and wall-to-wall fans. A great place to catch an A-list act up close, but get there early 'cause everyone already knows.

DRINKS

Sometimes the best way to get to know a town is just to sit down and have a drink with the locals. The following are a few suggestions of where to do so, scattered about town.

Downtown/Warehouse District

Swanky **Bar Congress** (512-827-2755; www.congressaustin.com), located next to Congress and Second Bar and Kitchen (see page 41) on the ground floor of a posh high rise, serves up some of the fanciest cocktails in Austin. Drinks here aren't cheap, but neither are they ordinary. Cocktails are a mix of top-shelf ingredients, old-school skill, and plenty of creativity. Follow up with nibbles—the chicken fried olives, stuffed with pimento blue cheese, are succulent, savory, and salty.

Bringing a little spice to Downtown, gourmet hot dog joint **Frank** (see "Local Flavors," below) serves up some ultra-creative and super-tasty drinks on Colorado near Fifth. Like bacon? Try the Red Headed Stranger, a combination of house-made, bacon-infused Tito's Vodka, and Bloody Mary mix, that's garnished with bacon, cheddar cheese, jalapeño stuffed olive, and peperoncini. Frank is open for Happy Hour and dinner, but not late night bar hours.

A quick glance at the menu and it's obvious that **Max's Wine Dive** (512-904-0111; www.maxswinedive.com) on San Jacinto isn't a dive at all. Instead you'll find fantastic southern comfort food and fancy drinks to go with. Diners rave about the jalapeño and buttermilk-marinated fried chicken that's crispy, juicy, and spicy all at the same time; Max recommends having it with champagne.

Rainey Street, located in a little slice of downtown sandwiched between Lady Bird Lake and I-35 south of César Chávez, offers a trio of bars. **Lustre Pearl** (512-469-0400; www.lustrepearlaustin.com) is ensconced in an old house; the living room is now the bar, and the backyard is a hipster hangout where you'll find a juke box, ping pong, and an onsite taco truck, not to mention plenty of picnic tables, lawn chairs, and a few hula hoops scattered underneath the white lights in the trees. **Clive Bar** (512-494-4120; www.clivebaraustin.com) has that country-meets-chic-meets-cool vibe. The inside is cozy, with intimate tables, votive candles, and artsy recycled bottle chandeliers, and the spacious deck out back is a charmer.

Clive has a nice selection of brews on tap. **Bar 96** (512-433-6604; www.96 austin.com) is the most laid-back of the bunch, with plenty of board games, beer, food truck food, and sports on the big screen. Basically, stopping by Bar 96 feels like crashing a twentysomething friend's house.

The Warehouse District has matured into a trendy place to stop in for a drink.

Part bar, part café, part coffee shop, and part lounge, **Halcyon** (512-472-9637; www.halcyonaustin.com), on West 4th at Lavaca, caters to a laid-back crowd with everything from liqueurs to lattes, with plenty of long necks and a chocolate espresso martini thrown in. The make-your-own s'mores are a hit. Down the street, **Ginger Man** (512-473-8801; www .gingermanpub.com) offers a huge selection of bottled microbrews, even more on tap rotation, a wide variety of local labels and national favorites, and a pleasant, low-key environment to drink them in. The mixologists at posh **Péché** (512-494-4011; www

.pecheaustin.com) on West 4th specialize in "pre-prohibition style cocktails" with top-shelf gin, whisky, vodka, rum, tequila, and even absinthe. Try the mussels in vodka and lemon broth or the crispy fries sprinkled with black truffle salt.

Nearby, the **Málaga Tapas Bar** (512-236-8020; www.malagatapasbar.com) on Second Street just west of Guadalupe has a sophisticated, loftlike atmosphere complete with hardwood floors, exposed brick, and walls of built-in wooden wine racks. The menu includes various tastings, such as the *queso de cabra frito*—breaded and fried goat cheese cakes with a red onion marmalade, drizzled with honey—all perfectly complemented by the 50-bottle menu of wine by the glass. Candlelit tables add romance. A few blocks away on the corner of 4th and Nueces, **Mulberry** (512-320-0297; www.mulberryaustin.com) works well for evening drinks paired with bacon-wrapped, gorgonzola-stuffed figs or a mix-n-match cheese plate. Brunch-goers single out the brioche French toast with cardamom syrup as a favorite. Snug and intimate, Mulberry is a nice spot for a date.

On the super-casual-but-not-divey side, stop in **Opal Divine's Freehouse** (512-477-3308; www.opaldivines.com), on Sixth Street at Rio Grande, for a good selection of wine and spirits, including 65 kinds of single-malt scotch, not to mention an assortment of mixed drinks and a range of specialty beers for those who like to mix it up. The large menu is filled with burgers and Tex-Mex items, and the casual outdoor seating is a plus.

South Congress

South Austin has plenty of places to stop in for a drink. Step off busy South Congress Avenue and into the serene courtyard of the **Hotel San José** (see "Pick Your Spot," above), where everyone is welcome for drinks. **Hopdoddy** (see page 43) has a nice selection of craft beers on tap, chosen to complement its fantastic gourmet burgers. Try a watermelon martini at the **South Congress Café** (see page 45) or a stiff, unsweetened, minty mojito at **Güero's Taco Bar** (see page 44). **The Continental** (see page 57) and the **Broken Spoke** (see page 55) top the list of dive bars that double as venerable music venues.

Head west to South First Street and pop in at **Freddie's** or **Shady Grove** on Barton Springs, both of which offer casual drinks and food with plenty of shade trees under which to enjoy them. Epicureans will enjoy **Barley Swine** (512-394-8150; www.barleyswine.com), a cozy gastropub on South Lamar featuring a fantastic drink menu with a nice representation of local brew and ingenious "small plates" to match. Shop for home furnishing with a glass of wine in hand at **Aviary** (512-916-4445; www.aviarylounge.com), the boutique/wine bar hybrid in South Austin. A host of special events and tastings showcase the lounge's wine list, appetizers, and free spirit.

UT/Hyde Park

Predictably, the watering holes around the university cater to students; the offerings mature the deeper you press into Hyde Park and surrounding neighborhoods.

Spider House (512-480-9562; www.spiderhousecafe.com), a student hangout located just north of the University of Texas campus near the intersection of Guadalupe and 30th Streets, serves some food but also dozens of hot and cold caffeinated drinks, frozen fruit smoothies and shakes, bottled beer, draft beer, and a coffee martini known as the Brown Recluse. Grab a L'Orangina—Orangina plus a splash of gin or vodka—or a glass of its refreshing signature sangria, and relax on the backyard patio under the oaks.

Nearby, **Trudy's** (512-477-2935; www.trudys.com) is a student favorite, mixing strong drinks and some good, gooey Tex-Mex alongside. Diners agree that the stuffed avocado is a must. Pair it with a Mexican Martini or a house margarita for the full Trudy's experience.

Just north of campus, the **Crown & Anchor Pub** (512-322-9168; www.crown andanchorpub.com) has pool tables, video games, dart boards, and plenty of seating. You'll also find good grub and plenty of beer to wash it down with—30-plus taps and a hundred bottles and pitchers of local brew.

Tucked into a neighborhood a block west of Central Market on Lamar and 42nd Street, a short but well-removed drive from the downtown bar scene, the **Draught House** (512-452-6258; www.draughthouse.com) seems like a leap across the pond. The British feel of this pub and beer garden tends to be a good fit for folks who prefer a neighborhood watering hole. There are dozens of beers on tap—both local and guest brews—and plenty of bottles to choose from.

In nearby Hyde Park, the offerings at **Vino Vino** (512-465-9282; www.vinovino tx.com) include fantastic wines, artisanal cheeses and plump mussels served with hot frites and a dollop of aioli. Try the orange olive oil cake with citrus tuile and avocado ice cream for dessert. Prices, but not quality, come down during Happy Hour, making it a great time to stop in. Both **Asti** (512-451-1218; www.astiaustin

.com) and **Fino** (512-474-2905; www.finoaustin.com) are sophisticated restaurants and wine bars serving upscale trattoria food and luscious desserts for both lunch and dinner. Drinks, noshes, and great Happy Hour specials make each appealing.

East Austin

A selection of trendy dive bars have sprung up along East Sixth Street, part of East Austin's rapidly evolving nightlife scene. The **Liberty** (512-600-4791), the **Grackle** (512-520-8148), and the quirky **Shangri-La** (512-524-4291; www.shangrilaaustin .com) have cheap beer, pool tables, outdoor space, and a great Asian fusion food truck onsite. Go more upscale and enjoy wine, cheese, and charcuterie on the lovely patio at **Uncorked** (512-524-2809; www.uncorkedtastingroom.com). The pricey **East Side Showroom** gastropub (512-467-4280; www.eastsideshowroom .com) has fantastic food, drinks, décor, live music, and the feel of an old-school speakeasy.

The Great Outdoors

Outdoor adventures and activities

Austinites just like being outdoors, in the year-round fantastic weather, on the miles of trails, and in the swimming holes. There are many opportunities for recreation in the city, and when you factor in the proximity of the Highland Lakes and the state parks of the Hill Country (see Hill Country chapter), the list of options grows exponentially.

Central Austin

Zilker Metropolitan Park and Preserve (512-867-3080; www.austintexas.gov) is Austin's playground. The 351-acre urban park just south of Lady Bird Lake and the Colorado River encompasses the Zilker Botanical Gardens, Zilker Nature Preserve, and Barton Springs Pool. It is dotted with sports fields, picnic tables, children's playgrounds, and a miniature railroad, the Zilker Zephyr. The park hosts many of the city's music, arts, and cultural events, including the Austin City Limits Music Festival and the Zilker Park Kite Festival. Miles of hike-and-bike trails traverse the park and connect with those of its neighbor, Lake. Zilker Park is a stop on the free Tour the Town weekend bus service. Parking is free on weekdays; on Saturday, Sunday, and holidays from March through Labor Day there is a $3 fee per car, collected at any gate, and valid throughout the day at any parking lot within Zilker Park. **Zilker Nature Preserve**, an expansive 60-acre preserve with meadows, a trickling stream, and an outstanding view of Austin from the Overlook Trail, is located just west of Loop 360.

    Zilker Botanical Garden (512-477-8672; www.zilkergarden.org), with its verdant terraced gardens, winding stone paths, and great views of the city and hills, is a pleasant place to stroll. Educational features prove there's more to the garden than just smelling the roses. The Green Garden features native and adapted plants and flowers best suited to the Central Texas climate, while the Hartman Prehistoric Garden conceals a life-size bronze sculpture of *Ornithomimus*, the dinosaur whose tracks were discovered here in 1992, nestled in among plants representing the Cretaceous period.

    The hot Texas sun can be a great equalizer. **Barton Springs** (512-867-3080;

Ornithomimus in the Hartman Prehistoric Garden of the Zilker Botanical Garden

www.austintexas.gov) attracts just about everyone in Austin with a swimsuit and a few dollars to pony up for a chance to cool off. It has always been a gathering place. Native Americans believed it held healing powers, and the Spanish, impressed and inspired by it, set up temporary missions here in the 1730s. The springs became a city park in 1917, and dams were added in 1929 and 1932, creating the swimming area. Today, Barton Springs is still a constant and bracing 68 degrees, a fact people approach with strategies ranging from dipping a toe in the cool dark water to belly flopping off the diving board. The expansive, grassy lawn rimmed with trees is a big draw. Unless you are a dog-lover, consider paying the fee for entrance to the gated portion of the springs, where the water is deep and the grassy knoll clean. The shallow free-and-open-to-the-public section below the dam tends to be overrun with canines fetching, splashing, and frolicking with their owners. And while the dog population runs high, the Barton Springs salamander has declined to the point of critical endangerment in this, its only known habitat. The little lungless salamander is now a protected endangered species, which means that Zilker Park's managers, scientists, and various environmental agencies are doing all they can to support its survival.

Take a ride on the little green **Zilker Zephyr**. This miniature train makes a leisurely 25-minute loop through the park, past Barton Springs and Lady Bird Lake before heading back to the playground in front of the Barton Springs Pool entrance.

Scoot underneath MoPac and you'll find the **Austin Nature and Science Center** (512-974-3888; www.austintexas.gov) just west of Zilker Park. School-age children enjoy this hands-on place, where you can dig up bones in the Dino Pit, be an "eco-detective" on the path around the nearby pond, use a science lab, and see some native Texas animals up close, courtesy of the center's program to care for animals who cannot be returned to the wild.

Right across the street the **SPLASH! Into the Edwards Aquifer** (512-478-3170; www.austintexas.gov) interpretative center at the old Barton Springs Pool Bathhouse does a nice job of explaining the fragility of the region's underground ecosystem through interactive exhibits.

When the city of Austin reconstructed the Congress Avenue Bridge in 1980, its architects unwittingly created a perfect **Mexican free-tailed bat** (www.batcon.org) habitat. Before long, close to a million migratory bats began using the nooks and crannies under the bridge decking as their summer home. From April to October, the bats live, give birth, and raise their young under the bridge, taking flight each night at dusk to scour the greater metro area for tens of thousands of pounds of insects *per night;* they head back to Mexico at the first nip of winter winds.

Tumbling water at Zilker Botanical Garden

Once Austin's biggest nuisance—early on there was talk of poisoning the colony—the bats are now its most innovative form of pest control, not to mention one of its most asked-about attractions.

The best time to see the bats is in August. Call the Bat Hotline at 512-327-9721 for information about observing the colony from the *Austin American-Statesman* Bat Observation Center, 305 S. Congress Ave., or the *Bat Boat,* a nightly cruise run either the Capital Cruises Boat Tours (www.capitalcruises.com) or the Lone Star Riverboat (www.lonestarriverboat.com).

The Umlauf Sculpture Gardens (512-445-5582; www.umlaufsculpture.org) is the home of the works of artist Charles Umlauf. A native of Michigan, Charles Umlauf moved with his wife, Angeline, to Texas in 1941, when he took a teaching position with the fledgling University of Texas art department. Forty years and dozens of awards and accolades later, he retired, and in 1985 he and his wife donated their home, studio, and 168 pieces of art to the city of Austin. In 1991 a new museum was built on neighboring land, and today visitors are invited to tour both its interior and grounds. Themes of children, mothers, and docile animals dominate Umlauf's works, and the resulting sculptures tend to be sweet, tender, and lyrical—an especially nice fit for the lush gardens in which they are displayed.

West Austin

Built in 1916, the concrete expanse of **Deep Eddy Pool** (512-472-8546; www.austintexas.gov) was the first outdoor pool in Texas and once part of a larger resort area that included rental cottages, bustling concession stands, and a Ferris wheel.

While all those amusements are long gone, the main attraction remains—the water. The pool is spring-fed, with areas for laps, wading, and just splashing around. The fantastic combination of swimming and a movie make the family-friendly Splash Party Movie Night a big hit in the summertime. The Friends of Deep Eddy (www.deepeddy.org), a crew of dedicated volunteers, have recently undertaken a thorough restoration of the 1936 bathhouse aimed at bringing it back to its former glory. Amenities such as family restrooms, wheelchair and stroller-accessible ramps, and more landscaping will keep the pool and its environs as well used and well loved in the future as they are now.

South Austin

The **Austin Zoo** (512-288-1490; www.austinzoo.org) is really more of an "educational sanctuary" dedicated to the rescue and rehabilitation of animals and education of the public. The zoo was originally known as the Good Day Ranch, a fitting moniker, since 90 percent of the animals at the zoo are rescued, in many cases from the unfortunate "roadside attraction" outfits that dot Texas's highways. There are lions, bears, monkeys, exotic birds, zebras, emus, Texas longhorns, a little petting zoo, and a sweet miniature train, which takes visitors on a 2-mile journey through the surrounding countryside. The zoo is neither large nor elaborate, but well intentioned; consider the price of admission a donation to a worthy cause.

Lady Bird Johnson Wildflower Center

The **Lady Bird Johnson Wild-flower Center** (512-232-0100; www.wildflower.org) is a lovely swath of nature in the midst of the growing Austin suburbs. Proving that it is never too late to follow a dream, on her 70th birthday, December 22, 1982, Lady Bird Johnson and her friend, the actress Helen Hayes, started the center to protect and preserve North America's native plants and diverse natural landscapes. Lady Bird is quoted as once saying, "Ugliness is so grim, a little beauty can help create harmony." Always one to follow words with action, Lady Bird was a tireless environmentalist, promoting the simple idea that we are all custodians of beauty as nature intended it. While its lovely gardens are populated by plants and flowers native to Texas, diligently tended by the center's staff and volunteers, the

Hiking, Biking, Running, Strolling

While Zilker Park provides plenty of opportunities for recreation, outdoor enthusiasts will also enjoy the other gems of Austin's extensive system of parks, hike-and-bike trails, and greenbelts. The city's Parks Department Web site has excellent maps of the greenbelts; see www.austintexas.gov for more details. The following list is not exhaustive, but includes highlights. All these listings offer activities appropriate for any ability level.

Barton Creek Greenbelt This enormous greenbelt, spreading south from Zilker Park then west of Loop 360, includes climbing walls, swimming areas, hike-and-bike trails, and abundant natural scenery.

Bright Leaf Park (www.brightleaf.org) A 200-acre natural area located in central northwest Austin, north of Camp Mabry, offering guided hikes only.

Hike and Bike Trail at Lady Bird Lake (www.ci.austin.tx.us/parks/trails) This hike-and-bike trail runs along the shores of Lady Bird Lake and is dotted with drinking fountains and rudimentary restrooms. A favorite trail for runners and dog walkers.

Mayfield Park Twenty-two peaceful acres with easy-to-navigate trails located beside Laguna Gloria.

McKinney Falls State Park (512-243-1643; www.tpwd.state.tx.us) Straddling the banks of Onion Creek, McKinney Falls is 13 miles southeast of Austin off US 183 and offers swimming, hiking, fishing, camping, and picnicking. When the river is high, the falls are lovely, but drought can lessen them to a trickle.

Mount Bonnell The 785-foot-high mount is a popular place to watch the sun set over the hills. Climb the steep stairs, and behold the wide views of Lady Bird Lake and the West Lake Hills.

Shoal Creek Greenbelt connects with the Hike and Bike Trail at Lady Bird Lake see above) and continues for 4 miles following Shoal Creek. The disc golf course in Pease Park is very popular with twentysomething Austinites.

Veloway (www.veloway.com) A 3-mile paved loop designed specifically for bikers and inline skaters. The trail traverses parkland, and its entrance point is across from the Lady Bird Johnson Wildflower Center.

center, through its Web site and hotline, is a clearinghouse of invaluable information to gardeners throughout the U.S. and Canada. Beyond flowers, the center also models both new and recycled ideas, such as its rainwater harvesting system, which diverts water from the roofs of its structure into several cisterns, supplying 10 to 15 percent of the center's annual water demand. The Wildflower Café serves drinks, sandwiches, and treats, and the gift shop, Wild Ideas, has nifty nature-themed items.

North Austin
Pioneer Farms (512-837-1215; www.pioneerfarms.org) is a collection of pre–Civil War structures, plus some new ones made to look old, arranged on a parcel of land

to re-create some of the look and feel of pioneer life. Within each barn, home, and shop, volunteer interpreters dressed in period costumes go about their work cooking, blacksmithing, spinning cotton into thread, making cheese, and woodworking. The General Store sells reproduction toys. Die-hard history buffs might enjoy taking a class at Pioneer School. Topics range from Dutch-oven cooking to the efficiency of the foot-powered lathe.

RECREATION

A tremendous online resource for all outdoor recreation in Texas is www.texas outside.com.

Baseball

Round Rock Express (512-255-2255; www.roundrockexpress.com). The thrill of minor league baseball. The Express play at the Dell Diamond, located on US 79 in Round Rock, just north of Austin.

Bicycling

Bicycling, both road and mountain biking, is big in Central Texas, especially in Austin and the Hill Country. Rentals are available through Bicycle Sport Shop (512-477-3472; www.bicyclesportshop.com) and University Cyclery (512-474-6696; www.universitycyclery.com).

Cyclist in Austin

Helpful Web sites include:

Austin Cycling Association (www.austincycling.org)

Austin Ridge Riders (www.austinridgeriders.org)

Bike Texas (www.biketexas.org)

Cycle Texas (www.cycletexas.com)

Bird Watching

Austin is a great spot to catch a glimpse of rare, migratory, and native birds. Online, Texas Parks and Wildlife, www.tpwd.state.tx.us, and the Travis County Audubon Society, www.travisaudubon.org, offer a wealth of information. See "Suggested References" in the Information chapter for a selection of bird-watching guides.

Boating, Canoeing, and Kayaking

Canoes, kayaks, and paddleboat rentals are available on Barton Creek or Lady Bird Lake. Fees range from $10–25 an hour.

Austin Canoe and Kayak (512-719-4386; www.austinkayak.com)

Capital Cruises (512-480-9264; www.capitalcruises.com)

The Rowing Dock (512-459-0999; www.rowingdock.com)

Zilker Park Boat Rentals (512-478-3852; www.zilkerboats.com)

Camping

Emma Long Metropolitan Park (512-346-1831; www.austinparks.org) is a favorite, as is **McKinney Falls State Park** (512-243-1643; www.tpwd.state.tx.us), just south of the city. **Camp Ben McCulloch** (512-858-2084; www.campben mcculloch.com) in Driftwood, southwest of the city, was once a reunion camp for Confederate veterans and is now a historic site, campground, and host of the annual Old Settler's Music Festival (see "Festivals," above). The various state parks in the Hill Country, Krause Springs, and the public and private parks surrounding the Highland Lakes offer a variety of camping options (see individual entries in Hill Country chapter).

Climbing

Cypress Valley Canopy Tours (512-264-8880; www.cypressvalleycanopytours.com) Gliding canopy tours in the Hill Country 30 minutes west of Austin. Tour participants use steel zip lines to travel between treetop platforms among old-growth cypress.

      Mountain Madness Rock Climbing School (512-590-2988; www.mtmadness .com) Weekend classes held at Enchanted Rock State Natural Area near Fredericksburg.

Disc Golf

Disc Golf is based on the rules of golf. Players throw a Frisbee-like disc toward a basket hanging approximately 2 feet from the ground, in an effort to "sink" the disc. Points are added for extra throws over par, and the courses tend to have 18 holes, though some have nine and others 27. Disc golf is extraordinarily popular in

Austin; free courses scattered throughout the city. Find out all you need to know about disc golf at Disc Nation (512-280-1115; www.discnation.com).

Fishing

Fishing in Central Texas is excellent, though developed or privately owned shoreline can make it difficult to find a spot to sink your lure in Austin. Emma Long Metropolitan Park on Lake Austin is a popular fishing spot, as are the Highland Lakes. Check www.texasoutside.com, ww.tpwd.state.tx.us, www.txfishing.com, or www.austinkayak fishing.com. You don't need a license to fish from the shore in a Texas state park.

Football

University of Texas Longhorns (512-471-3333; www.texassports.com) Austin doesn't have a pro team, but it does

Lake Austin

have the UT Longhorns, who play at the Texas Memorial Stadium. Hook 'em Horns!

Austin Wranglers (512-491-6600; www.austinwranglers.com; the Erwin Center, 1701 Red River St.) The Wranglers are the newest members of the professional Arena Football League.

Golf

Avery Ranch Golf (512-248-2442; www.averyranchgolf.com) Excellent public golf course in northwest Austin.

Lakeway Golf Club (512-333-0343; www.lakewaygolfclub.com) Semiprivate club and a local favorite.

Swimming

People have been dipping their toes in the water around Austin for centuries. If you're looking to cool off in the city, try Barton Springs or Deep Eddy Pool (see "The Great Outdoors," above). Outside the city, Hamilton Pool (see "Take a Dip," below), a natural grotto and waterfall, is about a 45-minute drive, as is Hippie Hollow (see "Highland Lakes" in Hill Country chapter), everyone's favorite nudist hangout on Lake Travis. Krause Springs, (see "Take a Dip") in Spicewood, also has camping.

Tours

Whether by foot, boat, amphibious vehicle, or Segway, touring Austin outside a car can give you a whole new perspective. The Austin Visitors Center (www.austin texas.org;) runs many worthwhile tours, all of which are listed on its Web site.

Take a Dip: Quick Getaways

When it's hot in Texas, it's get-in-a-swimsuit-and-get-in-the-water hot. Some folks make a beeline for Barton Springs (see page 62) or Deep Eddy Pool (see page 64), and others make a day trip to the Highland Lakes (see page 185) or tubing (see page 201) near New Braunfels. **Hamilton Pool** (512-264-2740; www.co .travis.tx.com), with its grotto and 45-foot waterfall, is another alternative. A well-marked trail leads from the parking lot to the pool. Bring your own food and water and arrive early, as the park closes when it reaches capacity. The park is approximately 30 miles west of Austin. From the intersection of TX 71 and US 290, take TX 71 to FM 3238/Hamilton Pool Road. Or, try **Krause Springs** (830-693-4181; www.krausesprings.net), a privately owned park with a large spring-fed swimming hole on Little Cypress Creek. With one of the nicest swimming holes around, combined with tent camping, Krause Springs is a great place to spend a hot day or two. From Austin take TX 71 west to Spicewood and follow signs.

Austin City Limits Tour (512-471-4811; www.klru.org) Studio tours available each Friday at 10:30 AM. Free.

Austin Eats Tours (512-963-4545; www.austineatsfoodtours.com) The perfect mix of walking, talking, and noshing, with historic facts, quirky stories, and lots of local flavor thrown in.

Austin Overtures (512-659-9478; www.austinovertures.com) Guides guests through town in its bright pink van with star-shaped hubcaps; check Web sites for details.

Alien Scooters (512-447-4220; www.alienscooters.com) Hour-and-a-half, eco-friendly tours of Austin on electric bikes that recharge using green energy.

Austin Duck Adventures (512-477-5274; www.austinducks.com) Drive around Austin in an amphibious British Alvis Stalwart before splashing into Lake Austin.

Austin Steam Train (512-477-8468; www.austinsteamtrain.org) Restored vintage trains run from Austin south to Manor and from Cedar Park to Burnet in the Hill Country. Trips seem best suited to die-hard train aficionados.

Capital Cruises (512-480-9264; www.capitalcruises.com) Sightseeing cruises leave Saturday and Sunday at 1 PM; bat-watching cruises leave nightly 30 minutes before sunset. Check Web site for dinner cruise details. Reservations recommended.

Gliding Revolution (512-495-9250; www.glidingrevolution.com) These tours on a Segway, the self-balancing, motorized two-wheel contraption, are rumored to be great fun; just be prepared for plenty of stares.

Haunted Texas Tours (512-853-9826; www.hauntedtexas.com) Tour paranormal Austin.

Historic Hyde Park Homes Tour (512-330-2228; www.hydeparkhomes tour.org) An architectural tour of Hyde Park held annually in November.

Lake Austin Riverboats (512-345-5220; www.austinriverboats.com) Relaxing riverboat tours.

Lone Star Riverboat (512-327-1388; www.lonestarriverboat.com) This old-fashioned, paddle-wheel riverboat cruises around Lady Bird Lake for a relaxing 90 minutes. There are also weekend bat-watching/sunset cruises; call for departure times. Reservations recommended.

SegCity (512-402-9299; www.segcity.com) More tours on that funky self-balancing machine, the Segway.

Texas State Capitol (512-463-0063; www.tspb.state.tx.us) See "Historic Places," p. 73.

Texpert Tours (512-383-8989; www.texperttours.com) A variety of tours throughout Austin and the Hill Country, hosted by Austin's own Howie Richey, whose knowledge of wacky stories and odd facts is astounding.

University of Texas Tower Tours (512-475-6633, 877-475-6633; www.ut.edu) For the best view of the UT campus and surrounding Austin, take a tour of the tower. Reservations are recommended; hours vary with the seasons.

Tubing

Without a doubt, tubing is one of the more popular outdoor activities in Central Texas, and New Braunfels is the best place to experience it (see page 201).

Shopping
In and around Austin

Austin has perfected the look of vintage urban chic. Shops are filled to the brim with coffee tables, clothing, housewares, signs, and any number of knickknacks from various eras. With other shops selling books, music, and folk art, as well as museum stores and galleries, Austin is great fun for folks who love the thrill of the hunt. Art Austin, www.artaustin.org, a collaborative effort to promote the visual arts in the city, lists additional art galleries on its Web site.

DOWNTOWN AND WEST AUSTIN

Antone's Record Store (512-322-0660; www.antonesrecordshop.com) Jazz, folk, bluegrass, tons of Texas music, and lots of great blues.

Book People (512-472-5050; www.bookpeople.com) Austin's much-loved independent bookstore and "an outpost for the literate." Almost daily readings, author visits, and public events make it a great destination for bibliophiles young and old. In addition to all manner of books spread out on two floors, Book People carries quirky Texas-themed gifts, both in its store and online.

By George (512-472-5951; www.bygeorgeaustin.com) In Austin since 1977, By George is a smart clothing store with distinctive style. Urban, sophisticated, and modern without being faddish, the designer clothing reflects the store's owners' personalities, and the store itself is a work of art. Locations on North Lamar and in SoCo.

Clarksville Pottery (512-454-9079; www.clarksvillepottery.com) What started in 1976 as a tiny pottery studio in Austin's artsy Clarksville has grown into a large professional gallery next to Central Market featuring ceramics, jewelry, art glass, and wood pieces all handcrafted by artisans from Texas and beyond.

Tesoros Trading Company (512-447-7500; www.tesoros.com) Purveyors of colorful folk arts, crafts, furniture, and jewelry from more than 15 countries, Tesoros has a wonderful selection of items from Latin America, including Lucha Libre (Mexican wrestling) collectibles.

Waterloo Records (512-474-2500; www.waterloorecords.com) A perennial favorite, Waterloo Records is a die-hard music lover's music store run by die-hard music lovers, a love affair in which sparks still fly. Though the store itself has evolved from its humble beginnings into something big and modern, its philosophy has not. The staff at Waterloo has encyclopedic knowledge of Texas music and would be thrilled to send you home with some local music you'll just love.

Women and Their Work (512-477-1064; www.womenandtheirwork.org) This intriguing art gallery hosts dozens of events each year featuring the visual art, dance, theater, music, literature, and film of female artists; check its Web site or call for current listings. The gift shop is packed with pieces from local artisans.

SOUTH AUSTIN

Stroll South Congress Avenue for antiques, resale, and vintage shops.

Allen's Boots (512-447-1413; www.allensboots.com) Allen's on South Congress carries a huge selection of boots, hats, shirts, and belt buckles for cowboys and cowgirls of all ages. Boots range from the modestly priced utilitarian ropers to the fashion-forward, best-selling Old Gringo Celeste Vintage Style # L171-2, a boot with turquoise-colored stars inlaid in warm brown leather, slightly distressed for comfort, which will set you back $300.

Mi Casa Gallery (512-707-9797; www.micasagallery.com) What began as one family's love affair with Latin America has grown into a large collection of international treasures ranging from the $3,500 French armoire to hand-hammered copper items from Santa Clara de Cobre, Mexico.

Quincy's Guitars (512-383-0456; www.quincysguitars.com) Quincy's Guitars is a dream for guitar aficionados. The shop has both the comfort of a living room, with guitar picks on the coffee table, and the reserve of a gallery, with Bourgeois, Collings, Goodall, National Reso-Phonic, and Webber guitars on display.

Yard Dog (512-912-1613; www.yarddog.com) This South Congress gallery gravitates toward folk, outsider, and contemporary art, pieces created by self-taught artists, and anything else that seems to fit its ethos. The small gallery shows national artists, and its exhibits tend to be dynamic and varied.

EAST AUSTIN

Big Red Sun (512-480-0688; www.bigredsun.com) Unique gifts, interesting objects for the home, and plenty of plants.

Flatbed Press (512-477-9328; www.flatbedpress.com). The Flatbed Press is both a publishing workshop specializing in etchings, lithographs, woodcuts, and monoprints and an art gallery exhibiting the same, as well as paintings, drawings, and photographs.

Culture

History, Heritage, and the Arts

HISTORIC PLACES

The Austin History Center is a good place to research the history of the city, and a visit to the Bob Bullock Museum will help you put the facts in the larger context of Texas history.

The Texas Capitol (512-463-5495; www.tspb.state.tx.us) sits on a high point in the city, with the University of Texas to the north and Congress Avenue descending gently southward from it to the Colorado River. The massive Renaissance revival–style building, built to replace its predecessor, which had been destroyed by fire, was completed in 1888 at a cost of over $3.5 million—not paid for in cash, but with the enormous parcel of land in the Texas Panhandle that became the legendary XIT Ranch. The largest capitol building in the nation, save for the National Capitol in Washington, D.C, the Texas State Capitol is big, bold, and—right down to the engraving of "Texas Capitol" on the *inside* of the 7-pound bronze hinges of the massive entrance doors—very Texas.

The Capitol's exterior walls are made of distinctive pink-hued granite known as "sunset red," quarried at Granite Mountain in nearby Marble Falls. The building is topped with a gleaming aluminum Goddess of Liberty, clutching a Lone Star in her hand. The original zinc figure was removed in 1985, painted white, and put on permanent display at the Bob Bullock Museum (see "Museums," below); her star rests at the Capitol Visitors Center. In 1995 the building underwent an extraordinarily expensive $98 million renovation and now sparkles inside and out, with original details restored. In the lobby Elisabet Ney's sculptures of Texas leaders Stephen Austin, Sam Houston, and Miriam "Ma" Ferguson, Texas's first woman governor and the country's second, are all on display, as are portraits of other notables and folk heroes such as Davy Crockett. Inside, centered in the impressive rotunda, a Lone Star of the Texas Republic looks down on a terrazzo floor mosaic of the seals of the six countries whose flags have flown over the state. The serene, parklike grounds, surrounded by the bustling city, are perfect for strolling, and the large shade trees and benches provide relief in the heat. The many monuments dotting the 22-acre grounds tell the stories of Texas and include statues

The Capitol

of an armed Alamo defender, Texas Rangers and cowboys, pioneer women, children, and a volunteer firefighter, war memorials, and even a replica of the Statue of Liberty; they are all detailed in a brochure available at the visitors center. Admission is free.

The **Capitol Visitors Center** (512-305-8400; www.tspb.state.tx.us/CVC) and gift shop is located in the faux-medieval General Land Office Building on the southeast corner of the Capitol grounds and is chock-full of information, booklets, pamphlets, videos, art exhibits, and Texas-themed merchandise. Whether your questions regard history, camping, bus tours, or public restrooms, the folks here have the answer, not just for the Capitol, but for Austin and Central Texas. Interesting exhibits include the O. Henry Room, where you can listen to information about the writer's life and works on old-fashioned telephones, a 1:16 scale model

Statue with a Lone Star atop the Texas Capitol

of the Capitol Dome, and a fascinating video that details the creative deal brokered between Texas and a group of Chicago businessmen that financed the construction of the Capitol in exchange for the land that became the XIT Ranch.

The gleaming-white, beautifully proportioned Greek-revival **Governor's Mansion** (512-463-5516; www.governor.state.tx.us/mansion/ or www.txfgm.org) was built by master builder Abner Cook and completed in 1856. The house proved so big that governors at first had a difficult time furnishing and maintaining it until Sam Houston, a man who liked to think big, moved in and had it properly appointed. Home to every Texas governor since 1856, the Governor's Mansion was nearly destroyed in a fire in June 2008; check either Web site for information about renovation progress. In the meantime, history buffs can head to the Capitol Visitors Center, described above, where an exhibit details history of the Governor's Mansion, including its restoration.

A division of the Austin Public Library, the **Austin History Center** (512-974-7480; www.austinlibrary.com/ahc) is centrally located on Guadalupe, a few blocks southwest of the Capitol, and certainly worth popping into. Well-presented collections of photos, news clippings, maps, and records trace the history of Austin through exhibits on African American History, the Women's Suffrage Movement, Austinites at Work, and Victorian Architecture.

MUSEUMS

While music has deep roots in Central Texas, the formal establishment of museums for the visual arts is still relatively recent. The city's two big museums, the Austin Museum of Art and the Jack S. Blanton Museum of Art, are less than 50

Remember East Austin

With so many of Austin's sights concentrated on the west side of I-35, the city's east side doesn't get as many visitors, but that doesn't mean there aren't interesting spots to check out, notably the Carver Museum and Cultural Center. Be sure to leave time to stop in at one of the neighborhood's eateries (see "Local Flavors," below) for a great taste of everyday Austin.

Originally built to house the French representative to the Republic of Texas, the **French Legation Museum** (512-472-8180; www.frenchlegationmuseum.org) comprises two buildings: the mansion and the kitchen. The mansion is the oldest building in Austin, having survived thanks to the good care of the Robertson family, who owned it from 1848 to 1940 and whose Victorian furnishings still grace the interior, and the Daughters of the Republic of Texas, who restored it in the 1950s. An example of French neoclassical architecture, the house feels very Continental, right down to the French wine cellar. The original kitchen burned down in 1880; the current building is a replica based on evidence from the archaeological record, and antique kitchenware adds authenticity. Docent-led tours bring the property to life. Each July, Bastille Day festivities add an air of celebration.

The George Washington Carver Museum and Cultural Center (512-974-4926; www.austintexas.gov) began in 1926 as a tiny library—no bigger than a house—serving the neighborhood's mostly African American population and has grown into a museum and cultural center celebrating African American heritage, the first of its kind in Texas. The centerpiece of the museum is its exhibit on Juneteenth (see "Festivals," below), which celebrates the announcement of the Emancipation Proclamation of 1862. A thoughtful exhibit featuring the history of 10 African Americans in Central Texas whose lives illustrate perseverance is also interesting. There is also a small interactive area for children, an art gallery, and the Boyd Vance Theater, which hosts music and film events throughout the year. Just a block farther east is the **Henry Madison Log Cabin** (512-472-6838; www.austintexas.gov), built in the 1860s by the man who would become the first African American city councilman in Austin.

The parklike **Texas State Cemetery** (512-463-0605; www.cemetery.state.tx.us), in the heart of East Austin, is the final resting place of many of Texas's leaders and personalities. Governors, authors, Texas Rangers, Confederate generals, and signers of the Texas Declaration of Independence are all buried here. Originally planned in 1851, the cemetery underwent a much-needed restoration, spearheaded by former Lieutenant Governor Bob Bullock (see p. 76), who has since been buried there, in the 1990s. The results include a gallery and sleek visitors center with displays and information designed to make the cemetery as educational as it is reverential. Genealogists will appreciate the very thorough online master list of burials.

years old, but their collections are still growing and their exhibition space is wonderfully intimate. Cultural museums, such as the Bob Bullock Museum, offer a dynamic introduction to the history and personality of the region, while interactive museums, such as the Children's Museum, are just plain fun.

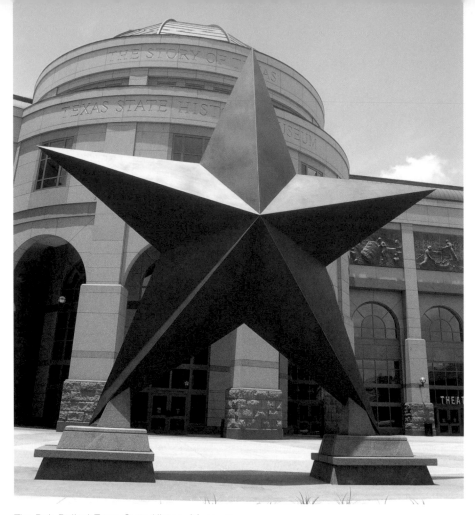

The Bob Bullock Texas State History Museum

Brush up on your Texas history at the Bob Bullock Texas State History Museum (512-936-8746; www.thestoryoftexas.com). The 35-foot-tall bronze star sculpture out front is your first indication that this museum thinks big. Spearheaded by former Lieutenant Governor Bob Bullock and opened in 2001, the Texas State History Museum has quickly become a must-see destination. Known for its elaborate and educational interactive exhibits, many of which challenge myths and misconceptions, the permanent collection of the museum is organized around the themes of Land, Identity, and Opportunity. Special exhibits have included "It Ain't Braggin' if It's True" which explores, among other things, the gray area between pride and swagger, and "The Faces of Texas," a lovely portrait series taken by Austin photographer Michael O'Brien. The vast sunsets, galloping herds of horses, and NASA space shuttles featured in *Texas: The Big Picture* are well suited to the enormous screen at the museum's IMAX theater. The Story of Texas Café on the second floor is a convenient spot to enjoy lunch or a snack, either inside or out on the balcony.

Directly across the street, on the edge of the University of Texas campus, the **Jack S. Blanton Museum** (512-471-7324; www.blantonmuseum.org) earns praise for both the focus and depth of its collection. The museum has a problem that every museum would like to have—collectors keep bequeathing them their collections. Consequently, what was a fledgling operation in the 1960s and '70s has grown to over 17,000 works of art and counting. The Blanton's 20th-century Latin American collection, for example, is almost unparalleled in the U.S. and one of a handful worldwide. Spacious, spare, and well lit, the environment at the Blanton showcases the artwork wonderfully and is both peaceful and provocative.

The Lyndon Baines Johnson Museum and Library (512-721-0200; www.lbjlibrary.org), on the eastern edge of the University of Texas campus near the Texas Memorial Stadium, is free and fascinating. With the benefit of hindsight and a few intervening decades, it is easy to appreciate Lyndon Johnson's life, times, and presidency, as they were some of the most tumultuous and formative years for the country. LBJ's terms as vice president and president encompassed the Cuban missile crisis, the civil rights movement, the assassinations of President John Kennedy, Robert Kennedy, and Martin Luther King Jr., and the Vietnam War. A Texan through and through, LBJ never forgot his childhood in the rural Hill Country, which fueled his passion for the enormous social reforms designed to bring about the "Great Society." A must for history buffs, who might also consider a trip to the LBJ National Historic Park (see Hill Country chapter).

A block away, **Texas Memorial Museum** (512-471-1604; www.utexas.edu/tmm), located in the Texas Natural Science Center, is dedicated to geology, paleontology, zoology, and anthropology, which translates into an eclectic mix of meteorites and dinosaur skeletons, a stuffed Mexican lizard, and Native American artifacts. The knowledgeable and personable staff enlivens what is otherwise a fairly dry presentation. A good museum for the super-curious. The small gift shop stocks some real gems for gift-giving.

Several blocks away, west of campus, you'll come across the **Neil-Cochran House Museum** (512-478-2335; www.nchmuseum.org). Built by the same architect responsible for the Governor's Mansion (see above), this Greek Revival–style mansion, dating to 1855, shares the neighborhood with others of its vintage, including the nearby Mansion at Judges' Hill. The home, which is shiny clean and filled with Victorian furnishings, offers a glimpse back in time to a historic Austin opulence.

The Austin Museum of Art and the Arthouse at the Jones Center recently partnered up, moved in together on Congress Avenue, and hyphenated their names, forming the new **AMOA-Arthouse** (512-453-5312; www.amoa-arthouse.org) and solving a predicament for each. In 2011 the Arthouse finished an expensive renovation, leaving it with posh digs, but little cash. At the same time, the Austin Museum of Art sold the real estate it had hoped to build on but never did, leaving it flush, yet homeless. Suddenly it made good financial sense for these two modern and contemporary art lovers to join forces, so they did. The Arthouse is still renowned for its biannual $30,000 Arthouse Texas Prize, the largest regional visual arts award in the nation, bestowed on a Texas artist whose innovation and talent have enriched the state's art scene.

Lovely **Laguna Gloria** (512-458-8191; www.amoa.org), part of the original AMOA, is still part of the AMOA-Arthouse relationship. The very talented Clara

Driscoll and her husband, Hal Sevier, onetime owner of the *Austin American* newspaper, built Laguna Gloria in 1916 and in 1943 donated it to the city of Austin, which established it as a museum in 1961. Situated on a bluff overlooking the Colorado River and the hills opposite, the Driscoll villa is surrounded by terraced gardens created by Clara herself and filled with native foliage. Tropical plants, statues and sculptures, and found objects such as a mission bell, an Italian wishing well, and other bits of whimsy dot the grounds. Contemporary works, such as the sculptures of Nancy Holt, Clyde Connell, and Jesus Morales, have been added more recently. The focus of Laguna Gloria is on its historic building and grounds.

Back downtown, the **Austin's Children's Museum** (512-472-2499; www.austin kids.org) is a bonanza for children in preschool and elementary school. Children can dress up for a Japanese tea ceremony, process milk in Miss Moo Moo's Dairy Processing Plant, or flip flapjacks and eat at the counter of the Global Diner. In addition to these permanent exhibits, featured exhibits tend to be very interactive and creative, illustrating simple science, math, or music principles. The gift shop is a great place to pick up an educational souvenir that your children will actually enjoy when the trip is over. The museum is located at the eastern end of the Sixth Street/Warehouse District, making it an easy place for families to pop into for a few hours and just let the kids be kids.

A few blocks away, what began in 1983 as a 300-square-foot gallery/studio has grown into one of a very few museums in the U.S. dedicated to traditional and contemporary Mexican and Latino art. The **Mexic-Arte Museum** (512-480-9373; www.mexic-artemuseum.org) has two exhibition spaces; the main gallery is reserved for major exhibits, and a smaller gallery houses the museum's Diversity and Emergence series, which highlights new talent. Exhibits can be political or personal, transcultural or transcendent, but they are always thought-provoking and timely. Recent shows have included such wide-ranging topics as "Los Hilos de Oaxaca," an exhibition of textiles and costumes vividly embroidered by different indigenous groups living in the Mexican state of Oaxaca, and a retrospective of the legendary Mexican political cartoonist, muralist, and printer José Clemente Orozco. The **Emma Barrientos Mexican American Cultural Center** (512-974-37722; www.austintexas.gov) on the shores of Lady Bird Lake has a busy schedule of exhibits, performances, theater, music, and films illuminating not only Mexican American but also Chicano and other Latino cultures.

William Sidney Porter was many things in his life. Although to officials in Austin he was a convicted embezzler, to the rest of us he is simply O. Henry or "master of the short story." The **O. Henry Museum** (512-472-1903; www.austin texas.gov/department/o-henry-museum) is housed in the charming 1886 Queen Anne–style cottage he lived in for two years at the end of the 1800s and contains a sparse collection of memorabilia from his life. A National Literary Landmark of the City of Austin, the O. Henry Museum offers writing programs and workshops and promotes all manner of wisecracking and witticism at the annual O. Henry Pun-Off (www.punpunpun.com) held in May. The museum is located on Fifth Street, between Trinity and Neches.

Moving to the Hyde Park neighborhood, the **Elisabet Ney Museum** (512-458-2255; www.austintexas.gov/department/elisabet-ney-museum) was the home of Elisabet Ney, a 19th-century German-born sculptor. After moving to Texas in

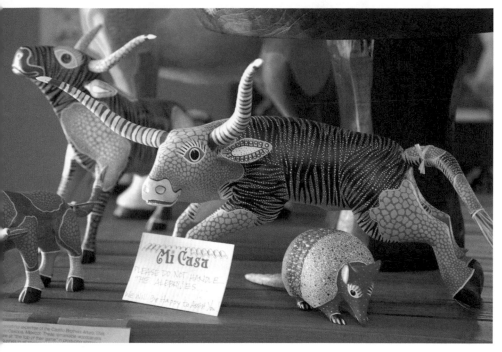

Folk Art from Oaxaca, Mexico

1872, Ney relocated to Austin in 1892, building herself a neoclassical studio in what was then rural Hyde Park. Ney's studio was a salon of sorts, with those who would become leaders of Texas frequently gathering to discuss ideas, politics, and, of course, art. In 1893 she was asked to sculpt life-size likenesses of Texans Stephen Austin and Sam Houston for the Chicago World's Fair; these sculptures are on display at the state Capitol in Austin and the national Capitol in Washington, D.C. Today, Ney's studio is a museum, owned by the city of Austin, containing a collection of her sculptures and portraits of notable European royalty and American leaders. A plaster model of her favorite sculpture, one of Lady Macbeth, is prominently displayed; its marble counterpart is at the Smithsonian American Art Museum in Washington, D.C.

THE PERFORMING ARTS

Austin just loves to express itself. From classic, contemporary, and country music to dramatic theatrical productions and dance, the city hosts performances practically every day of the year, and the newly renovated, centrally located, state-of-the-art Long Center for the Performing Arts is one hub of activity. The city's performance arts organizations are listed alphabetically below.

The **Austin Lyric Opera** (ALO) (512-472-5992; www.austinlyricopera.org) was founded in 1986 and has been producing outstanding opera ever since. Although the "Great Recession" hit the Austin Lyric Opera hard—it sold its home and performance space for close to $5.5 million—it didn't dampen its spirits. The Opera continues to charm audiences with spellbinding productions on stage at the lovely Long Center—a rebound that has been something to sing about.

The **Austin Symphony Orchestra** (512-476-6064; www.austinsymphony.org) typically plays a classical concert series from September through May, but they aren't shy about mixing it up with local talent. Crossover concerts—western swing, boogie, and roots-music band Asleep at the Wheel on one occasion and the Grammy-winning choral ensemble Conspirare on another—were huge hits. The ASO offers a 4th of July extravaganza of patriotic music and fireworks, a Halloween concert for families, Handel's "Messiah" at the holidays, and a popular Pops concert. All performances are at the Long Center for the Performing Arts.

Under the direction of Stephen Mills, **Ballet Austin** (512-476-2163; www.balletaustin.org) dances works such as Twyla Tharp's *The Golden Section,* a blithe rendition of *The Taming of the Shrew,* and the expected holiday tradition, *The Nutcracker.* This top-notch troupe impresses with stunning choreography, superb sets, gorgeous costuming, and plenty of passion. Ballet Austin Academy offers all manner of classes its dramatic studio space, where floor-to-ceiling glass walls make for good views—of the city from inside and the dancers from the street.

Esther's Follies (512-320-0553; www.esthersfollies.com) serves up satirical comedy performed in campy costumes, outrageous makeup, and wacky hairdos. From magic to impersonations, juggling to political parody, Esther's Follies is hysterical. The fact that there is a window onto Sixth Street on the back wall of the stage, through which pedestrians see performers and vice versa, only helps to blur the line between reality and ridiculousness.

Located in the little theater district along Congress Avenue, the **Hideout Coffee House and Theatre** (512-443-3688; www.hideouttheatre.com) hosts entertaining improv classes by day and hysterical improv performances by night. This little gem is located in a historic building in the informal theater district along Congress Avenue. It's no secret that shows sell out quickly, so buy tickets at least a day or so in advance to be on the safe side.

Home to the Austin Symphony, the Austin Lyric Opera, and Ballet Austin, the **Long Center for the Performing Arts** (512-474-5664; www.thelongcenter.org) rests center stage on the banks of Lady Bird Lake. A dazzling adaptive reuse of the distinctive, oval-shaped Palmer Auditorium, the Long Center is now spacious and modern, with roomy seating, fantastic acoustics, and expansive views the city.

The **Paramount Theatre** (512-472-5470; www.austintheatrealliance.org), on Congress Avenue, has been in the entertainment business since 1915, starting with vaudeville, then talkies, and now Broadway shows, classic films, and concerts. The regional hit *Greater Tuna,* a live comedy performance depicting small-town life in fictional Tuna, Texas, opened here in 1982 to rave reviews, and Lyle Lovett loves playing the Paramount when he's in town. The theater's enduring charm is in its detailed architecture, painted ceilings, twinkling chandeliers, balconies, and ushers—all hallmarks of a bygone era.

The **Salvage Vanguard Theater** (512-474-7886; www.salvagevanguard.org), in East Austin, has cut a path all its own, "defying theatrical tradition" without leaving audiences in the dust. Check its calendar for wacky improv, off-the-wall puppetry, contemporary dance, and vibrant multi-media presentations, with a few straight (-ish) plays mixed in. Located in dynamic East Austin, the theater is a good choice for an affordable, neighborhood-y night out for dinner and a show.

The University of Texas at Austin

Founded in 1883 with only eight teachers and 220 students, the University of Texas at Austin (UT) has grown into one of the largest universities in the country, with close to 50,000 students, numerous departments, and an enviable reputation that reaches far beyond its 350-acre campus.

UT is located just north of the Capitol, roughly bounded by Martin Luther King Jr. Boulevard to the south, I-35 to the east, and Guadalupe Street ("The Drag") to the west. The campus, a nice place to stroll, is home to the Blanton Museum of Art, the Harry Ransom Humanities Research Center, the LBJ Library and Museum, and the Texas Memorial Museum. The UT

The Mustangs, sculpted by Alexander Phimister Proctor

Tower overlooks the plaza at Guadalupe and 22nd Streets and offers a bird's-eye view of the city from its observation deck (accessible only by tour). In the fall, Texas Memorial Stadium fills up with football fans every time the university's Longhorns are in town, while the Cactus Café in the Texas Union Building hosts music concerts year-round. (See separate listings below for more information on all of the above.)

The University of Texas Performing Arts Center (UTPAC) (512-471-1444; www.utpac.org) is made up of several venues: Bass Concert Hall, McCullough Theatre, and Bates Recital Hall on East Campus across from the LBJ Library, just north of the Memorial Stadium; and, on West Campus, Hogg Auditorium near the intersection of 24th and Guadalupe Streets. UTPAC hosts an impressive lineup of touring talent, performing everything from dance, opera, and comedy, to rock, classical, and world music.

While the **Zachary Scott Theater** (512-476-0591; www.zachscott.com) can do all genres, the ones it seems to do best are the joyous, bittersweet, touching, and wonderfully exuberant musicals, and warm and witty comedies. A homage to Austin, *Keepin' It Weird* is so uproariously funny you'll barely flinch when you find out that the material used was culled from over two hundred interviews of residents and notables, all doing their part to keep life in Austin interesting.

Zilker Theatre Productions (512-479-9491; www.zilker.org) performs fun Broadway musicals under the stars in the summertime at the Zilker Hillside Theatre. The theater is essentially a grassy knoll, so bring your own blanket to sit on.

When writer/director Richard Linklater and cinematographer Lee Daniel joined forces to make *Slacker* (1991), they endeared themselves to a generation of twentysomethings trying to figure out what to do with their lives. Following up with *Dazed and Confused* (1993), Linklater garnered a national following and put Austin on the map as a city of slow and creative hipsters. Daniel's collaboration with director Margaret Brown, *Be Here to Love Me: A Film about Townes Van Zandt,* was a gem of a tribute to the beloved Texas singer-songwriter. The Austin Film Festival and Cinematexas Film Festival (see "Festivals," below) both offer yet more films to a city in which going to the movies is still about art.

The beauty of the **Alamo Drafthouse Cinema** (512-476-1320; www.draft house.com) is that it strives to fulfill the ultimate movie fantasy of great food delivered to your seat with permission to munch as much as you'd like throughout the movie. There are the usual appetizers—mozzarella sticks, jalapeño poppers, and fried pickles served with ranch dressing. You can order the classic Alamo Burger, an angus burger with lettuce, tomato, onions, American cheese, and chipotle mayo, or the vegetarian Splendor in the Grass pizza with zucchini, mushrooms, olives, tomatoes, garlic, and onions. Savor the Dolce Vita—chocolate ice cream bathed in a shot of espresso—and plan to stay up all night. The Alamo shows first-run movies all the time but also hosts special events like Anime Monday, Baby Day Tuesdays, and, on the last Thursday of the month, that essential flick shown by all great movie houses, *The Rocky Horror Picture Show.* Frequent theme nights pair food with film. Additional locations throughout the city.

What started as a bunch of friends watching movies together in 1985 has grown into the **Austin Film Society** (512-322-0145; www.austinfilm.org), a non-profit organization dedicated to the promotion of films and support of creative filmmaking. This translates into a huge range of films, from foreign to independent to documentaries, and some a combination of all, flickering across the screens of the various Alamo Drafthouse Theaters in the city. A must for film buffs.

FESTIVALS

Festivals are what Austin does best, and it hosts plenty of them. For specific information, check the calendars in the *Austin American-Statesman* or online at www.austin360.com.

Annual Festivals
The following organizations host a variety of events throughout the year.

Austin Food and Wine Alliance (512- 348-6847; www.austinfoodwine alliance.org) Celebration of wine, food, and Central Texas, with events in Austin and the surrounding Hill Country. Admission charged.

Austin Shakespeare Festival (512-470-4505; www.austinshakespeare.org) Experience the timeless works of Shakespeare. Performances throughout the year, season kicks off in September. Admission charged.

Monthly Festivals
The **Austin Farmers' Market** (www.austinfarmersmarket.org) Saturday-morning market at the corner of Fourth and Guadalupe Streets and Wednesday-afternoon

market at Whole Foods Market on Sixth Street and Lamar are not exactly festivals, but they certainly have a festive atmosphere.

February
Mid-Winter Music Festival (830-825-3108; www.aftm.us) A celebration of traditional, folk, and international music and dance organized by the Austin Friends of Traditional Music organization, which sponsors additional festivals throughout the year. Admission charged.

March
Austin Latino Comedy Fiesta (512-389-0892; www.lcp.org) Stand-up and sketch comedy hosted by Latino Comedy Project. Admission charged.

    Rodeo Austin (512-919-3000; www.rodeoaustin.com) Livestock show, rodeos, BBQ cook-off, and the popular kickoff event, the Cowboy Breakfast. Admission and free.

Super Fest

If you are lucky enough to be in town at the right time and get tickets, Austin's music festivals rock. Maybe it's the first breezes of spring that make everyone so frisky, but South by Southwest (see above), held in March, is just one big, weeklong party. Sure, it's technically more of a conference for those in the music, film, and multimedia industries where talent is "discovered" and deals are signed, but for the bar and club owners who have to clean up after the crowd leaves, it's just one long, beer-soaked bash. In September the Austin City Limits Music Festival is tamer, but it's growing fast as word catches on.

    South by Southwest (SXSW) (www.sxsw.com) A conference for film, multimedia, and music with performances and presentations. Admission charged.

    Texas Rock Fest (www.texasrockfest.com) Also known as the "The Heart of Texas Quadruple Bypass Music Festival" featuring plenty of indie talent. Admission charged.

    Zilker Kite Festival (www.zilkerkitefestival.com) A family-friendly festival with dozens of colorful kites dancing above Zilker Park. Free.

April
Art City Austin (512-609-8591; www.artallianceaustin.org) Featuring art, local food, and plenty of music. Admission charged.

    Eeyore's Birthday (www.eeyores.org) This groovy event benefits nonprofit groups in Austin and is more than 40 years old. Admission charged.

    Old Settler's Music Festival (www.oldsettlersmusicfest.org) International, national, and regional artists performing Americana music. Held in the Ben McCulloch Campgrounds in Driftwood, just south of Austin. Admission charged.

May
Austin Ice Cream Festival (www.icecreamfestival.org) Extra sweet since profits benefit local charities. Admission charged.

    Cinco de Mayo (www.cincodemayoaustin.com) Commemoration and celebration of the Mexican army's victory over the French at the Battle of Puebla on May 5, 1862. A joyous cultural festival featuring events throughout the city. Free.

Pachanga Music Fest (www.pachangafest.com) High-energy Latin music, food, and culture fest. Admission charged.

June

Juneteenth (512-974-4926; www.austintexas.gov) Remembering June 19, 1865, the day that slaves in Texas first received word of the Emancipation Proclamation. A spirited citywide celebration of freedom. Visit the George Washington Carver Museum and Cultural Center (see "Museums," above) in East Austin for more information. Admission charged.

Keep Austin Weird Festival (www.keepaustinweirdfest.com) "The ultimate toast to Austin." Cheers. Admission charged.

Republic of Texas Biker Rally (www.rotrally.com) A massive three-day fest of music and biker culture. Hop on a Harley and come on down. Admission charged.

July

Austin Chamber Music Festival (512-454-0026; www.austinchambermusic.org) Enjoy chamber music in various venues throughout the city. Free.

Bastille Day (512-472-8180; www.frenchlegationmuseum.org) A French-fest hosted by the French Legation Museum (see "Museums," above). Free.

Fourth of July Fireworks & Symphony (www.austinsymphony.org) Patriotic music and fireworks over Lady Bird Lake.

Zilker Summer Musical (512-479-9491; www.zilker.org) Outstanding family-friendly musicals performed outdoors. Free.

August

Austin Chronicle Hot Sauce Contest (www.austinchronicle.com) Beer, music, and lots of spicy sauce. Take a taste and feel the burn. Admission charged.

September

Austin International Poetry Festival (512-777-1888; www.aipf.org) Annual celebration of poets and poetry. Free.

Bat Fest (512-441-9015; www.roadstarproductions.com) Lots of arts, crafts, food, music, and fun on the Congress Avenue Bridge, with proceeds to benefit Bat Conservation International. Admission charged.

Diez y Seis Celebration (512-974-6715; www.diezyseis.org) A celebration of Mexico's independence from Spain on September 16, 1821. Celebrations at Republic Square, Fifth and Guadalupe Streets. Free.

Old Pecan Street Fall Arts Festival (512-485-3190; www.oldpecanstreet festival.com) Live music, arts and crafts, and a carnival for children. Admission charged.

October

Austin City Limits Music Festival (www.aclfestival.com) More than a hundred bands play to the crowds for three days straight. An Austin original. Admission charged.

Austin Film Festival (512-792-4795; www.austinfilmfestival.com) A multiday film festival attracting big Hollywood names and independent upstarts. Film buffs will enjoy the quality and range of the offerings. Admission charged.

Austin Gay and Lesbian International Film Festival/Polari (512-302-9889; www.polarifest.com) Edgy films tackling a wide range of topics. Admission charged.

November

Austin Celtic Festival (www.austincelticfestival.com) Celtic bands from Austin and around the world. Admission charged.

Austin Powwow and American Indian Heritage Festival (512-371-0628; www.austinpowwow.net) Spectacular celebration of Native American culture, the largest of its kind in the region, with food, music, and performances. Admission charged.

Dia de los Muertos/Viva la Vida Fest (512-480-9373; www.mexic-arte museum.org) "The Day of the Dead" is the ancient cultural tradition in which families "welcome back" departed loved ones, commemorating them through special altars and cemetery visits. Poetry readings and *calavera* processions, in which participants dress as skeletons, are especially moving. Free and admission.

East Austin Studio Tour (512-939-6665; www.eastaustinstudiotour.com) Enjoy a weekend visiting the open studios of East Austin artists. Free.

December

Armadillo Christmas Bazaar (512-447-1605; www.armadillobazaar.com) A casual, artsy market with lots of gifts ideas. Admission charged.

Fun, Fun, Fun Fest (www.funfunfunfest.com) A weekend of indie rock, hip hop, punk, electronica, and metal bands. Admission charged.

Trail of Lights and Zilker Christmas Tree (512-974-6700; www.austintexas .gov) Austin makes up for a lack of snow with a plethora of lights. Free.

2

San Antonio

PRIDE AND JOY

THERE IS SOMETHING SPECIAL ABOUT SAN ANTONIO. You notice it when you are there, and it stays with you when you leave. Even Mark Twain felt it, naming San Antonio one of America's "unique cities," along with Boston, New Orleans, and San Francisco. Both a crossroads and a destination, San Antonio has attracted people for centuries, and its roots are deep and widespread. It is in many ways the birthplace of Texas; as Frank Tolbert, a noted Texas historian and journalist, once said, "Every Texan has two homes, his own and San Antonio."

ROOTS

Native Americans were the first settlers of the area, drawn to the banks of the San Antonio River, or, as they called it, the Yanaguana, meaning "refreshing waters" or "clear waters." Indeed, San Antonio's raison d'être is water, flowing from the San Antonio and San Pedro Springs into the San Antonio and San Pedro Rivers, supporting the lush ecosystem of the surrounding Olmos Creek basin. Tools and other artifacts found in this region attest to over 11,000 years of human habitation, and it is known that Native Americans used this area as a popular meeting and camping spot and a productive area for hunting and gathering. Though drilling, damming, and diverting have altered the location, flow, and personalities of the area's waterways, it is still easy to envision the practicality, charm, and charisma the water held for those who encountered it. Gurgling springs, the rushing river, and the surrounding vegetation are the center around which the city's history, most of its contested issues, and civic pride have revolved.

While it is unclear exactly when the first explorers of European origin entered the region, what is known is that on June 13, 1691, a group of Spanish priests, en route to visit missions in East Texas, paused to camp at the clear-running river's

LEFT: Detail from the front of the Alamo

87

San Antonio Area

edge, beside a group of welcoming Native Americans. The day happened to be the Feast of Saint Anthony of Padua, and the priests, so taken with the area's beauty, decided to name it San Antonio de Padua. In the late 1700s, the French were eyeing Texas, and the Spanish moved to put down deeper roots. Between 1709 and 1722, organized Spanish expeditions, called *entradas,* started to search the region for strategic spots to claim in advance of any French incursions. By 1718, the Spanish had staked a claim in San Antonio and founded the San Antonio de Béxar Presidio. In the same year, Franciscans, anxious for citizens and converts, established the first of the five missions they would build in the area, including the Alamo. The inhabitants of the missions, in turn, built seven *acequias,* a series of interconnected irrigation ditches and aqueducts, linking the missions and transporting water from the San Antonio River and the San Pedro Creek to the outlying

farmlands, an outstanding feat of engi-
neering for its day. In 1731 the village of
San Fernando de Béxar was chartered
by Canary Islanders, who went on to
establish the San Fernando de Béxar
Cathedral, and in 1772 the small town,
by this time called San Antonio de
Béxar, was made the capital of Spanish-
ruled Texas.

When the Republic of Texas was
formed in 1836, just months after the
legendary battle of the Alamo, San
Antonio was chartered as the seat of
Bexar County. Located near a hotly
contested border, San Antonio endured
several Mexican invasions, and its population declined significantly until the
Civil War in 1861. After the Civil War,
San Antonio became a nexus of distribution, supplying the cattle-trail drives and
serving as a gateway to the Southwest.
Five railroad routes passed through
between 1877 and 1900, setting the city
on track to participate in the economic
growth and modernization of the nation
and hastening immigration. By the
1920s just over 161,000 residents called
San Antonio home, making it the largest
city in the state. The city was already a diverse mix of Tejanos, Mexicans, German
Americans, and Anglos from the American South when the Mexican Revolution
of 1910 fueled substantial Mexican immigration, enhancing the city's already inti-
mately intertwined history with Mexico.

Riverwalk Accessibility

The Riverwalk is recessed below
street level, and getting to it can
be a challenge for anyone with
restricted mobility. Strollers,
wheelchairs, and walkers are simply impossible to manage on the
steep, sometimes slippery, steps.
If you are planning some of the
details of your trip in advance and
online, consider printing a copy of
the "Accessible Riverwalk" map
found at www.sanantoniovisit
.com, under the "Plan" then
"Maps" sections.

While elevators dot the Riverwalk, other particularly convenient
locations include Crowne Plaza
Hotel, Hawthorne Suites Hotel,
Hilton del Rio, Holiday Inn Riverwalk, Hotel Contessa, the Hyatt,
La Mansión Del Rio, Rivercenter
Mall, the Westin, and in front of
the Aztec Theater.

THE RIVER

Over time, each group in each era has left its mark on San Antonio. From the
food and architecture, to historic sites and festivals, San Antonio is a fascinating
interplay of cultures and history. One of the city's most recognizable landmarks—
the lovely Riverwalk—is also one of its newest, though its story begins in the
19th century.

Back then, San Antonians relied on the river for drinking, swimming and
bathing, hydropower, and irrigation. By 1890, the need for more and more fresh
water had grown urgent, and many artesian wells were drilled into the Edwards
Aquifer. Snatching water directly from its source meant an inevitable decline in
water flow on the surface, and by 1896 the spring-fed river was in jeopardy, its current reduced to a gloomy trickle dotted with garbage. The social consequences
were steep for the diverse community of residents who would flock to the river to
swim and picnic along its shady banks. The final blow came, with a swift chop, in

Enjoying a boat ride on the San Antonio River

1904, as city workers used axes to fell two beloved willow trees in the name of
river "cleanup." After enraged citizens turned out in droves to berate their city and
its misguided plan, officials responded with promises to beautify and protect the
waterway. Civic associations formed and began to push for revitalization of both
the river and the public life that had flourished along it. In 1912 local architect
Harvey L. Page designed a plan for reinforcement of a 13-mile stretch of river
using what are known as "Surkey seawalls," which were to be traversed by decorative bridges and lined with benches.

     Mother Nature, it seems, had other plans. Six major floods between 1914 and
1921 destroyed any progress on the plans, testing the city's resolve. Some even
suggested simply covering the river with concrete and using it as a sewer, an idea
met with little enthusiasm. Then came the Big One. On September 10, 1921,
while the city slept, an enormous flood swept through the area, killing 50 people,
steeping downtown in 2 to 10 feet of water, and making it crystal clear to the
entire city that water must first be managed before it can be enjoyed. So the
Olmos Dam was constructed in 1926, and a cut-off channel, allowing excess water
to bypass downtown, was completed in 1929—projects that together provided
flood control. Then, a young architect, Robert H. Hugman, stepped forward with
an ingenious plan. Designed specifically to showcase the river, his proposal of narrow pedestrian walkways, shops, and restaurants built to hug the bends and curves
of the waters flowing 20 feet below street level was inspired by the old cities of
Spain. Unfortunately, the Great Depression derailed this new plan, and a few new
flower beds were planted along the river instead.

In 1936, the 100th anniversary of the Republic of Texas, a rush of civic pride washed over the city; by 1939 construction had begun on Hugman's plan for the Paseo del Rio, the San Antonio Riverwalk. The Work Progress Administration (WPA) managed the project, and on March 13, 1941, the WPA gifted the completed Riverwalk, with 17,000 feet of sidewalks, 31 stairways, and 4,000 plantings, to the city of San Antonio. Although 50,000 people came out to cheer for its dedication on April 21 of that year, the Riverwalk didn't come into its own until the 1968 HemisFair, during which it finally became an icon of the city.

PRIDE AND PRESERVATION

By 1930 both Houston and Dallas had surpassed San Antonio in population and economic clout. Geographically, San Antonio remained within the boundaries of its original Spanish charter until 1940, when the automobile hastened suburban growth.

Economically, San Antonio relies on military bases, educational institutions, and its medical complexes for stability. Good weather, access to health care, and a large veteran community, not to mention outstanding golf, have made San Antonio a popular retirement area. Another big segment of its economy is tourism, and San Antonio is well aware of the value of its many cultural and historic sites, neighborhoods, and festivals. With a rich history to care for, San Antonio has been a leader in preservation; the San Antonio Conservation Society, founded in 1924, has become a force to be reckoned with. Strict preservation codes, tempered by tax

Musicians on the Riverwalk

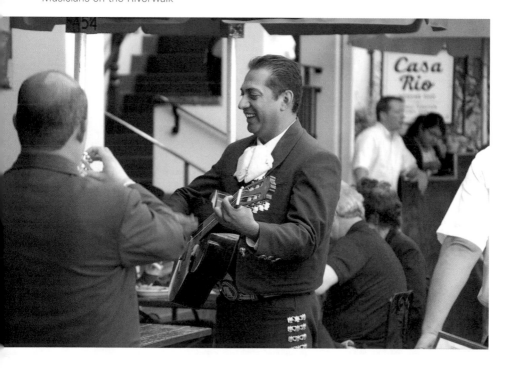

incentives for rehabilitation and preservation, have enabled individual buildings, even entire neighborhoods, to retain their unique features and identities. Festivals such as the San Antonio Annual Livestock Show and Rodeo in February, the wildly popular Fiesta San Antonio in April, the Tejano Conjunto Festival in May, and the Texas Folklife Festival in June bring out the city's best. A dynamic and diverse city, with lots of personality, and a river running through it, San Antonio is the pride and joy of Texas.

NEIGHBORHOODS

Many of San Antonio's sights, historic and cultural, can be found in the compact downtown surrounding the Riverwalk. Once you procure parking, this area is very easy to navigate on foot. Outside downtown, driving to and from the recommendations listed in this book is a nice way to explore the city's unique neighborhoods.

Downtown and the Riverwalk
Downtown is the area roughly contained by McCullough Avenue to the north, I-35 to the north and west, I-37/US 281 to the east, and West Durango Boulevard to the south. It is urban, with traffic, noise, and limited parking. Visitors can easily eat, sleep, and sightsee exclusively in this area.

King William District and Southtown
The King William District is the neighborhood south of Durango Boulevard, bounded by the river to the west and South Alamo Street to the east. German immigration to the neighborhood in the 1840s earned it the nickname "Sauerkraut Bend." Originally a fashionable area with large, single-family homes, the area slumped in the 1920s, and by the 1940s many of the homes had been converted to apartments. Located just a stone's throw from downtown, the neighborhood

Public art along the Riverwalk

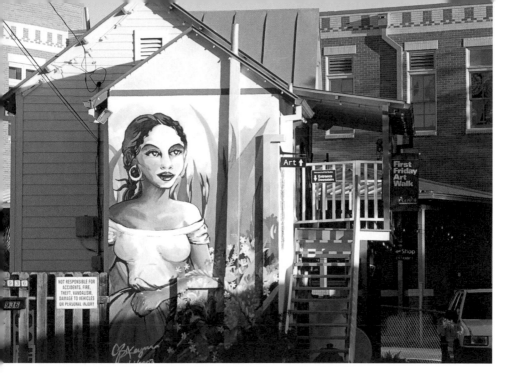

Mural on a building in Southtown

caught the spirit of renovation and preservation in the 1950s; in 1967 it earned the distinction of being the first Historic Neighborhood District in Texas. Today, the neighborhood is a lovely mix of restored larger homes, more modest abodes, atmospheric B&Bs, several small businesses, art studios, and popular restaurants, all nestled under huge pecan trees.

Directly east, the area south of South Alamo Street is known as Southtown. This neighborhood of art galleries and studios is particularly interesting to wander through during festive First Fridays (see "Galleries," below), when establishments stay open late.

TRANSPORTATION

Getting Around San Antonio

Public transportation offers an enjoyable way to get around in San Antonio. The city's public bus system, **VIA** (210-362-2020; www.viainfo.net), runs a network of routes throughout the city, and two are particularly useful to visitors. First, four VIA streetcars, reproductions of vintage open-air models, crisscross downtown along four different routes taking in most area attractions. Second, the No. 7, "Sightseer Special," ferries visitors to far-flung sites and attractions. All VIA buses are handicapped accessible. Fare: 80 cents a ride or $3 for a convenient one-day pass.

Or try a water taxi! **Rio San Antonio** (210-244-5700; www.riosanantonio.com) provides both river taxi and tour services (see "Tours," below) on the San Antonio River. You can purchase tickets from the drivers onboard, at a kiosk, or online. Fare: $5 for a one-way trip, $10 for a 24-hour pass, and $25 for a three-day pass.

Pick Your Spot

Best places to stay in and
around San Antonio

Since much of the activity in San Antonio revolves around the Riverwalk, it is no surprise that many visitors spend the night as close as possible to the water. While the area is dominated by large chain hotels, boutique hotels just blocks away offer variety. One of San Antonio's best-kept secrets is its network of bed and breakfasts scattered throughout the historic neighborhoods, just minutes from the city center. The San Antonio B&B Association, or SABBA (www.sanantoniobb.org), is a self-regulating group that ensures standards are kept up. To offer extra incentive and to compete with hotels along the Riverwalk, many B&Bs offer free WiFi and parking, modernized baths, and occasional discounts if you are traveling on a weekday or for business. Unlike chain hotels, however, B&Bs frequently require a two-day minimum stay on weekends, possibly more during holidays such as Fiesta (see "Festivals," below). Prices tend to rise and fall with the seasons.

When choosing an area of town, keep in mind that the Riverwalk tends to stay open late for dining and drinking, and people like to visit San Antonio to have a good time. If you are used to city sounds, the resulting noise level may not bother you, but if you require silence to sleep, you might consider a hotel in a quieter neighborhood several blocks away or a B&B with strictly enforced quiet hours. In addition, downtown hotels often charge hefty parking fees; be sure to inquire when making your reservation.

Guests with limited mobility may find the larger hotels to be the best fit, especially those along the Riverwalk, where they may have elevator access to the walk itself. The city's B&Bs are located in older homes that cannot always be retrofitted appropriately, but that said, if a certain property catches your eye, by all means call and inquire, as special arrangements can sometimes be made.

DOWNTOWN AND RIVERWALK

While run by the national corporation Omni Hotels, the historic Spanish Colonial–style **La Mansión Del Rio** (210-518-1000; www.omnihotels.com) maintains a distinctiveness. The building, once a Catholic school, dates back to 1852, and its hacienda-style courtyards, lush vegetation, and bubbling fountains exude the charm of a bygone era. Details such as exposed ceiling

La Mansion del Rio Hotel along the
Riverwalk

Downtown San Antonio

beams and brick walls capture the look and feel of old San Antonio. As with all older hotels, room sizes vary, ranging from spacious to cozy. The on-site restaurant, Las Canarias, serves a memorable Sunday brunch buffet that you can enjoy outside on the tiled veranda or inside in the atmospheric dining rooms.

Directly across the river is the

Mokara Hotel and Spa (866-625-1212; www.mokarahotels.com), which impresses guests with a combination of luxury and a slow-down-and-smell-the-roses friendliness. The hotel is stylish and sophisticated, with plenty of thoughtful touches, great service, and attention to detail. Rooms are spacious and airy, with simple furnishings and comfortable beds. Bathrooms have a separate Jacuzzi tub and shower, with big, fluffy robes and slippers at the ready. There is a full-service spa for pampering, a pool for relaxing, and a bowl of fresh fruit in the lobby. Mokara is pricey, but guests claim it's worth the splurge.

Around the corner, you'll find the **Hotel Valencia** (210-227-9700; www.hotelvalencia-riverwalk.com). Modern and hip, this boutique hotel isn't just a building, it's architecture. The Valencia is stylish, sophisticated, dramatic, and dimly lit. The down comforters, pillows, and seven layers of Egyptian cotton linens on each bed are thick and luxurious, and the sparse, uncluttered décor feels refreshing and romantic. Outdoor space is limited, with no pool and a tiny "balcony" that may best be described as a ledge outside some rooms. The Valencia is on busy Houston Street, so be prepared for some noise. Have a drink at the bar (see "Nightlife," below) and decide for yourself.

Several blocks away, the **Hotel Contessa** (210-229-9222; www.the hotelcontessa.com) is a 12-story, all-suite hotel and conference center right on the Riverwalk. Each spacious room has a separate parlor (with sleeper sofa) and bedroom, with comfy mattresses and crisp linens, and flat-screen televisions. The Contessa is designed with lots of open space, and noise can travel throughout it, especially on weekends, so consider requesting a room on one of the upper floors if you're a light sleeper. The exercise room is small but adequate, as is the rooftop pool, which comes with super views. Prices vary depending on the view; one features Marriage Island, just behind the property, where San Antonio's first Catholic Mass was held in 1691 and couples still say their nuptial vows today.

Heading toward the Alamo, you'll pass the **Riverwalk Vista** (866-898-4782; www.riverwalkvista.com) on Losoya Street. Completely unlike any other hotel in San Antonio, the Riverwalk Vista is part B&B, part boutique, and part Riverwalk venue, and it strikes a wonderful balance for travelers looking for personality, style, and location. Each of the hotel's 17 rooms feels like a bedroom in a city loft. Enormous 4-by-10-foot windows let in plenty of light, wood floors add charm, and some of the rooms have exposed brick walls. Chic and sparsely decorated, the rooms have wooden beds, down comforters, and leather chairs that work beautifully with the warm earth-tone walls and black-and-white artwork. Modern slate-tiled showers, a 26-inch flat-screen TV, and a teddy bear waiting on each bed round out the amenities.

Just a few steps away from the Riverwalk, you'll find two of San Antonio's most historic hotels: the Emily Morgan and the Menger Hotel. A tall, wedge-shaped Gothic-revival building built in the 1920s—a former medical facility whose exterior is festooned with ailing gargoyles—the **Emily Morgan** (210-225-5100; www.emilymorgan hotel.com) has a coveted location directly across from the Alamo. While the hotel has been updated, older hotels such as these have idiosyncrasies, such as fickle showerheads, well-worn tiling, and noisy heating systems. Overall, the Emily is a slice of history and character for travelers who prefer homespun hotels to big chains and expect quirks, including, reportedly, ghosts.

On the other side of the Alamo, you'll find the **Menger Hotel** (210-223-4361; www.mengerhotel.com), built in 1859, which, like the Emily Morgan, is so steeped in history that there are tales of ghosts haunting its halls. As

The Menger Hotel beside the Alamo

with most hotels of this vintage, the Menger's front entrance is grand while its rooms and bathrooms are small, especially by today's standards. On the plus side, the beds are comfy, the rooms cozy, the location fantastic, and the courtyard and poolside relaxing. Past guests include Mae West, Babe Ruth, and Teddy Roosevelt, so you can rest easy knowing you're in good company. Another perk is the Menger Bar (see "Nightlife," below), built in 1887 as a replica of the taproom inside the House of Lords in London and the venue from which T.R. reportedly rustled up his Rough Riders; it's still a fun place for a drink.

As you will quickly discover, many establishments in San Antonio love to include the famous Riverwalk in their name, regardless of where they are located. The InterContinental Hotels Group–owned **Hotel Indigo** (887-859-5095; www.ichotelsgroup.com) is situated, quite literally, on the Riverwalk, just farther north than you may have expected—a block north of the Southwest School of Arts and Crafts, to be exact, and nowhere near the restaurants and attractions. Those who enjoy a little peace and quiet, however, should take heart; the Hotel Indigo is situated on a flourishing stretch of the river, with lovely views of lush greenery, birds, and flowers. It isn't unnecessarily fancy, just new, clean, very functional, and spacious—a good value and perfect for families. From the hotel, it's a pleasant 20-minute stroll along the Riverwalk into downtown or a quick trip via River Taxi.

The nearby **Hotel Havana** (210-222-2008; www.havanasanantonio.com) is stylish and hip, with an old-school vibe and plenty of panache. The hotel was built on a pretty piece of property overlooking the river in 1914 and has maintained its Mediterranean Revival charm ever since. Rooms are simple and serene, with well-worn wood floors, sparse furnishings, white bedspreads and vintage Cuban artwork on the walls. Spend the night or just stop in for drinks at the Ocho Lounge (see "Drinks," below).

Architectural detail in the King William District

KING WILLIAM DISTRICT AND SOUTHTOWN

The lovely King William District, just a few blocks' stroll from the river and lively South Alamo Street, is home to several delightful B&Bs.

Cross over Cesar Chavez Boulevard and stroll south on Washington Street and the first B&B you'll happen upon is **Ogé House** (210-223-2353; www.nobleinns.com)—pronounced Oh-jay—nestled among the trees along the banks of the San Antonio River. Built in 1857, this lovely mansion is both listed in the National Register of

Historic Places and designated a Texas Historical Landmark. Once the home of Texas Ranger, cattle rancher, and businessman Louis Ogé, the Ogé House embodies the grandeur of bygone Texas, with tall ceilings and windows, verandas on each of its three stories, and fireplaces in many of its rooms. The same owners operate several other luxurious, though much smaller, B&Bs throughout the area; see www.nobleinns.com for more details.

The **Brackenridge House** (210-271-3442; www.brackenridgehouse .com) is located on Madison Street. The neatly kept rooms in this historic home are individually decorated with cheerfully painted walls, well-chosen

Who is King William?

As the story goes, King William Street, once the main thoroughfare of the neighborhood, was originally christened Kaiserwilhelm Strasse, in honor of King Wilhelm I of Prussia, by the German immigrants who settled here. During World War I, political tensions between America and Germany boiled over, and the name was changed to Pershing Avenue. Several years after the war, the name was restored, this time in its Anglicized form, King William Street. In 1967 the King William District was designated the first Historic Neighborhood District in Texas.

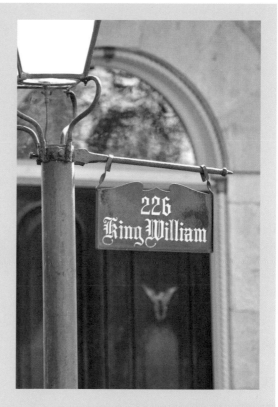

King William District

antiques, and colorful carpets over hardwood floors. Some rooms have quilts, others have kitchenettes, but they are all cozy as can be. In the morning, breakfast is a three-course affair, served with fancy crystal and china in the dining room and including all sorts of treats to start the day off right, like strawberries with whipped cream, cherry scones, and zucchini, sausage, and cheese mini quiches.

A Yellow Rose Bed and Breakfast (210-229-9903; www.ayellowrose.com) is just across the street. The home you see when you walk up is the owner's; the guest rooms are tucked back behind, each with its own door to the porches and garden. The rooms are large—especially the roomy Carriage

House Suite, which has two separate beds—and are clean, entirely comfortable, and have an air of familiarity. With large bathrooms, comfy sitting areas, books to peruse, and large beds for lounging, A Yellow Rose feels private and relaxing. Breakfast is not included in the price, but is available, so be sure to inquire when you book.

Nearby, on Beauregard Street, **Eva's Escape at the Gardenia Inn** (210-223-5875; www.evasescape.com) feels right at home in a stunning Greek Revival–style home built in 1905. The interior features gleaming woodwork set against crisp white walls in rooms decorated with richly colored rugs, upholstery, and artwork. Rooms tend to be large, light, and airy, with lustrous wood floors, antique beds, and deep claw-foot tubs. The Desert Blossom Suite can sleep five guests in its two connected rooms, making it a good choice for families or friends traveling together, and children over 12 are welcome.

Continuing along South Alamo, you'll come to **King William Manor** (800-405-0367; www.kingwilliammanor .com), a pleasant bed and breakfast in an 1892 Greek Revival–style mansion expanded in 1901 with a cottage addition. Rooms are casual, comfortable, uncluttered, and slightly modern, with clean lines and cheerful colors. The property includes a breezy veranda and pool, and breakfasts are provided by the Liberty Bar (see "Local Flavors," below) next door.

MONTE VISTA AND OLMOS PARK

Heading away from the city center and into San Antonio's more residential neighborhoods, you'll find a nice selection of quiet, quaint bed and breakfasts.

A standout is the **Ruckman Haus** (210-736-1468; www.ruckmanhaus .com), a comfortable craftsman-style B&B tucked away on a quiet side street off San Pedro Avenue. Its owners, the very affable Ron and lovely Prudence, are as gracious as can be, and their thoughtfulness is evidenced throughout the home. Rooms are decorated thematically; the pretty blue and yellow French Room, for example, is light and airy with gleaming hardwood floors, and the large Sun Room has its own rooftop deck. Guests are welcome to help themselves to an evening glass of wine in the kitchen, read in the living room, or relax on the deck or the backyard patio. With generous home-cooked breakfasts, including real cream

for your coffee, it's easy to feel right at home. Special rates are extended to visitors traveling alone on business. Many, once they've had a taste of life at Ruckman Haus, never return to the chain hotels. A real treat and a terrific value.

Two blocks north and three blocks east is the **Inn at Craig Place** (210-736-1017; www.craigplace.com). The Inn was built as a private home in 1891 and maintains an air of refinement and romance. The rooms are spotless and have luxurious linens on the beds and fireplaces for ambiance. Enjoy fantastic gourmet breakfasts in the mornings and a cool drink on the wraparound porch in the evening. The inn is so spacious and elegant that it has become popular for small weddings, relaxing honeymoons, and couples (there have been several) who decided to skip the hoopla all together and elope straight to Craig Place.

Two blocks farther east is **1908 Ayres Inn** (210-736-4232; www.1908 ayresinn.com). Designed by local architect Atlee Ayres, the inn has undergone a meticulous remodeling courtesy of its current owners, Michael and Hector, and its architectural details shine. Updates like memory-foam mattresses, iPhone docking stations, LCD TVs, and recessed lighting provide modern comforts without compromising the home's historic look and feel.

Approximately five blocks north, **Bonner Garden** (210-733-4222; www.bonnergarden.com) was built in 1910, modeled after a 17th-century Italian villa, and is filled with history and character. Once home to Texas artist Mary Bonner, the building has been lovingly restored by a succession of owners and is now run by Margi and Jim Herbold. Bonner's artwork and that of her French mentor hang throughout the house. Each of the

The table, set for breakfast, at a local bed and breakfast

home's six rooms has its own personality; the Studio, with exposed stone walls and hand-carved Mexican furniture, is both rustic and cozy, while the Portico Room has crisp, white woodwork and an airy ceiling mural. Outdoors, large shade trees and a refreshing, European-style swimming pool make this a great place to hide from the heat.

OUTER SAN ANTONIO

On the outer edges of San Antonio are two popular resorts. **The Hyatt Hill Country Resort and Spa** (210-647-1234; www.hillcountry.hyatt.com) is a self-contained resort with a distinctly Hill Country feel just minutes west of downtown San Antonio. With amenities like a spa, a golf course, a 4-acre water park, pools, numerous restaurants, a slow, artificial river for tubing, and pristinely manicured grounds, this place is made for those who like to combine relaxation and recreation, especially families. With so much here to do, you may find you check in and never go out, spending day after day at the pool just lazing around. Once you've worn yourself out, retire to the guest room with its understated earth-tone fabrics, wooden furniture, and sumptuous beds to sleep off the experience. If you visit the Hyatt Hill Country Resort and Spa, be sure to wear your pants with deep pockets; with all the additional fees, this place can get pricey.

Built high on a hill on the site of a former limestone quarry—*la cantera*—the **Weston La Cantera Resort** (210-558-6500; www.westinlacantera.com) is 20 minutes from downtown but in a world all its own. The resort's two world-class golf courses (see "Fore!"

below), including the challenging and spectacular Palmer Course, are a big draw, and the patrons who come to play are quite serious about their game. Consequently, the mood doesn't feel quite as relaxed as at the Hyatt. Six

pools, tennis courts, spa services, and three hot tubs round out the offerings. For accommodations, you can choose between a typical Westin guest room in the main complex or a *casita*, "little house," in Casita Village.

Local Flavors

Taste of the town—local restaurants, cafés, bistros, etc.

In a culture of chain restaurants and fast food, San Antonio has a satisfying number of *homegrown* restaurants and old-time establishments that have been favorites forever, as well as exciting new eateries that diners are always eager to try. In general, the Riverwalk is a mix of high-end restaurants, some of which are real culinary gems, and more predictable eateries catering to out-of-town visitors. In an effort to pre-serve the historic nature of the River-walk, the city of San Antonio has recently sought to limit the number of chain restaurants that can operate on its famed waterside in favor of high-lighting local eateries. And you cer-tainly don't have to go far to find restaurants with character and history. Just blocks away, the business section of downtown San Antonio is home to some much-loved standbys, which pack in the locals on lunch breaks. Visi-tors looking for a memorable dining experience may want to travel the short distance to the artsy King William Dis-trict or the Alamo Heights neighbor-hood, where a rise in diversity of both cuisine and clientele make dining more interesting.

In San Antonio, people like to eat out in style. For pricier establishments, "business casual" is generally appropri-ate. Families are welcome, particularly

at the city's many casual restaurants, which are often family-run themselves and quite kid-friendly. If you are on a schedule or dining with a large group, consider making reservations or calling ahead to ensure your meal goes smoothly.

The restaurants below are either local favorites or are frequently and enthusiastically cited "best of" citywide. San Antonians are justifiably proud of the uniqueness of their city, and they love frequenting the restaurants that contribute something special to the city's culinary scene.

DOWNTOWN AND RIVERWALK

The many convenient eateries lining the Riverwalk are perfectly enjoyable places to stop in; some are even desti-nations unto themselves. Several of the best downtown restaurants cater to the business lunch crowd.

Chef/owner Bruce Auden, four-time James Beard Award nominee, hit it big with **Biga on the Banks** (210-225-0722; www.biga.com). Auden's menu changes daily and features plenty of southwestern flavors. Start with the house apple-smoked salmon nachos, topped with chipotle cream cheese and escabèche vegetables, and move onto the achiote roasted pork tenderloin, which is served with plantains, corn sauté, avocado salsa, pickled onions, and cinnamon sauce. The popular sticky toffee pudding with English cus-tard hints at Auden's roots in Britain.

With all entrées averaging $32 and appetizers starting at $8, Biga isn't for everybody every day, but it is a boon for foodies, those celebrating special occasions, and anyone looking for a memorable meal. Reservations recommended.

Boudro's (210-224-8484; www .boudros.com) manages to keep both visitors and locals happy with its cheerful, modern atmosphere and tasty food. The flavors here are big and bold, with hot chiles and Cajun spices used liberally. The guacamole appetizer, made at your table, is as fresh as can be and always a big hit. The big, juicy steaks, Gulf Coast seafood, and the not-to-be-missed prickly-pear margaritas are all a taste of Texas, and the lime chess pie is a knockout. While dinner with drinks, dessert, and tip can easily put you over the $40 per person mark, the lunch menu will set you back just a fraction of that. Altogether, Boudro's is a predictably delicious local favorite for dinner as well as a solid value for a midday meal on the Riverwalk.

Upstairs on Presa Street, you'll find Boudro's relative, **Zinc Wine Bar & Bistro** (210-224-2900; www.zinc wine.com), a polished bistro that's popular for late-night martinis and apps. The guacamole—assembled tableside from Boudro's recipe—is outstanding, the rustic, gourmet pizzas are fantastic, and the super juicy Zinc Burger, with melted smoky cheddar and spicy tomato aioli, tops the list of diners' favorites. Since Zinc is primarily a wine bar, don't be shy about asking for recommendations. Equal parts trendy and down-to-earth, Zinc's intimate, upscale atmosphere is paired with reasonable prices, making it a fantastic bargain.

Around the corner on Commerce Street, you'll find **Schilo's Delicatessen** (210-223-6692; www.schilos.com) serving the sort of food necessary to survive hard labor and cold German winters—hearty and economical pea soup, plump kielbasa, pungent krauts, plates of rye bread with butter, and thick, dark beers. In sunny, urban San Antonio an old-style German deli may seem out of place until you learn that the Schilo family arrived in San Antonio via Poland and Germany in 1914 and have been feeding the good people of this city since 1917. In that time, many of the recipes have remained the same, and the prices seem barely to have matched inflation. In a part of town where a decent breakfast can be hard to come by, Schilo's is a real find, serving diner-style classics like two eggs, bratwurst, your choice of hash browns or grits, biscuits or muffins, and coffee for less than $7. If you are searching for a bit of historic San Antonio, step into Schilo's and split a pitcher of frosty homemade root beer in one of the well-worn wooden booths. In case you need to ask a local for directions, Schilo's is pronounced "she-lows," not "shy-lows."

Private and intimate, the **Fig Tree Restaurant** (210-224-1976; www.fig treerestaurant.com) offers fine dining from its perch near La Villita, high above the noise and crowds of the Riverwalk. The restaurant is located in a graceful, mid-19th-century home, and the elegance continues onto the outdoor terrace, surrounded by lush landscaping and trees festooned with twinkling white lights. The menu matches the ambiance, with delicately seasoned dishes and lovely presentation. Though the filet mignon, New Zealand lamb rack, and wild Tasmanian salmon are fantastic, diners also single out the jumbo Gulf shrimp cocktail, the Gulf lump crab cakes, truffled mashed potatoes, and the Bananas Foster for superlatives.

On a quieter stretch of the Riverwalk, **Bella on the River** (210-404-2355; www.bellaontheriver.com) is about as charming as they come. This little grotto of a restaurant has stone walls, wooden ceiling beams, candlelight, live music in the evenings, and outstanding Italian cuisine. Dishes are deceptively simple and perfectly prepared. The goat cheese ravioli, butternut squash soup, pasta with sautéed Texas Gulf shrimp, and pistachio cake are all exceptional. Even the bread—served with a little plate of olive oil, rosemary, and smashed sweet, roasted garlic—is delicious.

Nearby, Ácenar (210-222-2362; www.acenar.com) serves up colorful, Latin cuisine in its vibrant dining room or fantastic outdoor patio overlooking the river below. Diners rave about the fried oyster appetizer, served on yucca chips with a sweet and spicy sauce, cilantro pesto, and little chunks of grilled fresh pineapple. The *lomo de puerco,* pork tenderloin with a fantastic *mole* and a sweet potato spinach tamale beside it, is fantastic. A nice spot for a meal and a good choice for drinks.

Branching out from the most heavily touristed spots, stroll along Museum Reach to the **Pearl Brewery Complex** (www.atpearl.com) at the northern reaches of the Riverwalk or head south to the **King William District** and **Southtown** (see p. 105) for delightful—and delicious—dining.

Mi Tierra (210-225-1262; www.mitierracafe.com) demurely calls itself a café, but this Tex-Mex bakery and restaurant should be called Mi Tierra World. Festive hats and decorations stream from the ceiling, mariachi bands cycle through, and the waiters with overflowing trays of food weave their way in and out of the crowd. The restaurant is open 24 hours a day, offering a slightly overpriced menu packed with Tex-Mex favorites, and is always bustling, which it has been since

Treats at Mi Tierra Café

it opened in 1941. The bakery, on the other hand, is very reasonably priced, and the lines move quickly. In addition to baked goods such as the traditional pumpkin or sweet potato empanadas (turnovers) or churros (a fried stick of dough often dusted with sugar), there is a pineapple biscuit, which is best likened to a scone, and a pecan praline that is not to be missed. Take a minute to ogle the pastries, cookies, and treats at what feels like a mile-long counter, then order a wide selection to sample as you wander the nearby Market Square.

Looking for a 3-pound, Texas-sized cinnamon roll? Look no further than **Lulu's Bakery & Café** (210-222-9422; www.luluscafeinsa.com). While there is nothing glamorous about the location or the décor, Lulu's charms with enormous portions of some of the best-loved comfort foods—including plate-sized chicken-fried steaks smothered in queso—that garner "best of" awards yearly. Lulu's baked goods, including its famous behemoth of a cinnamon roll that drips with icing and is served with a knife, are a delight. Split it four ways and you'll still have leftovers. Open 24/7.

KING WILLIAM DISTRICT AND SOUTHTOWN

King William District and Southtown have some much-loved restaurants that possess as much character and charm as the neighborhood itself.

From the minute you tuck into the chips and salsa, you'll notice something different about **Rosario's** (210-223-1806; www.rosariossa.com). For instance, instead of the ubiquitous red salsa, Rosario's serves a signature tangy chipotle version that rings true to its roots deep in Mexico. Everything on the menu is super fresh and home-made, with a modern sensibility. The *Enfrijoladas Santa Clara* (chicken enchiladas with a zippy cumin chile sauce) and the fish tacos are just two of the many favorites that have diners returning again and again. The restaurant is usually hopping with professionals just off work, couples stopping in for drinks, families with children of all ages, and tourists and residents alike. While it can get a bit loud, Rosario's is also the sort of place where you can have a wonderfully intimate meal while surrounded by the din of happy diners. Consider arriving early to avoid a wait, and as the menu gently reminds diners, good food takes time, so allow for a leisurely meal; the outstanding results, at modest prices, will make you happy you did.

Family-owned and -operated since 1967, **El Mirador** (210-225-9444; www.elmiradorrestaurant.com) is deeply rooted in San Antonio. Owners Don Julian and Doña Maria hail from Salinas and Victoria, Texas, and Guanajuato, Mexico, respectively, and their family recipes exemplify Tex-Mex cuisine. Diners who grew up eating the handmade tortillas at El Mirador now bring their children to taste chicken enchiladas served with a choice of chile, *mole,* or *frescadilla,* a sauce made of spinach, tomatillos, and green chiles. The *sopa tarasca* is a hearty blend of tomatoes and beans and is both creamy and savory and a meal unto itself, as is almost any soup featured on the revolving menu of homemade family favorites. Eat inside El Mirador's casual and cheerful dining rooms or outside on a patio so lush with vegetation you'll hardly notice it juts out into a parking lot.

Located along busy South Alamo Street, **Azúca Nuevo Latino** (210-225-5550; www.azuca.net) offers an indoor/outdoor experience of the food,

A side of chips and salsa

music, and drinks of Central and South America and the Caribbean. While entrées can be pricey, some of the simplest menu offerings are the tastiest. The black bean soup with pico, crunchy chicharrones, and sour cream and the yellow fin tuna with a lime, aji amarillo, and green onion marinade, are both delicious. With fresh mojitos and salsa and merengue dancing into the evenings, Azúca is a fun place to spend an evening in Southtown.

Nearby, **La Frite Belgian Bistro** (210-224-7555; www.lafritesa.com) marries European bistro-style dining with the charm of the King William District, offering a full menu of Belgian cuisine. Belgian cuisine? Who knew? Turns out there are crisp salads, savory crepes and tarts, and a variety of seafood, including succulent mussels. The *mussels marinieres*—with onion, garlic, and white wine—are out of this

world, served with a pile of wonderfully crispy fries that are the best of Belgium on a plate. The menu changes seasonally; the $38 prix fixe menu changes daily.

Just a few years ago, the **Liberty Bar** (210-227-1187; www.liberty-bar .com) was located on a nondescript street, tucked under an elevated highway, and leaning, as a result of flood damage years ago, quite literally and rather dramatically to the left. And somehow this suited it just fine, since while the setting was casual, the food was refined—not expensive, fussy, or extravagant, just very simply inspired and wonderfully cooked—and its quirky building was part of its charm. Flash forward, and the Liberty Bar is now happily ensconced in a bright, coral-colored former convent, with the words "St. Scholastica" inscribed on the lintel over the front door. Again, this suits the Liberty Bar just fine. Diners haven't missed a beat in the move, arriving for delicious dishes like roasted hazelnut with prosciutto, apples, and Pecorino cheese, *chile relleno en nogada* (a poblano pepper in walnut sauce), lamb burgers, mesquite-grilled smoked pork sausages, pot roast sandwiches, and homemade fettuccine with garlic. The weekend menu is light and delightful, and the wine list at all meals is particularly well considered. Proving you can always "bloom where you're planted," the Liberty Bar is in full blossom on South Alamo Street.

Tucked on Beauregard Street just off South Alamo, the **Mad Hatters Tea House and Café** (210-212-4832; www .MadhattersTea.com) is a lovely spot for tea and a tête-à-tête, either outside at a bistro table under shade umbrellas or in the armchairs dotting the cheerfully painted and eclectically decorated interior. The inventive menu includes grilled bacon-wrapped artichoke "lollipop" appetizers and entrée salads, including the tea-smoked chicken breast salad with chile roasted pecans and tea vinaigrette and the warm pork tamale salad with a creamy chipotle dressing. Don't be fooled by the humdrum name of the grilled spinach and chicken salad sandwich—it is a signature dish and a favorite of devotees. Saturday breakfast is especially popular; they often run out of the eggs Benedict early. Not surprisingly, The Mad Hatters loves tea parties, and you can order high tea, afternoon tea, or kids' tea served on a three-tiered tea service.

Since it changes seasonally, it's a little difficult to nail down the menu at **The Monterey** (210-745-2581; www .themontereysa.com), the pricey little gastropub on South Alamo. Here's a taste: Roast potatoes with bacon and grapefruit? Maybe you'd fancy the

beef heart tartar with cheddar egg yolk? Or the porkbelly with miso caramel? Finish up with a tart and sweet blackberry granita, topped with a dollop of black pepper cream. To describe food at Monterey as "creative" is an understatement.

Carl Hilmar Guenther came to America seeking fortune and found it when the flour mill he built in the mid-1800s, Pioneer Flour Mills, prospered. **Guenther House** (210-227-1061;

Cowgirl hat in San Antonio

Tex-Mex in San Antonio

San Antonio is known for its plentiful Mexican and Tex-Mex food. Compared to the established El Mirador, Mi Tierra, and popular Rosario's, the eateries listed below are located somewhat off the beaten tourist path and frequented mostly by locals. From the cloth tablecloths at La Fogata to the paper napkins at Guajillo's, the atmosphere varies widely, but the food is consistently delicious. While every San Antonian has a favorite, the restaurants below always seem to top the list; they are presented here in alphabetical order.

Los Barrios (210-732-6017; www.losbarrios1.com) Los Barrios does everything so well, from predictably great enchiladas to the more obscure Argentinian churrasco steak with chimichurri sauce, that they've put it all in a cookbook.

La Fogata (210-340-1337; www.lafogata.com) Fresh, homemade northern Mexican cuisine served in a refined tropical setting. The dessert empanadas are delicious.

La Fonda on Main (210-733-0621; www.lafondaonmain.com) La Fonda has been feeding San Antonio since 1931. Tortilla soup, light and flavorful, with tender chicken, fresh avocado, and crispy tortilla strips, exemplifies the menu. An atmospheric dining room and hacienda-style patio make dinner special.

Guajillo's (210-344-4119; www.guajillos.net) The green *mole*, made with chilies and pumpkin seeds, is a must. A clean, casual, no-nonsense place north of town.

La Hacienda de los Barrios (210-497-8000; www.lhdlb.com) In a residential neighborhood north of Loop 1604, La Hacienda is owned by the enterprising Barrios family (see Los Barrios, above), who bring their well-honed techniques and time-honored recipes to the upscale menu.

Jacala Mexican Restaurant (210-732-5222; www.jacala.com) Jacala serves puffy tacos and spinach quesadillas, just as they've done since 1949.

El Jarro de Arturo (210-494-5084; www.eljarro.com) Outstanding upscale Mexican food made with high-quality ingredients has made El Jarro de Arturo a local favorite for decades.

Picante Grill (210-822-3797; www.picantegrill.com) Across the street from the Witte Museum, the Picante Grill makes fabulous fajitas and spicy hot salsa.

www.guentherhouse.com) is the home Guenther built for his family in 1860s; a popular restaurant and gift shop live here today. Guenther House serves a lovely lunch, including its champagne chicken enchiladas, but diners are also milling about outside waiting for a table because of the baked goods on the all-day breakfast menu. The buttermilk biscuits with sausage gravy, the sweet cream waffles, served with or without strawberries and whipped cream, and the enormous cinnamon rolls and sticky buns are a big draw. Guenther House's art nouveau interior and outdoor garden seating are both special and casual, making it a crowded, family-friendly favorite; you may want to consider eating here off-hours to avoid a long wait.

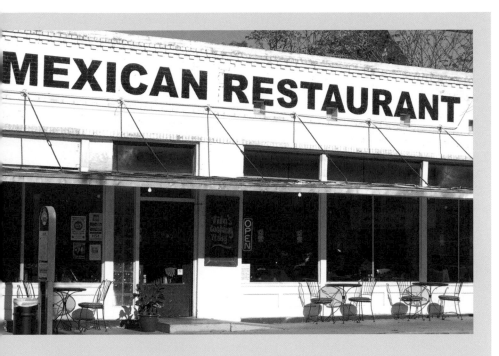

Pico de Gallo (210-225-6060; www.picodegallo.com) Owned by the same folks who keep Mi Tierra (see "Local Flavors," above) going all night long, this restaurant pleases crowds with its simple breakfasts, traditional Mexican dinners, accomplished mariachi band, and in-house bakery.

Taco Haven (210-533-2171; www.tacohavenpresa.com) From the *migas* to the tacos, Taco Haven's fresh, homemade tortillas make every dish delicious.

Teka Molino (210-344-7281) In business since the 1930s, Teka Molino makes up in food for what it lacks in atmosphere. Order at the counter, pick up your meal when it's ready, and dig into the sort of Mexican food that makes San Antonio proud.

Tomatillo's (210-824-3005; www.tomatillos.com) Hot, hot sauce, meal-sized appetizers, and maragaritas make Tomatillo's a popular happy-hour destination.

MUSEUM REACH/ PEARL BREWERY

San Antonio's newest addition to the Riverwalk, **Museum Reach**, was completed in 2009, successfully connecting the downtown portion with the Pearl Brewery Complex, a little under a mile and a half to its north. Stop by the **Pearl Brewery Farmer's Market** (www.pearlfarmersmarket.com) for fresh produce, flowers, food, and treats every Saturday from 9 AM to 1 PM.

Interrupt your stroll along the Riverwalk with a detour to **Ocho Lounge** (210-222-2008; www.havana sanantonio.com) in the Hotel Havana (see page 98). For breakfast, evening drinks, or anytime tapas-style snacks, try dishes like Havana papas bravas—roasted poblano peppers, caramelized onions, queso fresco and aioli, and Fruita Mixta (juicy fruits sprinkled with jalapeños , agave nectar, chile powder, and mint).Pretty and chic with great Riverwalk views, Ocho's atmosphere can't be beat.

Il Sogno Osteria (210-223-3900; www.atpearl.com) pairs upscale Italian cuisine with the trendy Pearl Brewery vibe. While the restaurant itself is a newcomer, owner Andrew Weissman isn't—he has two James Beard Award nominations to prove it. Rustic favorites like osso buco, delicate home-made pastas, and wood-fired pizzas seem elegant at Il Sogno Osteria. The antipasto selection—available in three- or five-dish options—is wonderful, and they have a wine to go with everything; just ask for a recommendation. Save room for the dreamy Nutella tarte. No reservations here. It's first come, first served, so go early.

Weissman's second eatery, the Sandbar Fish House & Market (210-212-2221; www.sandbarsa.com) features seafood as fresh as it gets. The white wine–poached Arctic char, with caviar and creamed leeks, literally melts in your mouth, as does its signature onion tart. While the menu is upscale—with fancy prices to match—the atmosphere feels a bit more casual.

BRACKENRIDGE PARK AND ALAMO HEIGHTS

Just a short drive from downtown, Brackenridge Park is less urban, yet home to several one-of-a-kind restaurants with a city feel. Farther north, Alamo Heights is even more polished.

Janie's Pie Factory (210-826-8715; www.janiespiefactory.com) is a mecca for pie lovers where the dessert is sold whole or by the slice. Janie's has won numerous local and national awards but hasn't let the fame stop them from staying a homegrown, hometown favorite. Janie's also sells quiches and casseroles to go, should you find yourself in need of enough chicken Tetrazzini or Texas zucchini bake to serve four. Janie's is located on Nacogdoches Road near the corner of North New Braunfels, and they also sell their pies at the Pearl Brewery Farmer's Market on Saturday mornings.

Cappy's (210-828-9669; www.cappysrestaurant.com), located in a brick building dating from the 1930s in the Alamo Heights neighborhood, serves an upscale menu at fairly modest prices. Two dishes are so popular they are served for both lunch and dinner: the Mustang Chicken, which packs a punch with fresh horseradish and Dijon cream and the Southern classic, pecan-crusted catfish. The casual, cheerful interior and leafy patio only enhance the dining experience and keep Cappy's a neighborhood favorite. Nearby, Cappyccino's (see "Drinks," above) is a great out-of-the-way place for evening drinks.

For classic—and classy—Tex-Mex, leave the Riverwalk behind and head a short way up Broadway into the Alamo Heights neighborhood to Paloma Blanca Mexican Cuisine (210-822-6151; www.palomablanca.net). Start with the basics: homemade chips and salsa and a side of guacamole made with a spritz of orange. Move on to something as simple as a chicken enchilada, which comes with your choice of crema de chipotle, crema de cilantro, salsa de mole, or a tangy tomatillo sauce, and prepare to be impressed. The menu is extensive, filled with all sorts of combinations and a wide variety of vegetarian and gluten-free options. The lush patio is a delight and the dining room strikes the perfect balance between rustic

The Cove

Since the following place defies categorizing, it is here, in a box all its own.

Everyone likes to slip into the Cove (210-227-2683; www.thecove.us). The funky, heartwarming spot near San Antonio College has become known as much for its great food, friendly service, and outstanding live music as for its odd mix of additional offerings. The Cove has an extensive, healthy, and affordable menu; eating a grilled-fish taco served with cilantro coleslaw and a signature poblano cream sauce is a terrific way to pass the time while doing your laundry. That's right, laundry. The Cove's 34 washers and 30 dryers get lots of use. Almost as much use as the basketball court out back, or the child-friendly playscape, or the self-serve, four-bay car wash. The Cove has everything you've never thought of, plus a pool table, video games, art on the walls, and wine and cheese tastings. At night, the nice long beer list takes center stage during "happy time" (Tuesday–Friday 3–7) when all domestics are $1.75. Things heat up around 8, when music lovers show up for the live blues, jazz, and acoustic folk concerts. The Cove is a San Antonio classic; stop in for some hospitality and go home full, clean, and satisfied.

and refined. Paloma Blanca is worth both the drive and the price.

MONTE VISTA, OLMOS PARK, AND BEYOND

Monte Vista and Olmos Park are distinct historic neighborhoods, organized around the north–south thoroughfare of McCullough Avenue. Some eateries in this section are literally within those boundaries and some are nearby; all are north of I-35.

Green Vegetarian Cuisine (210-320-5865; www.greensanantonio.com), on North Flores Street, has made a name for itself as one of the healthiest, tastiest, and friendliest eateries in the city, winning over vegetarians, vegans, and omnivores alike with salads, sandwiches, reworked soul food, and pared down Tex-Mex favorites. Crowd-pleasers include the portabella "steak" with caramelized onions and mashed potatoes and the mushroom stroganoff served over spaghetti. Be sure to leave room for a cupcake.

Pull up to the curb and you'll think King's Court Frankfurters (210-737-7774; www.frankfurterexpress.com) is nothing special—and from the outside it isn't. But one bite of one of its high quality dogs and all bets are off. With over two dozen options to choose from—and vegetarian versions of most—and an enormous topping bar, it's no wonder these frankfurters are a local favorite. Live a little and try "The Danger Dog"—a quarter-pound beef frank wrapped in bacon, deep fried, topped with grilled onions and chili, and served with a fresh serrano pepper.

Chris Madrid's (210-735-3552; www.chrismadrids.com), on Blanco Road, is the place to go for burgers in San Antonio, and people do, all day long. Choose from their many topping combinations, which include Porky's Delight, with cheddar and bacon, and the Flaming Jalapeño, with mustard and piles of jalapeños that will clear your sinuses for a week. The Tostada Burger, with mounds of refried beans, chips, onions, and cheddar cheese, is a crowd-pleaser despite its dubious reputation. The freshly made burgers come in two sizes, regular and macho, and are served in a casual, no-frills atmosphere.

Continue north on Blanco Road, veering east onto West Avenue, to **Magnolia Pancake Haus** (210-496-0828; www.magnoliapancakehaus.com), where you'll find hot and fluffy buttermilk, blueberry, chocolate chip, and pecan pancakes, and even a hot apple *munchener apfel pfannekuchen*, a Bavarian puffed pancake served with powdered sugar and whipped cream, for breakfast and lunch.

Pressing farther north still you'll come to **Silo Elevated Cuisine** (210-483-8989; www.siloelevatedcuisine .com). Enter this old farmers' market on the ground floor, now a martini bar, and take the elevator up to the main dining room. Menu mainstays include chicken-fried oysters served with applewood bacon, sautéed spinach, and apples with a mustard hollandaise sauce, and the Asian-inspired mango-wasabi crab cakes, both of which are crowd-pleasers. Embellishments such as the mint marigold béarnaise, a cognac cream sauce, foie gras port sauce, and a spicy dried cherry sauce bump the dishes up to new heights. Even though the restaurant is located on North Loop, on the outer edges of the city, the prix-fixe lunch is very popular.

Nightlife

Best places to go after hours

Nightlife in San Antonio is quite tame; simple pleasures such as sitting out under the stars, sipping a drink on the patio of just about any restaurant along the Riverwalk, are sure to make for a relaxing evening. Strolling the sidewalks of the historic King William District, gallery hopping on First Fridays (see "Galleries," above), or just lingering over dessert at a local bistro are activities San Antonians enjoy on nights out. Visitors will find that the city offers a nice selection of live music, from jazz ensembles to *conjunto* music, energetic performing arts organizations, and dynamic festivals whose exuberant celebrations can last well into the evening. For variety's sake, locals don't think twice about driving the 30 miles north on I-35 to historic Gruene for dinner and dancing in Gruene Hall (see page 205). For up-to-the-minute information on San Antonio's nightlife, pick up a copy of either the *San Antonio Current* or *San Antonio Express-News*, or access the information online at www.sacurrent.com and www.mysanantonio.com.

MUSIC

Popularized through the Public Radio International syndicated jazz broadcast *Riverwalk, Live from the Landing*, the seven-piece Jim Cullum Jazz Band (JCJB) has been making outstanding music in San Antonio since 1963. JCJB plays **The Landing** (210-223-7266; www.landing.com) at the Hyatt Regency Hotel Monday through Saturday starting at 8 PM; reservations are recommended for weekend performances. The local jazz group Small World takes the reins on Sunday night. If you can't make the performance, you can catch it on KSTX 89.1 FM Saturday at 7 PM and Sunday at noon, or listen online at www.riverwalkjazz.com.

Bella on the River (210-404-2355; www.bellaontheriver.com) is a tiny Italian

Piano player at Jim Cullum's Landing

restaurant (see "Local Flavors," below) that provides the perfect backdrop for the jazz combos who frequent its small stage, and the perfect foil to the noisy wide-open patios of the Riverwalk. A cozy place to spend a rainy evening or a sticky summer night.

Built in 1902 as a Southern Pacific Railroad depot, **Sunset Station** (210-222-9481; www.sunset-station.com) is located in the St. Paul Historic District near the Alamodome. The structure has been extensively renovated and is now a multipurpose entertainment venue, with an old-time saloon and plenty of space for the wide-ranging, big-name concerts it is known for hosting. Check the Web site for event details.

With a very '40s feel, **Luna Fine Music Club** (210-804-2433; www.lunalive .com) pairs top-notch musicians with a slightly more upscale ambience than other area clubs. The acoustics of the club benefit blues, jazz, Latin, soul, swing, and world music equally, making it a music-lover's delight. A classic mix of music, dancing, and cocktails in North Central San Antonio, Luna is a local favorite.

The **Bonham Exchange** (210-271-3811; www.bonhamexchange.net), located near the Alamo, is known for over-the-top celebrations, booty-shaking contests, and hot dancers. This gay/lesbian bar and club is popular with anyone looking for a fun night out.

Rosario's (210-223-1806; www.rosariossa.com) anchors the Southtown social scene. Arrive early, order dinner, eat at your leisure, and then join the margarita-fueled throngs on the dance floor for live salsa, pop, or contemporary Latin music. The combination of free live music every Friday night, a great Southtown location, and fantastic food all week long (see "Local Flavors," below) are just some of the many reasons to stop in at Rosario's.

Located in the Blue Star Arts Complex, the **Blue Star Brewing Company** (210-212-5506; www.bluestarbrewing.com) has a similar, albeit more polished, warehouse feel, with high ceilings, exposed brick, lots of wood, and enormous stainless steel vats of brew. The pub grub menu has appetizers of onion rings, mushrooms, or calamari dipped in the brewery's own beer batter and fried, plus burgers, pizzas, and fish-and-chips. A half-dozen handcrafted beers are brewed on site, from the mild golden lager and amber ale to the full-bodied King William Ale and the deep, rich signature stout. For nondrinkers, the homemade pints of root beer and cream soda are sweet stand-ins. Check the Web site for a roster of concerts "live from the deck."

Just off Broadway and just south of Brackenridge Park, **Sam's Burger Joint** (210-223-2830; www.samsburgerjoint.com) mixes it up all week with swing dancing on Monday, poetry slams on Tuesday, blues on Thursday, and hard rocking all weekend. No need to eat before you go; Sam's sells enormous, juicy burgers.

Part neighborhood hangout, part modern-day saloon, part pool hall, and part college bar, the **Bombay Bicycle Club** (210-737-2411; bombaybicycleclubsa.com) delivers it all in Alamo Heights. "Bays" is a drop-in sort of place where just about anybody can jump into a game of pool, throw some darts, catch some Spurs basketball on the flat screen, or just chill with a drink and a juicy burger.

Cowboys Dancehall (210-646-9378; www.cowboysdancehall.com), a warehouse-sized combination dance hall and indoor rodeo, is country western through and through. From the George Strait and Dwight Yoakam concerts to the live pro bull-riding shows, Cowboys is the place to go for dancing, cold beer, and a Texas-sized Good Time. Check the Web site for concert and event schedule. Tucked beside Loop 410 at I-35.

A honky-tonk northwest of town, **John T. Floore Country Store** (210-695-8827; www.liveatfloores.com) has had patrons singing, dancing, and whooping it up with folks like Willie Nelson and Patsy Cline for over 60 years. Floore's isn't as old as the historic dance hall in Gruene (see page 205), but it is much bigger and the boot scootin' is every bit as fun. Take Bandera Road northwest to Helotes, just past Loop 1604.

DRINKS

You can duck into anyplace on the Riverwalk for a beer and a view, but if you are looking for character, history, or a just a place the locals love, give these a try.

For history's sake, take a break from the margaritas on the crowded Riverwalk and duck into the dimly lit **Menger Bar** (210-223-4361; www.mengerhotel.com) for a stiff shot of whisky in the shadow of the Alamo. Rumor has it that here Teddy Roosevelt offered free drinks to men who would, after throwing back a few, readily join his Rough Riders and head off to fight in the Spanish-American War. Built in 1887, with a design based on the taproom in London's House of Lords, the bar is quiet and relaxed, with dark cherry-wood paneling, beveled glass mirrors from France, and other Victorian embellishments.

Established in 1933, the **Esquire Tavern** (210-222-2521; www.esquiretavern -sa.com) is still a local haunt, with a nice little patio overlooking the river and jukebox full of Texas tunes. Located near the corner of Commerce Street and St. Mary's, the Esquire is great place to enjoy drinks and a burger while sitting elbow-to-elbow with anyone from anywhere.

Located at street level—just a stone's throw from the Riverwalk, but easily missed on Presa between Commerce and Market—**Zinc** (210-224-2900; www.zinc wine.com) is a casual wine bar that's consistently a local favorite. Share appetizers over martinis or split the juicy Zinc Burger, topped with smokey cheddar and spicy tomato aioli, or a gourmet pizza and a bottle of something special.

Looking for something a bit more "loungey"? Head over to **Swig Martini Bar** (210-476-0005; www.swigmartini .com), where you'll find specialty martinis, cocktails, live music, and that thrill of yesteryear, cigars. With a slightly upscale look, but a down-to-earth attitude that makes most everyone feel welcome, Swing is located on Crockett, between Presa and Navarro.

The Hotel Valencia is home to **Vbar** (210-227-9700; www.hotelvalencia -riverwalk.com), just the spot to enjoy a little tapas, sip a cocktail, and take in the scenery—both the river and fellow well-dressed patrons. Couches, fun music, and a stone terrace directly on the Riverwalk keep the mood light.

Farther north, the **Ocho Lounge** (210-222-2008; www.havanasanantonio.com) in the Hotel Havana exudes a sophisticated, old world, Latin-inspired vibe. The décor looks the part, with antique sofas and armchairs, tiled floors, marble counters, and a dramatic, almost vaulted, glass ceiling soaring above. Candlelight, glowing chandeliers, and a peek at the river add romance.

The Great Outdoors
Outdoor adventures and activities

The San Antonio Botanical Gardens (210-207-3250; www.sabot.org) and Lucille Halsell Conservatory are located north of the city, just a few blocks east of Broadway near the Witte Museum and Brackenridge Park and en route to the McNay Art Museum. The entrance to the 33-acre property is through the stone Daniel Sullivan Carriage House, which was built in 1896 and moved, stone by stone, to its present location in 1988. The building also houses a gift shop and a small, casual restaurant offering simple, healthful, and filling dishes, some of which come garnished with fresh, edible flowers.

A welcome sight on a hot day

The Botanical Gardens are fascinating for flower enthusiasts, and though the variety and volumes of blooms you see will depend on the time of year you visit, there is something flowering year-round in the warm Texas climate. One of the most fascinating gardens here is the Garden for the Blind, centered on a gurgling fountain and planted with flowers and plants known for their smells and textures, such as the fragrant "root beer plant" and fuzzy lamb's ears, all labeled in braille on metal markers.

A highlight of any trip is bound to be the award-winning Lucille Halsell Conservatory, designed by the noted Argentinean architect Emilio Ambasz and opened in 1988. The conservatory is actually a complex of glass structures in which plants grow in their natural ecosystems; each is designed to re-create various climates from around the world. The building regulates the environments through the ingenious use of light and heat, and the results are wonderful to wander through.

San Antonio and Kumamoto, Japan, are sister cities, and gardeners came from Japan to San Antonio to help design the authentic and lovely Kumamoto En Japanese Garden, jam-packed with highly symbolic plants, structures, materials, and gestures. The double granite bridge clearly connotes mutual respect, understanding, and friendship.

Brackenridge Park (210-207-7275; www.sanantonio.gov) is a 343-acre urban park 2 miles north of downtown San Antonio beside and behind the Witte Museum on Broadway. The park first opened in 1899, and it has aged since then, gracefully. Home to the popular San Antonio Zoo, the tranquil Japanese Tea Gardens and the neighboring Sunken Garden Theatre, and the Brackenridge Golf

Course, the park is also dotted with play structures, picnic tables, and ball fields. The *Brackenridge Eagle,* a replica of an 1863 Central Pacific Huntington steam engine, pulls a miniature train filled with children around a several-mile track (210-735-7455; hours vary seasonally). The San Antonio River, which flows from an artesian spring just north of the park, meanders through, as do shady paved walking paths.

The **San Antonio Zoo** (210-734-7184; www.sazoo-aq.org), like many zoos in America, is undergoing major restructuring of both the physical space and the philosophy of keeping animals in captivity. The zoo's master plan, "2020 Vision," will transform it into five zones, each representing a different continent and its respective ecosystems. While the zoo is still enacting this plan, and some of the facility feels old-school by today's standards, the brand-new Africa Live! exhibit is quite dynamic and features animals in their natural habitat, surrounded by native plants and with much more room to roam; its "African Plains" extend around a man-made watering hole, from which various species come and go freely. Additionally, the new barnyard-themed petting zoo is fun for tykes, and the butterfly exhibit, recently rebuilt after a 45-foot-tall red oak tree toppled over and destroyed it in 2005, is of particular local interest. Opened in 2000, Cranes of the World is a verdant environment for all sorts of cranes, including the endangered whooping crane. Wear comfortable shoes for walking, and take a cue from the animals and drink lots of water.

The **Japanese Tea Gardens** (210-212-4814; www.sanantonio.gov), situated in what was once an abandoned rock quarry, have been utterly transformed into one of the most lush and peaceful places in San Antonio. The park was the brainchild of City Parks Commissioner Ray Lambert, who about a hundred years ago came up with the wacky plan of creating a "lily pond" in a quarry. Turns out that where there's a will, there's a way. Especially if you are a penny-pincher. Lambert used prison labor to shape the rocks into paths. He asked city residents and companies to donate supplies and plants. He used palm fronds from city trees to roof the pagoda. In the end, he had spent only $7,000 when the park opened in 1919. The park got a $1.5 million facelift in 2008, its year-round gardens, koi ponds, bridges, 60-foot waterfall, and shaded

Entrance to the San Antonio Zoo

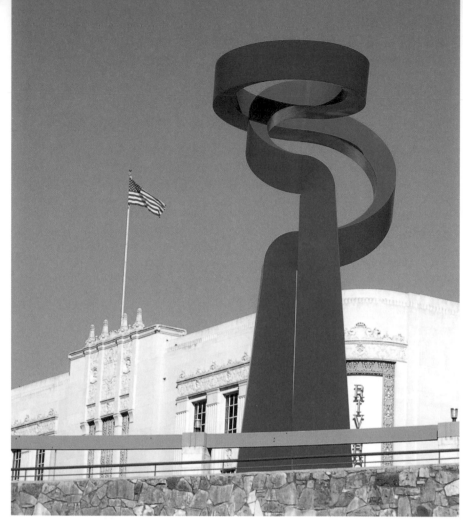

Torch of Friendship, created by Mexican artist Sebastian and donated to the people of San Antonio by the people of Mexico in 2002

paths all restored to tip-top shape. Next door, the outdoor Sunken Garden Theatre (see "The Performing Arts," above) is known for its Shakespeare productions.

Five and a half miles of trails weave throughout the hilly and heavily wooded 232-acre **Friedrich Wilderness Park** (210-207-5320; www.fofriedrichpark.org), an oasis in otherwise rapidly urbanizing Bexar County. The park is a popular spot for both birders and hikers, and its paths are clearly marked and designated by difficulty levels 1–4. All grade 1 trails are accessible by wheelchairs and strollers. First Saturday Interpretive Hikes take place on the first Saturday of each month. Two additional natural areas offering trails and fresh air near San Antonio are Medina River Natural Area and Crown Ridge Canyon Natural Area. See www.sanatural areas.org for more details on all San Antonio natural areas.

Located just outside San Antonio, the **Government Canyon State Natural Area** (210-688-9055; www.tpwd.state.tx.us) was purchased in 1993 and opened to the public for the first time in the fall of 2005. Trails are still being blazed through the park's 8,600 acres, but some are completed and ready for use, as are picnic areas and restrooms.

While you cannot swim in the 600-acre **Mitchell Lake** (210-628-1639; www .tx.audubon.org) you can spot, if you're lucky, more than 300 species of birds as you hike its protected wetland trails. Managed by the Audubon Society of Texas, the lake is somewhat off the beaten track but worth the trip for birders and nature lovers.

Talk to a native of San Antonio and they'll say that while the amusement parks are fun, **Natural Bridge Caverns** (210-651-6101; www.naturalbridgecaverns.com) is really fascinating. A National Natural Landmark, this place will exercise your vocabulary, reminding you that stalactites hang down, stalagmites rise up, and a sluice is a series of troughs leading from a water-filled tower. The standard North Cavern Tour is an informative 75 minutes that will take you a half-mile underground. The very challenging Adventure Tour is open to only the physically fit, who will enjoy the challenge of hours climbing, crawling, and rappelling in a room that is otherwise off limits. Kids will love the Watchtower Challenge, a massive outdoor climbing wall with two zip lines, and the chance to pan for treasure.

RECREATION

A tremendous online resource for all outdoor recreation in Texas is Texas Outside, www.texasoutside.com.

Bicycling
Bicycling, both road and mountain biking, is big in Central Texas, especially in the Hill Country; helpful Web sites include:

San Antonio Wheelmen (www.sawheelmen.com)

South Texas Off-Road Mountain Bikers (www.storm-web.org)

Bird Watching
San Antonio is a great spot to catch a glimpse of rare, migratory, and native birds. Online, Texas Parks and Wildlife, www.tpwd.state.tx.us, and the Audubon Society of San Antonio, www.saaudubon.org, both offer a wealth of information. See "Suggested References" in the Information chapter for a selection of bird-watching guides.

Camping
Camping around San Antonio is best accomplished in New Braunfels (see page 199).

Fishing
Fishing in Central Texas is excellent, though your best bet is to head west to Medina Lake, north to Canyon Lake or the rivers in New Braunfels, or to a Texas state park where you don't need a license to fish from shore (check www.tpwd.state.tx.us for details). See "Attractions, Parks, and Recreation" and "Texas State Parks" in the Hill Country chapter. Other online resources include www.texasoutside.com, www.txfishing.com, and www.austinkayakfishing.com.

Though Mark Twain once remarked that golf is just "a good walk spoiled," San Antonians seem to like the walk just fine. The dips and rises of the Hill Country lend themselves perfectly to the game, and some of the courses have been built in old, abandoned quarries, a nice reuse of land. With near-constant sunshine and courses ranging from the charming and historic municipal Brackenridge Golf Course to the breathtaking Palmer Course at La Cantera, it is no wonder that San Antonio has become a destination for serious and recreational golfers alike. The courses listed below rank as some of the best; expect to pay $50–100 and up. For a complete interactive online listing of local courses, visit www.golfsanantonio.org, a nonprofit organization that uses golf to both educate children and enhance charitable giving in San Antonio or www.visitsanantonio.com.

Brackenridge Golf Course (210-226-5612; www.alamocitygolftrail.com) With all the great golf to be had in greater San Antonio, one of the charms of this course is that it has that comfortable, well-worn, communal feel of an old-school municipal course. It was designed in 1915 by the fascinating and charismatic A. W. "Tillie" Tillinghast, who was also the mastermind behind what we now consider classic courses across the country—Newport in Rhode Island, Quaker Ridge in Scarsdale, New York, and his triumphant Baltusrol in Springfield, New Jersey. Golf enthusiasts may enjoy reading about his legacy at www.tillinghast.net.

Canyon Springs Golf Club (210-497-1770; www.canyonspringsgc.com) Canyon Springs is situated on the site of an old homestead, and many of the current buildings are constructed using rocks that were originally part of the 50-mile dry-stack wall encompassing the property. The unique loop design of the course means the scenic views are completely unobstructed.

The Quarry Golf Club (210-824-4500; www.quarrygolf.com) The atmospheric back nine is situated inside an old quarry and surrounded by 100-foot-high walls of rock. Elsewhere there are terrific views of the city, particularly at dusk. From downtown take US 281 out of the city and exit right at Basse Road.

The Westin La Cantera Resort (210-558-6500; www.westinlacantera.com) Built high on a hill on the site of a former limestone quarry, called *la cantera*, this resort is 20 minutes from downtown but in a world all its own. A golfer's fantasy, the resort boasts two championship 18-hole golf courses, which have earned it kudos from national magazines such as *Golf Magazine* and *Condé Nast Traveler.*

Professional Sports

The Alamodome (210-207-3663 or 800-884-3663; www.alamodome.com) hosts the high school Texas Football Classic in September and the Alamo Bowl in December (see "Festivals," above).

The AT&T Center (210-444-5000; www.attcenter.com) is host to most sporting events in San Antonio. Texans love their sports; in San Antonio, the sport is basketball, thanks to the three-time NBA champion **San Antonio Spurs** (www.spurs.com) and the **San Antonio Silver Stars** (www.wmba.com/silverstars), the women's basketball team with an enthusiastic following. The **San Antonio Rampage**, the minor league ice hockey team, (www.sarampage.com), keeps things chill.

Swimming

San Pedro Springs Park (210-207-7275; www.edwardsaquifer.net), San Antonio's oldest park, the second-oldest in the nation after Boston Common, San Pedro Springs Park is popular today primarily for its swimming area, which consists of a natural spring-fed body of cool water lined with trees and stone walkways.

Theme Parks

One of the reasons Central Texas is such a popular family getaway is the proliferation of amusement, theme, and water parks just outside San Antonio that are also easily accessible from both Austin and the Hill Country. By March or April, all are open for the season; most cut back to weekends only after Labor Day. If possible, consider planning your trip early or late in the season, avoiding July and August, for a more manageable visit; in the summer months the parks can be crowded, their sidewalks sizzling hot, and their food, snacks, and cool drinks expensive. Arriving early in the day helps beat both the throngs and the heat, but some park-goers achieve the same result by arriving in the mid-to-late afternoon, once most everyone else has worn themselves out. Arriving early may also help you snag a decent parking spot, but it won't help you avoid the $10–15 parking fee. All of the

Hats from Mexico for sale in Market Square/El Mercado

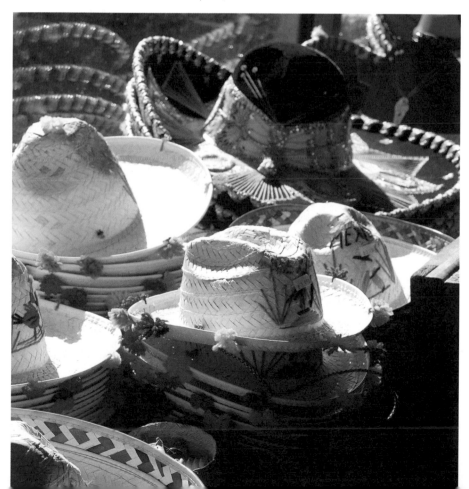

parks recommend you wear comfortable shoes and pack sunscreen, a hat, extra towels, and even a change of clothes. For swimming, proper swimsuits are essential; park-goers in anything else may be turned away. In all cases, purchasing tickets on the Internet tends to save both time and money.

German for "slippery road," **Schlitterbahn** (830-625-2351; www.schlitter bahn.com) is the place for soaking-wet, family-style fun. The park is consistently voted one of the best water parks in the country, and there are some obvious reasons why. The park is expansive, built on two different locations along the Comal River, with shuttle service in between. There are numerous chutes (some spring-fed from the river), beaches, slides, pools, tubs, and playgrounds, all very well designed for a variety of age-appropriate thrills. Adventurers may wait over an hour to ride the Master Blaster, a jet-propelled water roller coaster, while others are perfectly content to float along in tubes on the low waves and currents of The Torrent. While plenty of food and drinks are on sale inside the park, you are actually allowed to bring your own (no alcohol or glass containers, however) into the park, where picnic tables are thoughtfully provided. Schlitterbahn has on-site lodging, which, while modest and well used, is certainly serviceable, with kitchens and BBQ areas for do-it-yourself meals.

Part of the larger Busch Garden's group of Sea World parks across the United States, **Sea World San Antonio** (210-523-3000; www.seaworldparks.com) is part amusement park, part water park, and part marine life education center. Smaller than Sea World in either Florida or California, the San Antonio park is more manageable, and tickets are somewhat less expensive. The amusement park includes water rides and roller coasters, all of which spin, drop, propel, twist, or lurch their riders in the name of fun. While Journey to Atlantis will leave you soaking wet, the Steel Eel might just leave you breathless. The water park section of Sea World—Aquatica—is tamer, with water slides and wave pools; it's an area easily enjoyed by family members of all ages. Marine life enters the picture, with rare opportunities to interact with the animals, or sit back and watch elaborate shows. The "Shamu-Believe" show is a huge hit with all ages and is awash with visual effects, music, video, and, if you are sitting in the first 14 rows, water. Another popular show, "Viva," features synchronized swimmers, high divers, and Pacific white-sided dolphins and beluga whales engaged in dramatic acrobatics.

The name says it all. This is **Six Flags Fiesta Texas** (210-697-5050; www .sixflags.com), not Disney, so expectations should be adjusted accordingly. The park is designed with rides for smaller children scattered in and among those for adults, making it easier for families to stay together and stay sane. Crowd-pleasers include the mile-long, super-smooth Superman Krypton roller coaster and the Texas Tree House, with its cowboy and his ominous 1,000-gallon hat. Award-winning shows and music performances, many of which retain a Texas twang, are fun, as are the holiday-themed events. While it might be nice to have a little less Tweety Bird—who came to stay when Warner Brothers bought the Six Flags group—the park is still a Texas good time.

Much more low-key than its high-energy neighbors, **Splashtown** (210-227-1400; www.splashtownsa.com) is a small, fun, easygoing water park just a few minutes north of San Antonio. Perfect for preschool and young children, Splash-town has a wave pool, huge slides, a water bobsled, and the gently flowing Siesta del Rio waterway for tubing.

SegCity (210-224-0773; www.segcity.com) Tours on this self-balancing, motorized two-wheel contraption are rumored to be great fun, but be prepared for plenty of stares. Variety of tours daily.

Rio San Antonio Tours (210-244-5700 or 800-417-4139; www.riosanantonio .com) Narrated cruises lasting 35–40 minutes and covering 2.5 miles of Riverwalk. Tickets available online or at ticket booths at the Rivercenter Mall (Commerce St. and Bowie St.), Holiday Inn Riverwalk (St. Mary's and College Sts.), and under the Market Street Bridge at Alamo Street. All ticket booths are near elevators for handicapped access. Rio San Antonio also runs a water taxi (see "Transportation," above). Open: Daily 9 AM–9 PM.

San Antonio Tours (800-804-9486; www.sanantoniotours.net) Bus tours of San Antonio, including an all-day tour of major sights, the IMAX theater, several missions, and a riverboat ride. Also bicycle tours of the city, walking tours of King William District, a "Ghosts and Legends" tour, and bus tours of the Hill Country. Discounted tickets available online.

Texas Trolley Hop (800-804-9486; www.sanantoniotours.net) Two 60-minute tours departing from the Alamo Visitor Center beside the Alamo. With the Hop Pass, visitors are allowed to use the trolley services all day.

Tubing
Nearby New Braunfels and historic Gruene offer outstanding tubing on the pretty Guadalupe and Comal Rivers. See page 201.

Shopping
In and around San Antonio

There are plenty of knickknack and souvenir shops in the neighborhood surrounding the Riverwalk and Market Square/El Mercado (210-207-8600; www.marketsquaresa.com), with plenty of Mexican imports for sale.

For clever and quirky gifts, try the gift shops at any of the area museums, and for handcrafted arts make a trip to the gift shop of the **Southwest School of Art and Craft** (see below). **Southtown** is a good neighborhood for gallery-gazing.

Brackenridge Park and Alamo Heights
From downtown, Broadway heads north past Brackenridge Park on its way to Alamo Heights. While the area surrounding Brackenridge Park and its attractions maintains an urban feel, Alamo Heights, San Antonio's original suburb and now its own city, is much more residential. Its large homes, upscale dining, and shopping are clustered around the intersections of Broadway, North New Braunfels Avenue, and Austin Highway south of Northeast Loop 410 near the McNay Art Museum.

Monte Vista and Olmos Park
Neighboring Alamo Heights to the west, this once-exquisite neighborhood has an uneven look and feel today, with lovingly restored mansions side by side with those that have fallen on hard times. A down-to-earth side of San Antonio, Monte Vista and Olmos Park are home to some well-loved restaurants and B&Bs.

Culture
History, Heritage, and the Arts

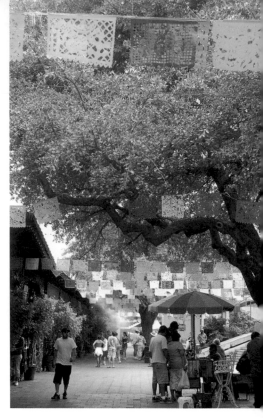

Most of San Antonio's sights can be found in three neighborhoods of the city—the Riverwalk, King William District, and Brackenridge Park—but don't miss the Mission Trail, the route linking the four historic missions on the outer edges of the city.

HISTORIC PLACES

Visitors may be surprised by the size of the **Alamo** (210-225-1391; www.the alamo.org). Rather than an imposing fort, the Alamo is a small structure whose architecture is indicative of its religious roots. Built from local rock, its intricately carved exterior is a light, sandy beige color that reflects the bright Texas sun. The Daughters of the Republic of Texas, women whose Texas roots run as deep as the Edwards Aquifer, are particularly proud of their role as custodians of the structure; they

Market Square/El Mercado

maintain it with care and demand utmost respect. To best understand the Alamo's significance, you must first understand its history.

The Alamo began as an idea when Antonio de San Buenaventura y Olivares, a participant in the entrada to establish missions in Texas, visited a spot just west of the San Pedro Springs on April 13, 1709, and dreamt of building a mission there. That dream was realized nine years later on May 1, 1718, when he erected a small hut of brush and grapevines, said Mass, and named his creation the Mission San Antonio de Valero. In 1719 the mission relocated to the east of San Pedro Springs; it was later uprooted and moved once more to the spot now occupied by St. Joseph's Church in San Antonio, where it was destroyed by floods in 1724. Finally, in 1744 the mission was built along the banks of the San Antonio River, only to be abandoned when Mexico secularized the missions in 1793. From these chaotic beginnings and amid rising tensions between area Anglos and Mexicans, the mission's function morphed from sanctuary for converts to an enclave of combatants. When the Mexican cavalry occupied the mission in the early 1800s, it was referred to as the *pueblo del alamo*—*alamo* being the Spanish word for cottonwood, so-called perhaps for the trees along the river—and the name stuck.

On October 2, 1835, turf wars between Mexicans and Anglos reached a boiling point when Mexicans demanded the town cannon from the nearby settlement of Gonzales, and were told, in no uncertain terms, "Come and get it." Needless to say, the Mexicans did and promptly lost the first battle of the Texas Revolution.

Emboldened by success, a hastily gathered group of barely 200 male colonists (and dozens of women and children), including the legendary Davy Crockett, Stephen F. Austin, William Travis, and the famous knife fighter Jim Bowie, seized San Antonio and settled into the abandoned mission, the Alamo, to wait for the inevitable Mexican retribution.

On February 23, 1836, an estimated 4,000 Mexican troops, under the command of the formidable Gen. Antonio López de Santa Anna, besieged the Alamo, capturing it after 13 days of constant battle and the deaths of all defenders. While the participants lost the Alamo and their lives (though some women and children were released), their actions became the stuff of legend. The event galvanized

The Alamo

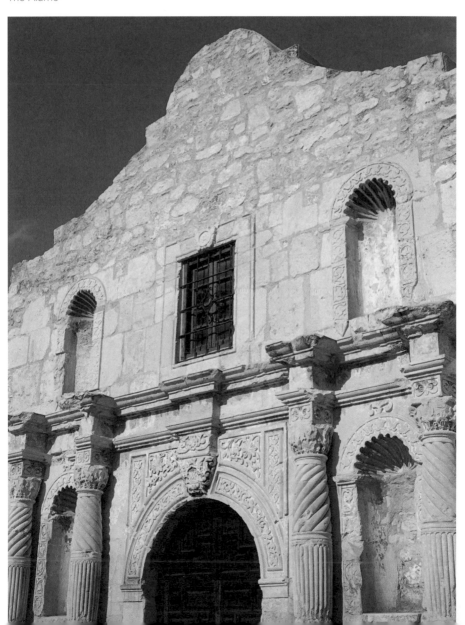

support for the ultimately successful revolution against Mexico, for which the phrase "Remember the Alamo" became a rallying cry. Or so the story goes. As with any historically significant battle, especially one as dramatic and pivotal as this, the facts are still debated. What remains is what the Alamo has come to represent: collective courage in the face of insurmountable odds.

Near the Alamo, the larger-than-life drama of the siege comes alive on a six-story screen accompanied by six-track stereo sound at the **Alamo IMAX Theater** (210-247-4629; www.imax-sa.com) in the Rivercenter Mall. Highly recommended for those whose Texas history has gotten a little rusty. Check the **San Antonio Living History Association**'s Web site, www.mysalha.org, for the schedule of dramatic live reenactments.

The Missions

The **San Antonio Missions** (210-534-8833; www.nps.gov/saan), now a national park, were built in the 1700s as part of Spain's efforts to colonize its northern frontier, Texas. The idea was to build self-sustaining communities, patterned after villages in Spain, that would provide support for continued colonization as well as formal education for Native Americans in the ways and religion of the country that now considered them subjects. While some Native Americans met the idea with resistance, others acquiesced, and construction began. The five expansive San Antonio missions were built in just 13 years, with presidios, or military outposts, established nearby for protection.

Memorial to those who died at the battle of the Alamo in 1836 ·

One of the extraordinary features of the missions are the *acequias*—aqueducts and irrigation ditches—running between them. While the Pueblo in New Mexico had already designed and built aqueducts, this technology would have been unknown to the nomadic Native Americans in Central Texas. Desperate to irrigate the arid land, the Franciscan missionaries, familiar with the aqueducts built by the Romans and the Moors, designed the system, part of which is still in use and can be seen at various locations along the Mission Trail, including Espada Park near Mission San José.

With housing, water, and farming in place, the missions functioned relatively well from 1745 to the 1780s.

Mission San Jose

Over time, though, attacks and looting by Native Americans, lack of recruits, and disease took their toll; in 1794 a decree from the government ordered the secularization of all missions, disbanding their communal structure.

Throughout the years, the missions have endured the passing of time, weather, and some misguided attempts at restoration. Though many of the details you see today are actually painstaking reproductions, the sheer beauty and scale of the endeavor is impressive.

Today, the individual missions are active parishes, with many descendants of the original parishioners among their members. Though visitors are welcome to attend Mass, the Park Service reminds guests to be respectful of weddings, funerals, or other functions, which may temporarily close the venue for several hours.

Leaving San Antonio and following signs for the Mission Trail, the first property you'll come to along Missis Road is **Mission Concepción** (210-534-1540; http://www.nps.gov/saan) at the corner of Felisa. A stone church bookended by a pair of bell towers, Mission Concepción is a spectacular example of Spanish colonial architecture, with intricate details, artwork, and design adaptations that illustrate

Hike and Bike Between

Allow at least three hours to visit the entire park: 1½ to 2 hours at Mission San José and the park's **Visitor Center** located there, then 30–40 minutes at each of the other three parks. The missions are approximately 2 miles apart, a short drive from one to the next. The brand new **Mission Hike and Bike Trail** has begun the process of reconnecting the missions, providing a safe way for visitors walk or bike alongside the San Antonio River between them. See www.san antonioriver.org for details.

the close relationship between the Native American, Spanish, and Mexican artisans who built it. Colorful and detailed frescos once covered both the front and interior of the church. While only a handful have survived the 250 years since they were created, those that do remain are a testament to the craftsmanship and artistry of their makers. Mission Concepción hosted any religious festivals, celebrations, pageants, and processionals, all designed to school new Spaniards in the ways of Christianity.

A few miles south is **Mission San José** (210-962-1001; http://www.nps.gov /saan), home to the Park Service's **Visitor Center.** Founded in 1720 by Father Antonio Margil de Jésus, its complex of bastions, a granary, and a church, surrounded by stone walls, was completed in 1782. Elaborate design features, such as the intricately carved wooden doors, poignant statuary, and ornate La Ventana de Rosa, the Rose Window, earned Mission San José the reputation of "Queen of the Missions." A thriving community of three hundred souls in its heyday, Mission San José was a model of success for the other missions.

It is still a very active parish, and visitors are welcome to attend Mass on Sunday. The noon "Mariachi Mass" is very popular; doors close once seats are filled, so plan on arriving early.

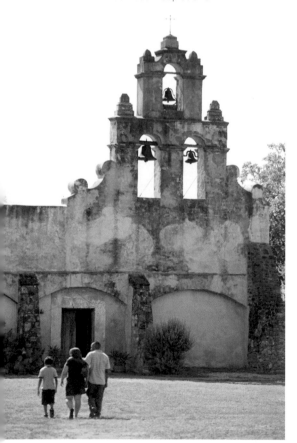

Mission San Juan Capistrano

Next in line is **Mission San Juan Capistrano** (210-534-0749; http://www .nps.gov/saan), founded in 1716 in what is now East Texas and moved to its present location in 1731. This mission is best remembered for its remarkable productivity, with orchards and gardens in its adjacent *labores* (farmlands designated for the mission's use) and herds of sheep and cattle. By the mid-1700s, Mission San Juan was a major supplier of produce not just to the local area, but to markets as far away as Louisiana and Mexico.

Duck under I-410 and make your way to **Mission San Francisco Espada** (210-627-2021; http://www.nps.gov /saan), the very first mission in Texas, originally founded in East Texas in 1690 and moved to San Antonio in 1731. The present-day building, completed in 1756, is clearly recognizable by its graceful *espadaña*, (bell tower) with three bells, which rises above its unique arched doorway; be sure to ask a park ranger about the mystery of its design. The wooden cross beside the door, as the story goes, was borne by parishioners processing and praying for rain. The diminutive and detailed

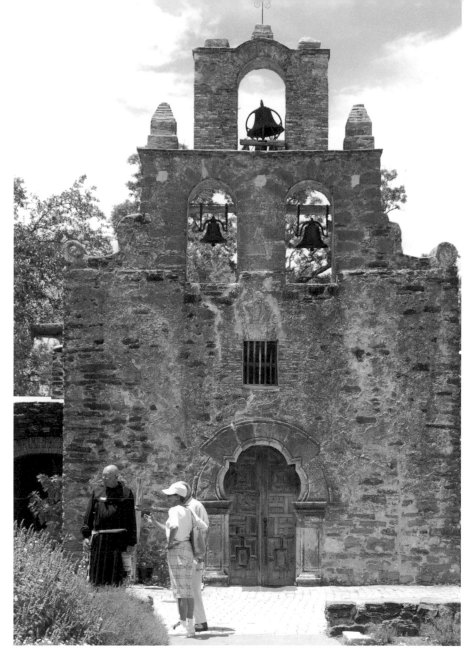

Mission San Franscisco de la Espada

chapel is intimate and tranquil. Mission Espada's *acequia madre* (the main aque-
duct) and nearby Espada Dam, built in the 1730s, are both still in use.

   Casa Navarro State Historic Site (210-226-4801; www.visitcasanavarro.com)
is a complex of white limestone, clay, and adobe structures, once home to promi-
nent Tejano businessman, statesman, and writer José Antonio Navarro, and of
interest to anyone wanting to dig a little deeper into the complexities of Texas

history. Navarro, who was born in 1795 and died in 1871, witnessed the most significant years in Texas history. He was one of the signers of the Texas Declaration of Independence in 1836 and a tireless defender of Tejano rights.

You can see the bell towers of the **San Fernando Cathedral** (210-227-1297; www.sfcathedral.org) a few blocks away. Established in 1731 by just over a dozen families from the Canary Islands, the cathedral that was designed to be in the center of town has certainly been the center of drama over the years. Jim Bowie was purportedly married here. Santa Anna used it as a lookout post and from its walls raised the flag that signaled the start of the Battle of the Alamo. The huge Gothic

The dramatic facade of San Fernando Cathedral

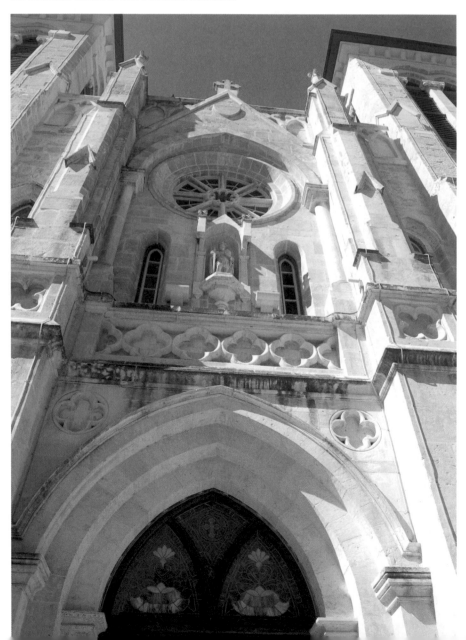

La Villita

Perched above the San Antonio River is the city's first neighborhood, **La Villita** (210-207-8610; www.lavillita.com), "little village." First, the Coahuiltecan Indians settled here. Later, Spanish soldiers built huts, which were washed away in a flood in 1819 and replaced with more substantial dwellings made of stone, adobe, and brick. In 1836 General Santa Anna used the area for his cannons in the Battle of the Alamo. In the late 1800s Germans and French immigrated to the area and brought with them their own architectural style, hence the Victorian elements still seen in La Villita. In the early 20th century the neighborhood fell into disrepair, but by the late 1930s talk of the Riverwalk project brought renewed interest in San Antonio's historic past, and La Villita was preserved as the urban center grew around it. These days, La Villita is called an artist community, though it feels more like one gift shop after the next. The area is pleasant, a welcome detour from the city's busy streets, and its Arneson Theatre (see p. 138) is well known for hosting music and cultural performances.

Revival–style cathedral you see today, built in 1868, integrates the original structure into its plan. In 1871 the original massive dome ceiling collapsed to be later rebuilt. In the 1930s remains uncovered on-site thought to be those of Bowie, Davy Crockett, and William Travis were laid to rest in a marble casket at the back of the church. After Texas joined the United States in 1845, the strong ties between San Fernando Cathedral and the community it served survived; they are still vital today, making the cathedral one of the most important, lasting Hispanic institutions in a rapidly changing city and state.

San Fernando Cathedral is host to music, concerts, and interdenominational events, and doubles as a community center and social services headquarters. In order to preserve the historic structure and add much-needed space for functions, San Fernando is currently raising funds for a massive renovation project scheduled to begin in the near future. A

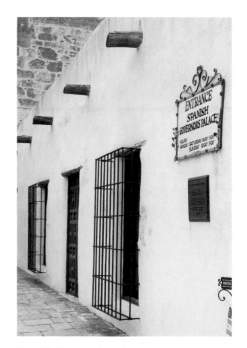

Spanish Governor's Palace

parish church, San Fernando conducts hundreds of baptisms, weddings, and funerals each year: If your visit coincides with one, the church respectfully asks that you return at a different time. The best way to visit just might be by attending Mass; see the Web site for details.

Across the street, the **Spanish Governor's Palace** (210-224-0601; www.spanish governorspalace.org), a National Historic Landmark, was actually the residence

HemisFair Park

The HemisFair, held April through October 1968 and planned to coincide with the 250th anniversary of the founding of the city, was an international exposition celebrating the shared cultural heritage of San Antonio and Latin America, organized around the theme of "Confluence of Civilization in the Americas." Canada, Mexico, Italy, Spain, France, and Japan were quick to host large exhibits; and some effort, including securing sponsorship from local foundations, had to be made in order for exhibits representing Nicaragua, Honduras, Guatemala, El Salvador, and Costa Rica to be realized. The Institute of Texan Cultures (see below) was constructed for this event, and its exhibits highlighting the contributions of various ethnic groups to the formation of modern Texas were a huge hit.

The construction of the fairgrounds was mired in controversy, as the land

Tower of the Americas, with a storm brewing

and headquarters of the presidio captain who was to watch over the Mission San Antonio de Valero—the Alamo. Built in the early 1700s, the building is the only surviving example of a Spanish aristocratic home in the United States. A small, white stucco building with very low ceilings and doorways, the abode is graceful in its simplicity; a small courtyard, fountain, and period furnishings lend themselves to the atmosphere, as does *La Compañía de Cavallería del Real Presidio de San Antonio de Béxar,* the living history group that gives performances on the final Sunday of each month. Acquired by the city of San Antonio in the 1920s, the home is currently under the auspices of the city's Parks and Recreation Department.

MUSEUMS

The **Institute of Texan Cultures** (ITC) (210-458-2300; www.texancultures.utsa .edu) was originally designed as a collection of exhibits for the Texas pavilion of the HemisFair held in San Antonio in 1968. The ITC is best described as an education center highlighting the contributions of the state's vastly diverse ethnic groups and, as their mission statement states, "the dynamics between cultural history and sciused was part of the "old city," home to 120 buildings in various states of upkeep and residents with an attachment to their neighborhood. Fair planners were able to have the area designated an urban renewal site and secured federal funding for the project. In the end only 22 of the original structures survived and were incorporated into the park, the rest destroyed; all the residents were relocated. The Tower of the Americas, a technological feat at its time, was built, and the Riverwalk was extended a quarter-mile to link the park to the greater downtown neighborhood. Though over 6 million visitors enjoyed the park during the HemisFair, the park failed to become the cultural or recreational center of the city, as planners had hoped. The Institute of Texan Cultures excepted, many of the buildings now serve functions that aren't recreational or cultural; for example, what was the United States' exhibit hall is now a federal courthouse.

Today, the park consists of 5 acres of grass, trees, and gardens crisscrossed with paths, dotted with fountains, and featuring an enormous wooden play structure for children. **The Instituto Cultural Mexicano** (210-227-0123; www.icm.sre.gob.mx/cul turamexsa) hosts films, music, salsa, merengue, and tango dance classes and is home to the small Casa Mexicana Gallery, which displays works of contemporary artists from Mexico. The **Tower of the Americas** (210-223-3101; www.towerofthe americas.com) has undergone an $11 million makeover designed to ignite more interest among both residents and visitors. The observation deck, **Flags Over Texas**, offers spectacular views of the city, and the 4-D theater, **Skies Over Texas**, will challenge your sensitivity to vertigo. At the deck's pinnacle, the newly opened rotating restaurant, **Chart House Restaurant** (210-223-3101; www.toweroftheamericas.com), is run by Landry's, with a seafood-centric menu and friendly, if somewhat slow, service. The ground floor café is open for coffee or cold drinks.

entific discovery." Though it was supposed to have only a six-month run, the effort was so well received that the ITC remains open to this day, now under the auspices of the University of Texas at San Antonio. Its exhibits, while fairly low-tech and not particularly flashy, are engaging, thoughtfully put together, and rich with historical detail. The esoteric surprises are fun, such as the small exhibit on the Wendish immigrants who came to Texas from what is now borderland between Germany and Poland. The staff is particularly knowledgeable and happy to answer questions. The institute hosts the fantastic Texas Folklife Festival every year in June (see "Festivals," below).

Stroll north along a more peaceful stretch of the Riverwalk, and you'll come upon the exquisite **Southwest School of Art and Craft** (210-224-1848; www.sw school.org), built in 1851 as the Ursuline Convent and Academy as part of an effort to renew Texans' interest in the Catholic Church. The Ursuline Academy remained until 1965, when it relocated and sold a portion of its property to the San Antonio Conservation Society, who in turn invited the Southwest School of Art and Craft to take up residency in the early 1970s. Possessing a creative appreciation of the property's beauty and significance, the school extensively renovated the complex while retaining its lovely sense of calm and quiet dignity. The school's

Inside the Southwest School of Art and Craft

gardens, courtyards, and chapel are serene. The graceful buildings were created using a technique known as *pisé de terre*, in which bricks are made by forcing clay, rock, and straw into wooden forms, allowing them to dry, and then skim-coating with plaster— it is the inspiration for modern-day rammed-earth construction. The resulting bricks are solid and thick so that they can resist the heat of the sun, and, when combined with creaky wooden floors, make for a very atmospheric interior. The structures are designated as a Texas Historic Landmark and are on the National Register of Historic Places. The Copper Kitchen Café (210-224-0123) serves simple, healthy meals, and its dining rooms have an austere beauty that harks back to convent days; the Gift Gallery (210-224-1848) has unique artistic gifts; the History Museum (210-224-1848) offers docent tours of the property on weekdays; and the annual Fiesta

After a day of saying "Please don't touch that, honey, this is a museum" and "Please don't climb on that, it is very fragile and of great historical significance," doesn't a museum for kids sound great? At the **San Antonio Children's Museum** (210-212-4453; www.sa kids.org) kids can be kids and all you have to do is just sit back and watch.

Quirky Museums

There are several museums in San Antonio that, depending on your interests, may intrigue.

Buckhorn Saloon and Museum (210-247-4000; www.buckhornmuseum.com) If you're not into alcohol and taxidermy this place may not appeal, but if you are, it's neat. The entrance is at the bar, and from there you can wander, drink in hand, into the museum, where all sorts of Wild West memorabilia share billing with the mounted heads of a wide variety of animals. Just in case you didn't think it was odd enough, check out the Curio Store.

O. Henry House Museum (www.ohenryhouse.org) A glimpse into the world of William Sidney Porter, who lived in this 1886 Queen Anne–style cottage from 1893 to 1895; but die-hard O. Henry fans will find the O. Henry Museum in Austin more satisfying (see page 78).

Arts Fair is a much-anticipated kickoff event for Fiesta San Antonio in April (see "Festivals," below).

Continuing north and slightly east along the Museum Reach extension of Riverwalk, the **San Antonio Museum of Art** (SAMA) (210-978-8100; www.sa museum.org) inhabits the large, industrial, almost fortress-like facilities of the former Lone Star Brewery. The bulk of the museum's holdings results from the combination of two major collections, one bequeathed by Gilbert M. Denman Jr. and the other the Stark-Willson Collection. The SAMA is noted for its outstanding collection of ancient Egyptian, Near Eastern, Greek, and Roman art; it is the largest collection of antiquities in the United States. Remarkable ivory carvings, detailed mummy masks, a flask with snake-shaped threads at its opening, and a camel cosmetic case are all good examples. The museum's Nelson A. Rockefeller Center for Latin American Arts has over 10,000 pieces in its collection. Pre-Columbian art, mostly from the first millennium AD, is well represented, and there is plenty of Spanish colonial art, particularly that which is religious in nature. For some, though, it is the pieces of folk art that really stand out—such as a fascinating display of colorful jaguar masks used in religious rituals from pre-Columbian days through the colonial era and still used in the villages of southern Mexico during certain celebrations. That it has endured for this long illustrates the staying power of imagery and its adaptability under outside influences and changing times. From the Riverwalk, take the #7 Sightseer Special bus (www.viainfo.net), a river taxi (www.riosan antonio.com), or rent a bicycle (www.sanantonio.bcycle.com), and plan on having lunch at the museum's bistro, Café des Artistes (www.cafedesartistes.com).

Located on Broadway, at the edge of Brackenridge Park (see p. 116), the **Witte Museum** (210-357-1900; www.wittemuseum.org) has a story or two to tell. Remarkably, San Antonio's natural history museum was born through the perseverance of a local schoolteacher. The teacher, Ellen Schulz, managed to raise $5,000 in the 1920s and purchase a large group of specimens, which were then put on display at the high school. An appeal to the city for assistance in building a proper museum yielded public funding and a $65,000 donation from a local businessman, Alfred G. Witte, who requested that the planned museum be built in Brackenridge Park and named for his parents. The Witte Museum subsequently opened its doors in 1926. In the 1970s the museum hired an art historian as director, and its focus began to shift, leading to the purchase and renovation of an old brewery to house its rapidly expanding collection of art and culminating in 1981 in the formation of the San Antonio Museum of Art (see above), an entity that would become independent in 1994.

Refocused on its original mission, the Witte is now a museum dedicated solely to the history, cultures, ecology, and science of South Texas and is most interesting

Interior of the San Antonio Museum of Art

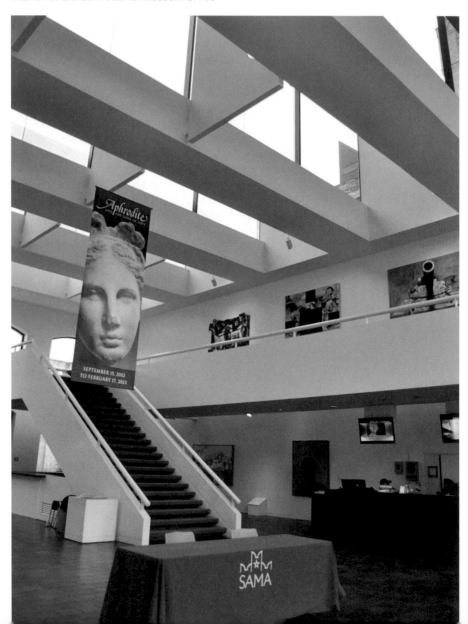

Galleries

Tightly knit Southtown has a growing number of galleries and creative shops, all within easy walking distance from one another. The highly respected **San Angel Folk Art Gallery** (210-226-6688; www.sanangelfolkart.com), in the **Blue Star Arts Complex** (www.bluestarart.org), displays a very nice selection of folk art pieces created by artists living in the United States, Mexico, and Europe. Also in Blue Star, **Stone Metal Press** (210-627-8170; www.stonemetal-press.com) displays works on paper, and **Garcia Art Glass** (210-354-4681; www.garciaartglass.com), nearby on South Alamo, sells vividly colored handblown art glass.

to children and their families. Full-scale dinosaur skeletons, including the enormous triceratops at the center of the gallery, detailed dioramas depicting what life may have been like for Native Americans in the Lower Pecos region, and displays of live bees, spiders, and snakes will all appeal to the curious. The colorful H-E-B Science Tree House features hands-on science exhibits. The museum has undergone a much-needed expansion and some of its most interesting and intriguing pieces, once in storage, are now on display in the brand new Kleberg South Texas Heritage Center.

Broadway continues north, merging with New Braunfels Avenue at the location of the wonderful **McNay Art Museum** (210-824-5368; www.mcnayart.org).

Pensive statue in front of the McNay Art Museum

The first modern art museum in Texas, the McNay is located in the Spanish Colonial Revival–style mansion of art-lover Marion Koogler McNay. Upon her death in 1950, she bequeathed the mansion, the gorgeous 23 acres on which it sits, the extensive art collection housed within it, and two-thirds of her fortune to the city of San Antonio, which opened the entire estate as a museum in 1954. A serious collector, Mrs. McNay had a wonderful eye; the museum houses some real gems, most of them American or European pieces from the 19th and 20th centuries. There are bold paintings by Paul Gauguin and Vincent van Gogh, watercolors by Mary Cassatt and Winslow Homer, and collections of pieces in various mediums that McNay acquired on trips to artist colonies in New Mexico in the 1930s. Over the years, gifts by various collectors have added major paintings by Georgia O'Keeffe and sculptures by Auguste Rodin and Alberto Giacometti, among others. In 1984 Robert L. B. Tobin donated a collection of eight thousand books, many on the theater arts, which are now part of a research library that bears his name. The Blanche and John Leeper Auditorium was completed in the early 1990s, paving the way for performances and concerts to be held at the museum. In many ways, the McNay is best known for the breadth and depth of the outstanding national exhibitions it is able to attract and host in its galleries in a given year. All told, a lovely museum, inside and out.

THE PERFORMING ARTS

San Antonio has fantastic theaters that are historic and atmospheric; most are multipurpose performing arts centers.

Alamo City Men's Chorale (210-495-7464; www.acmc-texas.org) Local gay men's chorus harmonizes in lovely holiday concerts and enthusiastic performances at the annual Pride Concert.

Arneson Theatre (210-207-8610; www.lavillita.com/arneson) The Arneson hosts events in its outdoor amphitheater on the banks of the Riverwalk at La Villita. Diverse offerings include the **Alamo Irish Festival** (www.harpandshamrock .org) in March and the **Fiesta Noche del Rio** (www.alamo-kiwanis.org), an August celebration of song and dance from Mexico, Spain, Argentina, and Texas, put on by the Kiwanis Club, with all proceeds benefiting local charity.

ARTS San Antonio (210-226-2891; www.artssanantonio.com) ARTS San Antonio brings comedy, musicals, and dance performances from classical to contemporary, with most taking place at the centrally located Convention Center.

The Blue Star Arts Complex (210-227-6960; www.bluestarart.org), or Blue Star for short, is both a building and a community. Blue Star the building is a historic 1920s warehouse that has been renovated, retrofitted, and readapted to serve as a residential, commercial, and art space, with lofts, studios, and several galleries. This effort was pioneered in 1985 by a community of artists and volunteers bound by their dream of providing exhibition space for contemporary artists; it made a big splash when it opened, and the ripple effects of revitalization were felt throughout its neighborhood, the King William District, and neighboring Southtown. Though Blue Star has matured into a sophisticated and sought-after contemporary art venue, one now run by a professional staff, it retains much of the earnestness of its grassroots days. With local, national, and international artists represented across the gamut of painting, etching, photography, and performance art—and its own on-site brew pub, the Blue Star Brewing Company (see "Nightlife," below)—Blue Star shines brightly in South San Antonio.

Carver Community Cultural Center (210-207-7211; www.thecarver.org) The Carver Center began as an African American public library in 1929, when segregation mandated separate facilities. The center soon grew into an epicenter of the arts, with performances by many of the greats, such as Ella Fitzgerald, Louis Armstrong, Charlie "Bird" Parker, and Cab Calloway. These days, the Carver is a historic venue that still hosts big-name national and international stars of dance and music, especially jazz.

Empire Theatre (210-226-3333; www.majesticempire.com) Nine feet of water poured into this theater during the flood of 1921, damaging much of its gilded 1890s interior. Over time, the Empire declined, and it closed in the 1970s. Rescued by the city with the help of Las Casas Foundation, the nonprofit organization responsible for saving some of San Antonio's most historic and treasured cultural institutions, the Empire reopened in 1998, restored to its original glory. Due to its outstanding acoustics, the Empire Theatre hosts mostly music.

Guadalupe Cultural Arts Center (210-271-3151; www.guadalupeculturalarts .org) The Guadalupe, as it is known, aims to "preserve, promote, and develop the arts and culture of the Chicano/Latino/Native American peoples for all ages and backgrounds" through the performing arts. And it certainly does. Among other things, the organization presents the city's annual CineFestival and Tejano Conjunto Festival (see "Festivals," below).

Josephine Theatre (210-734-4646; www.josephinetheatre.org) The Josephine is a small local theater with a lot of chutzpah. When the future of the theater company's 1947 art deco digs became uncertain in 2003, the spunky little company raised enough money to buy the building and continued right along, producing high-energy, feel-good musicals.

Jump-Start Performance Company (210-227-5867; www.jump-start.org) Located in the Blue Star Art Complex, the performances at Jump-Start are definitely energizing. Jump-Start recently staged The Return of the Shrew, a contemporary takeoff on Taming of the Shrew that involved lots of outrageous outfits and madcap escapades, as do most of their productions. Each year, Jump-Start and writer Sandra Cisneros pair up to host a special event, always a mélange of entertainment, refreshments, and well-chosen words; see the Web site for details.

Magik Children's Theatre (210-227-2751; www.magiktheatre.org) This is a terrific theater for children and families. Daytime and evening shows change monthly, and Shakespeare in the Park is a mid-summer's night dream in June.

Majestic Theatre (210-226-3333; www.majesticempire.com) The impossibly ornate Majestic Theatre was built in 1929, sadly closed in the 1970s, then triumphantly renovated and reopened in 1989. The home of the San Antonio Symphony (see below), the Majestic has an enticing roster, ranging from Broadway shows to ballet, classical, and contemporary music.

San Antonio Dance Umbrella (210-212-6600; www.sadu.org) This city organization promotes, encourages, supports, and hosts all aspects of dance in San Antonio. Its comprehensive Web site lists all dance performances throughout the city.

San Antonio Living History Association (210-255-1432; www.sanantonio livinghistory.org) A group of dedicated volunteers performs action-packed reenactments of historic battles, including the one for the Alamo. The events are interesting, free, and infrequent.

San Antonio Symphony (210-554-1010; www.sasymphony.org) For many years after its inception in 1939, the San Antonio Symphony traveled a bumpy road fraught with financial difficulties and changing leadership. Today the path is smoother, and music lovers can now enjoy the symphony's sharp performances in the sumptuous, historic Majestic Theatre.

San Pedro Playhouse (210-733-7258; www.sanpedroplayhouse.com) Actors at the San Pedro Playhouse have been onstage in this Greek Revival–style mansion in San Pedro Park for more than 70 years, putting on everything from *Hair* to *Hamlet*.

Sunken Garden Theatre (210-735-0663; www.sanantonio.gov) Another abandoned quarry put to good use, the Sunken Garden Theatre is located in Brackenridge Park, next to the Japanese Tea Garden. A lovely open-air venue for comedy, Shakespeare, and music performances.

Texas Talent Musicians Association (210-320-4200; www.tejanomusicawards .com). A nonprofit organization dedicated to promoting more understanding and appreciation of Tejano music, in part through its largest event, the Tejano Music Awards. The list of past winners reads like a Who's Who of the Tejano music scene.

CINEMA

Alamo Drafthouse (210-677-8500: www.drafthouse.com) The San Antonio branch of this Central Texas–based cinema chain is every bit as fun as the ones in Austin. Great flicks, with great food brought right to your seat. Everything from Angus burgers to fried pickles.

Alamo IMAX Theater (210-247-4629; www.imax-sa.com) The larger-than-life drama of the siege of the Alamo comes alive on this six-story screen accompanied by six-track stereo sound. Highly recommended for those whose Texas history has gotten a little rusty.

The Bijou at Crossroads (210-496-2221; www.santikos.com) The Santikos family has been bringing movies to San Antonio for over 80 years; they currently operate a variety of venues (including a drive-in), many of which serve hors d'oeuvres, burgers, gourmet pizzas, and spanakopita, the Greek spinach dish.

FESTIVALS

San Antonio is bursting at the seams with festivals, cultural events, market days, and music. Some may be worth planning a trip around, and others may just happen to coincide with your visit. These events always bring out the best in vivacious and community-minded San Antonio.

January

Riverwalk Mud Festival (210-227-4262; www.thesanantonioriverwalk.com) Celebrating the annual draining of the San Antonio River for cleaning, this festival features parades, pie, a pub crawl, and mud.

Martin Luther King Jr. March (210-444-2315; www.dreamweek.org) While most cities have special events on the weekend of Martin Luther King Jr. Day, San Antonio has one of the largest. Free.

February

San Antonio Stock Show and Rodeo (210-225-5851; www.sarodeo.com) A 16-day extravaganza of food, music, and rodeo performances. Admission charged.

Mardi Gras (www.thesanantonioriverwalk.com) Colorful barges and a variety of music along the river are the hallmarks of Mardi Gras in San Antonio. Held the weekend before Ash Wednesday. Free.

March

Remember the Alamo Weekend and Dawn at the Alamo (210-273-1730;

www.mysalha.org) Reenactment and interpretation of the events at the Alamo, both commemorative and educational. Free.

St. Patrick's Day (210-227-4262; www.thesanantonioriverwalk.com) Various events, including parades on both street and river, and the "Dyeing o' the River Green." Free.

Watercolor Month (210-207-6700; www.visitsanantonio.com) Watercolors of all sizes, styles, and subjects on display in galleries, museums, and other venues throughout town. Free.

April

Fiesta San Antonio! (210-227-5191; www.fiesta-sa.org) One of the country's oldest traditions of sheer cross-cultural fun, and the city's signature event. Food, art, fireworks, carnivals, sports, and music you can't help but dance to bring out some three million revelers to this weeklong, citywide party. Admission charged.

King William Fair (210-271-3247; www.kwfair.org) Held at the end of April, this fair encompasses several blocks of Madison, King William, and Washington Streets. With food booths, juried arts and crafts vendors, a children's area with pony rides and blow-up bouncy structures, and a parade. A great way to spend some time in the lovely King William District. Free.

May

Cinco de Mayo (210-207-8600; www.visitsanantonio.com) Commemoration and celebration of the Mexican army's victory over the French at the Battle of Puebla on May 5, 1862. A joyous cultural festival featuring events in Market Square and throughout the city. Free.

Tejano Conjunto Festival en San Antonio (210-271-3151; www.guadalupe culturalarts.org) A week of live music from traditional *conjunto* to progressive *Tejano* and everything in between, played by extremely talented musicians, in some cases living legends. Food, games, and dancing. Admission charged.

June

Texas Folklife Festival (210-458-2300; www.texancultures.com) A major four-day cultural extravaganza representing more than 40 ethnic groups, with plenty of food, dancing, music, and crafts to go around. The 2006 celebration had nine performance stages booked solid for the duration of the festival, with such acts as Scottish bagpipe bands; Lebanese, Flemish, and German folk dancers; Mexican ranchero songs; Latin jazz; and Chinese dragon dancers, all from groups with strong Texas roots. Food is as wide-ranging, from Czech *kolaches* to Polish *pierogis* to homemade flour tortillas. A truly amazing display of diversity. Admission charged.

Juneteenth (210-527-1830; www.juneteenthsanantonio.com). Remembering June 19, 1865, the day that slaves in Texas first received word of the Emancipation Proclamation. A spirited citywide celebration of freedom. Admission charged.

July

Fourth of July (210-227-4262; www.thesanantonioriverwalk.com) In San Antonio, Independence Day festivities center on Market Square, the Riverwalk, and blowout celebrations at the local theme parks. Admission and free.

Conjunto Music

As the Spanish moved across Texas in the early 1800s, they organized dances and concerts featuring the violins, guitars, and *pitos* (a wind instrument) specific to their musical traditions. By the 1860s, the rhythms of the waltzes and polkas of the European court had drifted from Maximillian-ruled Mexico north into Texas and were added to the developing style of *música tejana,* or Tex-Mex music. Then Germans arrived to live and work in South and Central Texas and northern Mexico, bringing with them the diatonic button accordion, the instrument that would revolutionize the music of the area.

Since the accordion allowed for a single musician to play both melody and harmony with one instrument, the popularity of the violins and pitos diminished. By the late 1880s, the *tambora de ranch* (goatskin drum) and the *bajo sexto* (12-string guitar) were added to the accordion to give more depth and complexity to the sound. By the 1900s, *música norteña* was played all over ranches and farms of South Texas and northern Mexico and at the *fandangos*, or get-togethers, featuring eating, dancing, and gambling, closely identified with working-class Tejanos.

In the early 1900s, as Tejanos moved to cities, they took their accordions with them and continued to play *conjunto* at home, parties, and neighborhood events. During the 1930s virtuoso Narciso Martínez, known as the father of modern *conjunto*, and San Antonian Santiago Jimenez popularized the genre through recordings and radio broadcasts. The legendary Tejana singer of this era, Lydia Mendoza, also known as the "queen of Tejano," sang her way to fame in the plazas of San Antonio.

San Antonio Conjunto Shootout (210-207-8600; www.visitsanantonio.com) A *conjunto* battle of the bands, held in Market Square, with food, refreshments, and dancing. Free.

Contemporary Art Month (www.contemporaryartmonth.com) The only monthlong contemporary arts festival in the nation, with more than 400 exhibitions in galleries, museums, neighborhoods, and studios. Admission and free.

Cactus Pear Music Festival (210-838-2218; www.cpmf.us) A chamber music festival in San Antonio and the Hill Country towns that steps in where the San Antonio Symphony leaves off in the summer. Admission charged.

Pridefest (866-535-8067; www.pridesanantonio.org) Local gay/lesbian groups celebrate this nationally recognized event with a block party and parade in HemisFair Park. Free.

August

Ford Canoe Challenge (210-227-4262; www.thesanantonioriverwalk.com) Participants race canoes from the Chamber of Commerce, around the Convention Center Lagoon, through the River Center Mall Lagoon, and back to the Chamber of Commerce. Free.

September

FotoSeptiembre USA (www.safotofestival.com) One of the largest photography

In the 1940s and 1950s, singer Valerio Longoria layered lyrics over the accordion, playing what would become known as *canciones rancheras*. These "ranch songs" were nostalgic pieces whose lyrics of love, loss, and simpler times resonated deeply with listeners. As *conjunto* matured, it never strayed far from its Tejano roots. Touring and playing for large groups along the migrant trail between Mexico and the United States in the 1950s and '60s, Tony de la Rosa added amplifiers to what had by then become the standard quartet: accordion, *bajo sexto*, bass, and drums.

In more recent memory, individual musicians have left their mark. Paulino Bernal, Roberto Pulido, and Rubén Vela each added his own innovations in the 1960s. Leonardo (Flaco) Jimenez, son of Santiago Jimenez, took the music to more mainstream audiences throughout the United States and Europe to much acclaim. The very open-minded Esteban Jordán stretched the limits of the genre, and his followers, such as Inocencia and Emilio Navaira and Río, have added saxophones, keyboards, and synthesizers, creating the new sounds of *conjuntos orquesta*.

San Antonio has long been the epicenter of *conjunto* music in Texas, and each May the Guadalupe Cultural Arts Center brings some of the biggest names and greatest talents to the city for the spectacular Tejano Conjunto Festival (see "Festivals," below). The event draws crowds of thousands of fans and features an outstanding lineup of top-notch musicians, including such luminaries as Fred Zimmerle, Eva Ybarra, Lupita Rodela, Laura Canales, as well as some of the musicians mentioned above. Conjunto music is sometimes referred to as *música alegre*, or happy music; after just a few notes you'll know why.

festivals in the country, with exhibits, workshops, and multimedia presentations. Admission and free.

Jazz'SAlive (210-212-8423; www.saparksfoundation.org) Outstanding performances from the nation's top jazz entertainers and local talent. Travis Park. Free.

Diez y Seis Events (210-207-8600; www.visitsanantonio.com) A celebration of Mexico's independence from Spain on September 16, 1821. Three days of parades, dance, and rodeos. Free.

Valero Texas Open at La Cantera (210-558-4653; www.lacanteragolfclub .com) One of the oldest professional golf tournaments and an official PGA tour event. Admission charged.

October

A Festival of Films (www.afestivaloffilms.com) This two-day festival produced by Texas independent filmmakers features independent films and workshops for filmmakers. Admission charged.

International Accordion Festival (210-573-6984; www.internationalaccordion festival.org) A three-day festival of dancing, food, and accordions. Free.

AT&T Championship (210-698-3582; www.pgatour.com) An official Senior PGA Tour golf tournament at the Oak Hills Country Club (210-349-5151; www .oakhillscc.com). Admission charged.

Cinefestival 2006 (210-271-3151; www.guadalupeculturalarts.org) Interna-

Altars for the El Dia de los Muertos, the Day of the Dead

tional film festival featuring Chicano/Latino/indigenous films at the historic Guadalupe Theater, with panels, workshops, retrospectives, and sidebar programs offered in conjunction. Admission charged.

November

El Dia de los Muertos (210-207-6700; www.visitsanantonio.com) "The Day of the Dead" is the ancient cultural tradition in which families "welcome back" departed loved ones, commemorating them through special altars and cemetery visits. Poetry readings and *calavera* processions, in which participants dress as skeletons, are especially moving. Admission and Free.

　　Culinaria Wine & Food Festival (210-822-9555; www.culinariasa.org) A celebration of food, wine, and San Antonio's position as culinary and cultural gateway to Mexico and Latin America. Admission charged.

　　Holiday River Parade and Lighting Ceremony (www.thesanantonioriver walk.com) Held the day after Thanksgiving, this twilight river parade lights up the Paseo del Rio. The more than 122,000 lights stay on until New Year's Day. Admission charged.

December

Alamo Bowl (210-226-2695; www.alamobowl.com) Post-season college football game featuring teams from the Big Twelve and Big Ten conferences at the Alamodome. Admission charged.

　　Bazar Sábado (210-978-8100; www.samuseum.org) Mexican folk art on display and for sale. Admission charged.

　　Celebrate San Antonio (210-227-4262; www.sanantonioriverwalk.com) New Year's Eve fireworks, live music, food, and family activities. South Alamo Street between Durango and Market Streets, La Villita, and HemisFair Park. Free.

　　Hecho a Mano/Made by Hand (210-271-3151; www.guadalupeculturalarts .org) An arts and crafts market featuring ceramics, jewelry, woodwork, fiber arts, clothing, metalwork, and more. Admission charged.

3

The Hill Country
TEXAS TRAILS

THE HILL COUNTRY OCCUPIES the eastern portion of the Edwards Plateau and is bounded by the Balcones Fault to the east and the granite domes of the Llano Uplift to the north and west. The green grazing terrain is textured with limestone rocks and boulders and pierced by outcroppings. The region is the perfect habitat for deer, coyote, squirrels, foxes, raccoons, skunks, and armadillo, as well as migrating birds and butterflies, and its many caves and caverns are home to millions of bats. Numerous state parks offer ample opportunity to view nature close-up. You could spend the day or a week in these hills, winding your way from town to town, past wildflowers, vineyards, and fields of lavender, watching the sun move across the enormous Texas sky.

BANDERA

The self-proclaimed "Cowboy Capital of the World," little Bandera has got some big boots to fill. Located approximately 50 miles northwest of San Antonio on TX 16, Bandera is named for nearby Bandera Pass, the natural V-shaped access point that allowed Native Americans, the Spanish, the United States Army, Texas Rangers, and even cattle during the cattle drives of the 19th century to pass through the rocky ridge separating the Medina and Guadalupe river valleys. Founded in 1852, Bandera was settled by Polish immigrants and was also home to a Mormon colony. Since the 1920s, Bandera and its surrounding countryside have played host to summertime visitors who enjoy the area's ranches, campgrounds, dance halls, and rodeos. Bandera is known for its dude ranches, twice-weekly rodeos from Memorial Day to Labor Day, summertime water fun in the Medina River and nearby Medina Lake, and scenic trails in the two state natural areas located nearby.

LEFT: Hill Country Vineyards

Hill Country Area

© The Countryman Press

Local Flavors

Taste of the town—local
restaurants, cafés, bistros, etc.

Brick's River Café (830-460-3200;
www.bricksrivercafe.com) may not win
you over with its location—beside a
hotel on the northern edge of town—
or décor, but one bite of the sweet
potato fries, hot ham and cheese sandwich on sourdough bread ("The
Brick"), or coconut cream pie and
you'll soften. Farther south along
Main Street, **Busbee's BBQ** (830-796-
3153; www.busbeesbbq.com) smokes
up hard-to-resist brisket, sausage, ribs,
ham, and chicken, all served on red-
checkered tablecloths. The homemade pecan pie and peach cobbler
provide the perfect finish. Nearby,
Old Spanish Trail (830-796-3836),
known to everyone as "OST," takes
the cowboy theme to new heights,
placing diners high in the saddles that
double as lunch-counter stools.
Chicken-fried steaks and enchiladas

Bandera General Store

are menu mainstays, the chuckwagon buffets are filling, and even the simple breakfast tacos hit the spot. With spurs on the wall, wagon wheels on the ceiling, and an entire room devoted to John Wayne, you'll never forget you're in the Cowboy Capital of the World.

The Great Outdoors
Outdoor adventures and activities

In town, the cypress-lined Medina River is an irresistible spot to cool off, though heavy rainfall can cause it to become temporarily hazardous. Rent tubes and kayaks from the **Medina River Company** (830-796-3600; www.medinarivercompany.com).

To the southeast, **Medina Lake** is a recreational lake with plenty of cabins and cottages for rent; check the Bandera Convention and Visitors Bureau's Web site, www.banderacowboycapital.com, for links to individual properties. Farther south, the 5,500-acre **Hill Country State Natural Area** (see "Texas State Parks," below), makes for terrific horseback riding, hiking, and views. To the west, the **Lost Maples State Natural Area** (see "Texas State Parks," below) is just gorgeous in the fall and has nice hiking all year round. The **Love Creek Orchards** (830-589-2202; www.lovecreekorchards.com) makes a nice lunch stop en route to Kerrville along lovely TX 16.

Culture
History, Heritage, and the Arts

Opened in 1933, the **Frontier Times Museum** (830-796-3864; www.frontiertimesmuseum.org) you see today is the result of decades of collecting; its eclectic mix of western memorabilia, artifacts from frontier times, and oddities such as a stuffed, two-headed sheep are sure to intrigue.

Polly's Chapel, a lovely little house of worship with a remarkable history, stands off TX 16, approximately 6 miles southeast of the city near Privilege Creek. Situated on a pretty piece of land in what feels like the middle of nowhere, the chapel is unexpected, to say the least. It was built entirely by hand by José Policarpo "Polly" Rodriguez more than 120 years ago. Polly was born in Mexico, moved to Texas as a child, and became a scout with the U.S. Army and eventually a Methodist minister. His spiritual awakening prompted Polly's desire to build the chapel, a labor of love he completed in 1882. The doors are usually left unlocked.

Once the sightseeing's done, join the local tradition of live music, mostly country and western and honky-tonk, and dance your boots off. Though hours may vary, there is always a dance hall open Wednesday through Sunday nights, with mellower bring-your-own-guitar jam sessions Sunday afternoons.

Beside the general store and down a flight of stairs, **Arkey Blue's Silver Dollar** (830-796-8826; no Web site, but you can find 'em on Facebook) is one of the last of its kind, a honky-tonk with sawdust floors, a pool table, lots of neon, live music, and cold Shiner longnecks all night long. Boot scoot to Arkey Blue and his Blue Cowboys, who play live every Saturday night. Quintessential Bandera.

A block away is the **11th Street Cowboy Bar** (830-796-4849; www.11thstreetcowboybar.com). A little wooden shack of a bar, the 11th Street Cowboy Bar is a huge, level social playing field, with a clientele as varied as the many, many bras which hang from the ceiling. Drink specials, free burgers, and steak nights may lure customers, but it's the fantastic live country and western and country swing music that keeps 'em there dancing into the night.

Rodeos
In Bandera, summertime is rodeo season; the big kickoff event is the **Cowboy Capital PRCA Rodeo** (830-796-7207; www.banderarodeo.com), held during Memorial Day weekend in Mansfield Park. Featuring cowboys competing for points to qualify for the National Rodeo Finals, this event always brings out some top-notch riders. Contact the Bandera Convention and Visitors Bureau (800-364-3833; www.banderacowboycapital.com) for more information.

Dude Ranches

Boots for sale

Out here in Bandera the itch to slide into a pair of jeans, put on cowboy boots, and start wrangling begins to need scratching. Below are some ranches where you can be a cowboy for a day.

Rates are roughly the same, approximately $120 per day per adult and $80 per day per child, plus or minus, depending on the season. Limited horseback riding, use of the ranch swimming pool, and participation in ranch-organized events tend to be included, though three meals may not. Often there is a minimum stay of two or three nights. Details vary; check Web sites and don't hesitate to call for clarification. Day visitors are welcome at some of the ranches for horseback riding at rates of approximately $30 per hour; call to inquire.

Dixie Dude Ranch (830-796-7771; www.dixieduderanch.com)

Mayan Ranch (830-796-3312; www.mayanranch.com)

Flying L Guest Ranch (830-460-3001 or 800-292-5134; www.flyingl.com)

Hill Country Equestrian Lodge (830-796-7950; www.hillcountryequestlodge.com)

Rancho Cortez (830-796-9339 or 866-797-9339; www.ranchocortez.com)

Running R Ranch (830-796-3984; www.rrranch.com)

Silver Spur Guest Ranch (830-796-3037; www.silverspur-ranch.com)

Twin Elm Guest Ranch (830-796-3628 or 888-567-3049; www.twinelmranch.com)

Every Saturday from mid-March through October, the Frontier Times Museum's Living History Project sponsors **Cowboys on Main** (830-796-3864; www.frontier timesmuseum.org) featuring storytellers, trick ropers, musicians, and cowboys on horseback. Spice things up in April with the **Annual Silver Sage Corral Benefit Chili Cook-Off**, hosted by the 11th Street Cowboy Bar, then cool off at the **Riverfest** (830-796-4447; www.banderariverfest.com) and its popular Everything But a Boat River Regatta, held in May.

BLANCO

A small ranching and trade town, Blanco got its start in 1858 and almost immediately entered into a power struggle with nearby Johnson City for the title of county seat, a distinction it held until 1890, when Johnson City prevailed. Blanco is typical small-town Hill Country, with a courthouse in the middle, shops all round, and hillside surrounding. Tubing in **Blanco State Park** and pie at the **Blanco Bowling Club** are mainstays, but what really puts Blanco on the map today is the **Blanco Lavender Festival** (www.blancolavenderfestival.com) and the proliferation of lavender farms sprouting up all around (see "Lavender," below).

Pick Your Spot:
Best places to stay in Blanco

The clever owners of the **Blanco County Inn** (830-833-4502; www .blancocountyinn.com) managed to take a run-of-the-mill motor court motel and turn it into something pleasant. The rooms have been renovated, each neat and clean, with personal touches such as quilts. Flowerbeds, tidy landscaping, and comfortable chairs scattered on the massive deck and underneath the property's huge shade trees beckon guests to come out of their rooms for a little sunshine and socializing.

Local Flavors
Taste of the town—local restaurants, cafés, bistros, etc.

It would be easy to drive straight past the nondescript **Blanco Bowling Club** (830-833-4416; www.blancobowling club.com). This very informal and friendly spot is popular with locals, and you can just walk on in and plop down at one of the formica tables in the wood-paneled dining room. While the hamburgers, hot roast beef sandwiches, chicken-fried steak, and various Mexican dishes are all tasty, leave room for a slice of the famous meringue pie, an essential part of the dining experience. The glazed doughnuts and cinnamon rolls served hot in the mornings are a perfect pairing for a cup of coffee. And, yes, there is ninepin bowling.

Several creative and healthy eateries have opened recently in Blanco, and one of them is **Zocalo Eclectic Café** (830-833-4300; www.zocalo blanco.com). The brainchild of a food-loving musician, Zocalo's menu meanders from thick, juicy burgers and

Stop by a farm stand for a taste of homegrown Texas.

Asian-inspired noodle bowls to quail with blue cheese couscous and fish tacos without missing a beat. Everything here is fresh, creative, and delicious. Lunch hours, some evenings, and live music events; check Web site for details.

Nearby, the delightful **Redbud Café Market and Pub** (830-833-0202; www.redbud-cafe.com) is located across from the courthouse in the center of town and owned and operated by local potters, Jon and Jan Brieger. In fact, their pottery shop (830-833-2860; www.briegerpottery.com) is right next door. On the menu, you'll find tasty chicken salad, hot pastrami Reubens on marble rye, pimento cheese sandwiches, homemade soups, quiches, and several delicious vegetarian options, including a grilled Portabella mushroom "burger" and an avocado and vegetable sandwich. The restaurant is open Friday and Saturday evenings, featuring Real Ale on tap, several Hill Country wines, and live music; check Web site for details.

Speaking of Real Ale, **Real Ale Brewery** (830-833-2534; www.realale brewing.com) is just a short jaunt up US 281. The brewery offers beer tastings on Fridays from 2–5 PM — the Fireman's #4 is often cited as a must-try—and brewery tours on Fridays at 3 and 4 PM.

Before heading out of Blanco, stop at the only street light in town and set your odometer to zero. Drive exactly 3.5 miles north and you will find yourself at **McCall Creek Farms** (830-833-0442; www.mccallcreekfarms.com), located on the east side of the highway. (If you are coming from the north, look for the farm 4 miles south of the US 281/US 290 intersection.) This small farm stand sells locally grown produce, cheeses and eggs, and locally made jams and preserves. They also make their own delicious homemade custard-based ice cream in vanilla, chocolate, and peach. Hill Country Lavender (see "Lavender," above) is located in the fields behind the farm.

Lavender

The Hill Country has several burgeoning lavender farms, thanks to growing condi-tions tailor-made to the herb and the insight of photographer Robb Kendrick, who noticed, while on a photo shoot in Provence, France in the late 1990s, the similarities of that region and the Hill Country where he lived. Robb solicited advice from French farmers and went home to experiment with the rocky limestone soil around Blanco. He and his wife, Jeannie Ralston, found that Provence lavender grew beautifully, and they started Hill Country Lavender, which sold lavender and offered seminars on lavender farming. At the same time, Richard and Bunny Becker, owners of Becker Vineyard, also returned from a trip to Provence and noticed the very same similari-ties. The Beckers planted a 3-acre field of the fragrant herb behind their winery. The Hill Country Lavender seminars made an impression on the locals; soon farms were taking root, growing both plants and the region's identity as the newly anointed "Lavender Capital of Texas." In fact, so many farms participated in the hugely suc-cessful, first annual **Blanco Lavender Festival** (www.blancolavenderfestival.com), held in June 2005, that the event has become a Hill Country favorite. Visitors are welcome to stop by the farms during the lavender blooming season—May, June, and July—and doing so makes a nice complement to the **Texas Hill Country Wine Trail** (www.texaswinetrail.com). Growing, blooming, and harvesting times vary, as do hours of operation, so call ahead to the farms you hope to visit.

Becker Vineyards (830-644-2681; www.beckervineyards.com) Behind its main wine-making operation in Stonewall, this lovely vineyard and winery has a 3-acre field of lavender that guests are invited to wander through, drink in hand.

The Great Outdoors

Outdoor adventures and activities

After a meal, consider stretching your legs at **Blanco State Park** (830-833-4333; www.tpwd.state.tx.us). With over 100 acres of land on either side of a bend in the Blanco River, Blanco State Park is one of the oldest in the state, known for great trout fishing, shaded campsites, and river tubing—a favorite Central Texas pastime—on warm Texas days. You'll find Blanco State Park located an easy four blocks south of the Blanco town square on Park Road 23. Inquire at the park store about tube, canoe, and kayak rentals and water safety tips. There are several other state parks within striking distance of US 281, and each offers a close-up look at a piece of the Texas landscape. A complete listing and maps can be found online at www.tpwd .state.tx.us.

BOERNE

Located in the San Antonio metropolitan area approximately 30 miles north of downtown, Boerne (pronounced BURN-ee) was settled in 1849 as a small agri-cultural community and maintains a small-town atmosphere with distinctly Ger-

Heron's Nest Herb Farm (830-833-2627; www.heronsnestherbfarm.com) A lovely farm just east of Blanco, with lavender trails and fields of echinacea, watered with a custom solar-powered rainwater drip-irrigation system and other off-the-grid farming techniques.

Hill Country Lavender (830-833-2294; www.hillcountrylavender.com) The first commercial lavender farm in Texas, Hill Country Lavender has a farm and store on US 281, and you can purchase their lavender-themed products at Brieger Pottery, located between the Post Office and the Bank on the north side of the square in Blanco.

Hummingbird Farms (830-868-7862; www.hummingbirdlavender.com) Five lovely acres of organic lavender located 9.5 miles west of Johnson City.

Miller Creek Lavender (512-934-1616; www.millercreeklavender.com) Miller Creek, positioned between Johnson City and Blanco, has 3.5 acres of lavender, a butterfly garden, and signature lavender margarita mix for sale.

Rough Creek Lavender (512-847-2888; www.roughcreeklavender.com) Rough Creek Lavender has 5,000 lavender plants, with alighting butterflies, for picking and frolicking among during blooming season. Located in Wimberley.

Sweet Dreams Lavender Farm (512-288-7270; www.sweetdreamslavenderfarm .com) This farm is a sweet-smelling escape just 15 minutes west of downtown Austin, a few miles from TX 71/US 290.

Wimberley Lavender Farm (830-833-1595; www.wimberleylavender.com) The Wimberley Lavender Farm is located on a bucolic hilltop between Wimberley and Blanco.

man roots. Its population fluctuated until the 1960s, when the completion of I-10 made it a bedroom community for growing San Antonio. Located on the banks of Cibolo Creek, Boerne makes a nice day trip from San Antonio or a jumping-off point into the Hill Country.

Pick Your Spot
Best places to stay in Boerne

Once a stagecoach stop, **Ye Kendall Inn** (830-249-2138; www.yekendall inn.com) is now a destination and a Texas historic landmark. Built in 1859, the solid limestone inn has a charmed atmosphere, with details such as a galvanized metal tub in the Texas Suite and rustic primitive décor in the Waco Cabin, a structure dating from the mid-1800s. Each of the inn's 34 very individualized guest rooms and cabins are well documented on its Web site, which is worth perusing before making your reservations. The on-site **Limestone Grill** (830-249-2138; www.yekendall inn.com) offers a sophisticated menu including Texas Gulf Coast shrimp and grits, flatbread pizzas, and a prime rib special every Wednesday night.

Local Flavors

Taste of the town—local restaurants, cafés, bistros, etc.

Heading south along Main Street, you'll come to the **Cypress Grille** (830-248-1353; www.cypressgrilleboerne.com), where everything from the luscious lobster, brie, and portabella lasagna smothered in smoked tomato cream sauce to the perfectly cooked prime rib is delicious. The décor is not as "fancy" as the food, but the atmosphere is very relaxed and enjoyable.

Several blocks farther, the **Creek Restaurant** (830-816-2005; www.the creekrestaurat.com) occupies several historic buildings—one was the baggage depot for the train station—along the banks of Cibolo Creek. The Creek serves fresh, healthy soups, salads, and sandwiches for lunch and steaks, seafood, and pasta dishes for dinner. The menu and the atmosphere are refreshingly simple and slightly elegant, putting the Creek on the top of the list of many locals' favorites.

Follow River Road a few blocks east to the **Dodging Duck Brewhaus** (830-248-3825; www.dodgingduck.com), a popular place to unwind creekside with a home-brewed beer, some fried green tomatoes, a jumbo pretzel and sausage bites, or spicy stuffed mushroom caps.

The **Hungry Horse** (830-816-8989; www.hungryhorsehillcountry.com) doesn't look like much, but folks say the chicken-fried steaks, creamy, bright yellow macaroni and cheese, fried onion rings, and corn muffins hit the spot. Portions are huge here; the "pony" size is a good fit.

Another casual eatery is the **Bear Moon Bakery** (830-816-2327; www.bearmoonbakery.com) where you can have breakfast, lunch—diners love the chipotle grilled cheese and the Reuben—or an enormous cinnamon roll or a slice of cake and a cup of coffee.

Two of Boerne's most popular restaurants are on its outskirts. **Po-Po Family Restaurant** (830-537-4194; www.popofamilyrestaurant.com), a roadside classic since 1929, is widely known for its crispy yet juicy fried chicken, catfish, and shrimp. Order from the standard menu or choose the all-you-can-eat specials available Monday through Thursday from 4 PM onward. You haven't seen a big group of souvenir plates until you've seen the display at Po-Po's. Located 6 miles

Gift shops in Boerne

Potted succulent

north of Boerne off exit 533/Welfare; reservations recommended. Though technically in Boerne, the **Welfare General Store and Café** (830-537-3700; www.welfaretexas.com) is located approximately 10 miles north of town, on the Waring-Welfare Road (SR 1621), just off I-10/US 87. Irre sistible gourmet food served in an irresistibly charming 1920s general store and post office. While the *Kart-offelpfannekuchen*—potato pancakes served with apple sauce or sour cream—and a half dozen versions of schnitzel are clear references to the region's German heritage, the Pad Thai knows no cultural bounds, and the steaks are pure Texas.

The Great Outdoors
Outdoor adventures and activities

While the aboveground geography of the Hill Country is fascinating, the eerie subterranean landscapes of the region's caves and caverns can be an interesting and fun diversion. The natural area in and around Boerne offers both.

Cascade Caverns (830-755-8080; www.cascadecaverns.com) is located approximately 3 miles south of Boerne; take exit 543 off I-10. Home to the endangered, albino Cascades Cavern salamander, Cascade Caverns is 140 feet deep and a half mile long. The highlight of the 45-minute tour is a peek at the 100-foot waterfall for which the cavern is named.

Naming was an issue from the beginning for the **Cave Without a Name** (830-537-4212; www.cavewithoutaname.com). In 1939, when a contest was held to name this cave, a boy remarked that it was "too pretty to name," and it is. To see for yourself, take FM 474 northeast for approximately 5 miles, then a right onto Kreutzberg Road.

From town, travel east on TX 46 for one mile to City Park Road, turn right, and follow to the **Cibolo Nature Center** (830-249-4616; www.cibolo.org). The four distinct ecosystems represented in the center's 100 acres make its pedestrian-only trails interesting and educational. Picnic tables and outdoor concerts invite visitors to stay the day, and the center's Mostly Native Plant Sale in April draws gardeners from near and far.

Nearby

From Boerne, travel north along FM 1376 approximately 13 miles to Sisterdale, stop in at Sister Creek Vineyards (see "Hill Country Vineyards," below) for a wine tasting, then head on to Comfort. Or head east on TX 46, then north on US 281 to Guadalupe River State Park (see "Texas State Parks," below). Alternatively, take TX 46 westward to pretty TX 16 and head north to Bandera and Kerrville, or, from TX 16 take CR 337 farther west to Lost Maples State Natural Area (see "Texas State Parks," below).

Culture
History, Heritage, and the Arts

German-themed festivals such as the **Berges Fest** (www.bergesfest.com), held on Father's Day weekend and featuring watermelon-eating contests and dachshund races, **Oktoberfest-Wurst Braten** in October, and **Weihnachts (Christmas) Fest Parade Weekend** in December celebrate the town's heritage, while **Cowboy Christmas** festivities exemplify the region's distinctly Texas twang. Check www.boerne.org for details of the city's festivals.

COMFORT

Located near the intersection of TX 27, US 87, and I-10, Comfort is a lovely Hill Country hamlet nestled along the banks of gentle Cypress Creek. Settled by educated, free-thinking Germans who arrived via New Braunfels in 1852, Comfort has always marched to its own drummer. Opposed to slavery, the town was sympathetic to the Union in the Civil War, and it lost many men to the cause at the Battle of the Nueces in 1862. To commemorate their bravery, the Treue der Union ("True to the Union") Monument stands on High Street between Third and Fourth Streets. Averse to central authority, the settlers organized a communal form of self-governance and didn't get around to building a church until 1892. Comfort has many examples of traditional *fachwerk* (half-timber construction) and Victorian buildings, and much of the town is listed on the National Register of Historic Places. Comfort has weathered its share of tragedy. In 1978 a flood destroyed many historic buildings in town, and in 2006 a fire leveled the beloved Ingenhuett Store (834 High Street), a general store owned and operated by the same local family since 1867 and very much the anchor of the town. Despite these losses, tiny Comfort is sweet comfort indeed. The business part of town is

Comfort, Texas

only a few blocks long and takes in several restaurants, cafés, and antiques shops, all with varying business hours. See the town Web site, www.shopcomfort.com.

Pick Your Spot
Best places to stay in Comfort

Comfort is a relaxing place to stay, as **Meyer Bed and Breakfast** (830-995-2304 or 888-995-6100; www.meyerbed andbreakfast.com), on High Street, will prove. This congenial B&B is a complex of buildings dating from the 1800s to the early 1900s, each with clean and comfortably worn rooms. Sizes range from snug to spacious, making Meyer a good choice for families and friends traveling together. The lovely common breakfast area is lined with windows overlooking Cypress Creek.

Several miles outside of town and perched high on a hilltop overlooking the fertile pastures—land that has been farmed for over a century—**Riven Rock Ranch** (830-995-4045; www.rivenrock ranch.com) is surrounded by cows, sheep, and plenty of solitude. Cottages—generally the size of an average house—are skillfully decorated with warm earth tones, rich textures, and original artwork. Fully equipped kitchens allow for self-sufficiency and the onsite restaurant, the **Terrace Grill**, open to the general public as well as guests, features juicy lamb burgers, wild boar schnitzel, melt-in-your mouth steaks, and gourmet pizzas served with stunning views of the valley. The Guadalupe River runs through the property, offering opportunities for fishing and canoeing.

Local Flavors

Taste of the town—local
restaurants, cafés, bistros, etc.

Most of Comfort's restaurants are located in a little cluster along High Street, the nexus of which is **High's** (830-995-4995; www.highscafeand store.com). It feels like everyone stops by High's at some point during the day to grab a muffin and coffee for breakfast, maybe a turkey sandwich with cilantro, orange and chipotle cabbage slaw for lunch, or a homemade key lime tart with a graham cracker crust in the middle of the afternoon. The food at this little deli is outstanding, but the friendliness of High's lovely owners is just as big a draw. Closed Wednesday.

For dinner, try the cozy **814 A Texas Bistro** (830-995-4990; www.814 texasbistro.com). The bistro, which has quilts hanging on the exposed brick walls and creaky wooden floors, turns out pricey gourmet dinners such as grilled molasses marinated Bandera quail and New York strip steak. Open for dinner and Sunday brunch; reservations recommended and BYOB. Closed Monday and Tuesday.

The Plaid Goat (830-995-2015; www.theplaidgoatcomfort.com) is open evenings for appetizers, desserts, and drinks. Nibbles and noshes include warm brie with toasted almonds and golden raisins, and skewered shrimp with mango salsa. Desserts range from a decadent German chocolate cake with a coconut-caramel-pecan ganache to shortbread with lemon curd and

High's on High Street in Comfort

lavender-infused berries. The ample wine list includes some local labels.

You can also have a sip at **Comfort Cellars Winery's** (830-995-3274; www.comfortcellars.com) tasting room in town, or head out to one of the many area vineyards; see box below.

Nearby

The outstanding meals at the Welfare General Store and Café (see "Boerne"), a 15-minute drive south, are worth every mile, and the road to Sister Creek Vineyards is a treat unto itself.

FREDERICKSBURG

Fredericksburg, named for Prince Frederick of Prussia, was founded in 1846 by John O. Meusebach and a group of 120 German immigrants who came to the area from New Braunfels as participants in the Adelsverein, the planned German settlement of Texas. At the time, as was the case in most of the Pedernales Valley, the

Sunday Houses

Devoutly religious, German settlers on farms and ranches outside Fredericksburg were determined to journey to town for church services, but the long distances, road conditions, and weather made this difficult. The solution was to build "Sunday houses." These tiny houses were built on small parcels in town and used by families coming to town for shopping on Saturday and church on Sunday. The houses were of frame construction, with steeply pitched roofs and decorative millwork. The lean-to kitchen was tacked on the back and sometimes the staircase was built on the outside of the home to save precious space indoors. Sunday houses were wildly popular between 1890 and 1910, and the ones that survive today are sprinkled throughout Fredericksburg and the Hill Country; many are used as B&Bs. In Fredericksburg, small groups of Sunday houses can be seen on West San Antonio Street, near St. Mary's Church on West Main Street, and on South Milam Street.

area that would become Fredericksburg was inhabited by Native Americans, in this case the Comanche. In 1847, Meusebach and the Native Americans hammered out the details of the Meusebach-Comanche Treaty, establishing peace in their shared valley—a remarkable feat given the times and circumstances.

The town, patterned after villages in Germany, was laid out with one long, wide road, Main Street, running parallel to Town Creek, and residents set about building the *fachwerk* homes that are now synonymous with Hill Country architec-

Fourth of July Parade in Fredericksburg

Hill Country Vineyards

The similarities between Texas and Tuscany are striking. Sure, you have to look past the cowboy hats and longhorn cattle to really notice them, but the distinct qualities of the limestone outcroppings, the berries growing wild along the roadsides, and the hot, hot sunshine shared by the regions are notable. And those similarities are not lost on Texas winemakers, who toil year-round to create a little bit of Italy in the Lone Star State. The region's rich alluvial soil is mixed with limestone, flint, and shale chips from rivers past and provides ideal conditions for growing grapes. For the past 40 years, vintners have coaxed their vineyards to take root in the Hill Country, and consumers and connoisseurs are now drinking the fruits of their labor.

All wineries offer tastings; some are complimentary and others charge a small fee, usually between $1 and $5. Those new to the experience of wine tasting will enjoy any of the wineries listed below, as they all have their individual strengths, charms, and personalities. Those with a more discerning palate might enjoy perusing the vineyards' comprehensive Web sites for specific labels or vintages before planning their trip. **Texas Hill Country Wineries** (872-216-9463; www.texaswine trail.com) comprises over 30 member wineries, some of which are listed alphabetically below. For up-to-the-minute information regarding festivals, special events, and the Wine and Wildflower Trail, a coordinated effort of all the vineyards, please check the Web site. Additionally, the wineries along US 290 have organized themselves online at **Fredericksburg Wine Road 290** (www.wineroad290.com).

Alamosa Wine Cellars (325-628-3313; www.alamosawinecellars.com) Perched at an elevation of 1,200 feet, Alamosa Wine Cellars overlooks San Saba County.

Becker Vineyards (830-644-2681; www.beckervineyards.com) Becker Vineyards has acres of grapes and fields of lavender.

Chisholm Trail Winery (830-990-2675; www.chisholmtrailwinery.com) A low-key winery in the hills west of Fredericksburg.

Comfort Cellars (830-995-3274; www.comfortcellars.com) Whether you are coming or going from Comfort, the scenic drive along CR 473 to Sisterdale offers great views of the Guadalupe River Valley.

Driftwood Vineyards (512-858-9667; www.driftwoodvineyards.com) This small, family-run vineyard debuted its first wine a decade ago.

Dry Comal Creek Vineyard (830-885-4076; www.drycomalcreek.com) The rooster you see on the roof is also featured on this vineyard's labels.

ture. The Vereins Kirche, a multipurpose building, served as school, church, fortress, and gathering place. Crops were planted, stores opened, and the town prospered.

The Civil War challenged the immigrants to square their communal beliefs with those of their new home country. Many were opposed to slavery and secession, with most supporting the Union, but all endured the hardships of Con-

Duchman Family Winery (512-858-1470; www.duchmanwinery.com) Duchman Winery, located in Driftwood, makes win using Texas-grown fruit exclusively.

Fall Creek Vineyards (325-379-5361; www.fcv.com) Started in 1975, Fall Creek Vineyards is known for its signature Meritus wine, which is a blend of cabernet sauvignon, merlot, and petit verdot.

Flat Creek Estate (512-267-6310; www.flatcreekestate.com) Located on former pastureland just west of Austin, Fall Creek Estate is a sophisticated yet casual 80-acre vineyard with endless views.

Fredericksburg Winery (830-990-8747; www.fbgwinery.com) This winery is right on Main Street in Fredericksburg.

Grape Creek Vineyards (830-644-2710; www.grapecreek.com) Take a tram tour of vines, a crush pad, and a tank room to see how wine is made, and enjoy a taste in the barrel room.

Lost Creek Vineyard (325-388-3753; www.lostcreekvineyard.com) A casual vineyard near the north shore of Lake LBJ.

McReynolds Wines (830-825-3544; www.mcreynoldswines.com) A very informal, family-run winery located between Johnson City and Spicewood.

Pillar Bluff Vineyards (512-556-4078; www.pillarbluff.com) Pillar Bluff specializes in French varietals.

Sister Creek Vineyards (830-324-6704; www.sistercreekvineyards.com) These friendly folks make European-style wines aged in oak barrels.

Spicewood Vineyards (830-693-5328; www.spicewoodvineyards.com) Spicewood Vineyards hosts a variety of dinner, dessert, and live music events.

Stone House Vineyard (512-264-3630; www.stonehousevineyard.com) Befitting its name, Stone House Vineyard occupies a lovely, white limestone winery on Lake Travis.

Texas Hills Vineyard (830-868-2321; www.texashillsvineyard.com) Texas Hills Vineyard built a rammed-earth tasting room to protect its wine and environment—a creative solution, with charming results.

Torre di Pietra (830-644-2829; www.texashillcountrywine.com) Patios, live music, and wine-filled chocolates only enhance the tasting experience.

Woodrose Winery (830-644-2539; www.woodrosewinery.com) A wonderful winery that's been growing by leaps and bounds.

federate martial law in 1862. The experience galvanized the German sense of self-determination; many residents spoke only German for decades afterward in an effort to distance and insulate themselves from national issues.

At the turn of the century, Fredericksburg was a manufacturing center, with various factories, quarries, and plants, but in the 1930s the town's reputation as a resort area began to grow. Today, Fredericksburg is known as a weekend getaway spot, with restful B&Bs, gourmet dining, and historic sites, surrounded by parks, wineries, and wildflowers. At times it can feel a little kitschy, but head off the beaten path and there's plenty of genuine Hill Country to be enjoyed.

Pick Your Spot

Best places to stay in Fredericksburg

The locus of Fredericksburg is Main Street, and the nearby neighborhoods are just teeming with B&Bs, guesthouses, and boutique hotels. Alternatively, the usual roster of chain hotels can be found along US 290 on the outskirts of the city. Fredericksburg is such a popular weekend destination that it's essential to book a room in advance, particularly during festivals.

Most of the establishments listed below are independently owned and operated by the very folks you'll meet when you call or visit. Another useful way to book a room is to use the following reservation services, which handle a wide variety of B&Bs and guesthouses: Gastehaus Schmidt (866-427-8374; www.fbglodging.com); Main Street Reservations Service (830-997-0153 or 888-559-8555; www.travel mainstreet.com). Most reservations require a two-day minimum.

Ab Butler's Dogtrot at Triple Creek (877-262-4366; www.abbutler .net) is a two-story cabin, built in Kentucky in the 1800s and moved to Texas in 1997. There are two suites, each with a wood-burning fireplace in the living room downstairs and a secluded bedroom and bathroom with Jacuzzi tub upstairs under the eaves. Rocking on the front porch under the shady oak trees, it's easy to feel like a pioneer—until a hot breakfast delivered to your room gently interrupts the fantasy.

Kevin and Lynn operate a spot-

lessly clean **Das Garten Haus** (800-416-4287; www.dasgartenhaus.com), with three private suites, each with a kitchen or kitchenette, and perks such as fresh flowers, homemade cookies, and popcorn. The delicious breakfasts, sometimes made with produce from the owners' gardens, are delicate and delicious, yet healthy and filling. Spend a minute poking around the lovely gardens, planned and nurtured by Kevin, a professional horticulturalist.

B&B in Fredericksburg

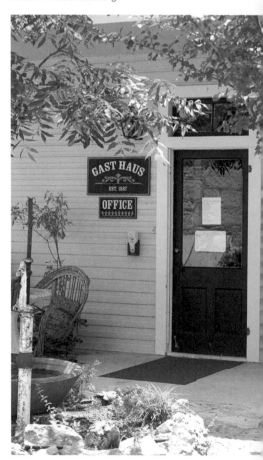

Wildflowers

Springtime in Central Texas is lovely. The sun is out, the birds are singing, and the humidity has yet to arrive. Also making an appearance are the millions upon millions of wildflowers that dot pastures and highway medians, line fences and riverbanks, and rise up with their colorful blooms turned sunward. By April, sometimes as early as March, these little native flowers—bluebonnets, Indian paintbrushes, and Mexican hats—seem to appear out of nowhere. In May, this first magical spray disappears and other, less well-known, though equally exquisite, native flowers bloom in their place. And so it goes, through summer, fall, and even a mild winter. In fact, in Texas the careful observer can find something in bloom all year long.

In Austin, the **Lady Bird Johnson Wildflower Center** is both beautiful and informative. If you are in the Hill Country, stop in at **Wildseed Farms** (see "The Great Outdoors," below) in Fredericksburg for a closer look, or drive the **Bluebonnet Trail**, a self-guided tour winding through Burnet (the Bluebonnet Capital of Texas), Marble Falls, and Llano and continuing on alongside the Highland Lakes (see individual listings below for all these places). Maps are available online at www.burnetchamber .org/bluebonnetmap.

Other scenic routes include the **Willow City Loop** outside Fredericksburg, **TX 16 South** between Kerrville and Medina, and along the **Devil's Backbone** in Wimberley. Or call the local wildflower hotlines for advice; the Lady Bird Johnson Wildflower Center (512-832-4037; www .wildflower.org) and the Texas Department of Transportation (800-452-9292; www.dot.state.tx.us) both have frequently updated recordings describing particularly colorful routes.

A word of warning, however. Before you pull off the highway and plop your children down for a photo amid the petals, please watch your step; wildflowers and fire ants seek the same habitat: a sunny, dry, hot field.

Texas Bluebonnet

Magnolia House (800-880-4374; www.magnolia-house.com) is full of 1920s charm and expertly managed by gracious owners, who woo guests with homemade cookies and delicious breakfasts from locally sourced ingredients. Warm, homey, and neat as a pin, this Prairie-style Craftsman B&B is tucked away on a quiet side street several blocks from the center of town. Magnolia House has plenty of repeat guests, and once you've experienced a relaxing getaway here it's easy to imagine why.

The Two Wee Cottages (830-990-8340; www.2weecottages.com), Granny Hein House and My Little House, are tucked in a little garden behind the host's home on Morse Street, eight blocks north of Main Street. The cottages have their own individuality; the Granny Hein House feels a tad more formal, with dark wood and an adorable old-fashioned kitchen, while My Little House is light and cheerful. Both cottages have hot tubs on private screened-in porches, hammocks large enough for two, and breakfast fixings in the fridge. The fresh baked goods make a lasting impression. Skip and Kate, the on-site hosts, are happy to offer recommendations for dining and entertainment.

The individualized rooms at Hoffman Haus (830-997-6739; www .hoffmanhaus.com), each with wood floors, high ceilings, luxurious linens, and several well-chosen pieces of antique or reproduction furniture, are both rustic and sophisticated. Rough-hewn beams, chinking, whitewash, and simple window treatments give the rooms a historical feel. Have breakfast in bed, then stroll the spacious gardens or rock in the rockers on the porch.

The Fredericksburg Inn and Suites (830-997-0202; www.fredericks

burg-inn.com) is a very casual spot, located just blocks from Main Street, that some guests try once and others return to again and again. The inn has fairly basic, clean rooms, a heated outdoor pool and patio, and a family-friendly atmosphere. By the same token, lots of children and adolescents, under various levels of supervision, can sometimes mean things are a little noisy, but if you go prepared for an environment that closely resembles summer camp, you won't be surprised. A good-natured good time at a great price makes the Fredericksburg Inn a solid value.

Adjacent to the small Gillespie County Airport, the Hangar Hotel (830-997-9990; www.hangarhotel.com) isn't just for aviation buffs. The appealing décor is reminiscent of the 1940s South Pacific, a theme that is carried through in the mahogany and rattan furniture, the armchairs covered in bomber-jacket leather, the hexagonal white floor tile in the bathrooms, and music playing in the common areas. The on-site Officers' Club serves drinks, while the Airport Diner has the classic curved ceiling and cozy booths, with a menu of burgers, malts, and onion rings to match.

Located just off RR 1376 on the way to Luckenbach, Settler's Crossing (830-997-2722; www.settlerscrossing .com) is a 35-acre spread that includes seven 19th-century cabins, some relocated from Indiana, Missouri, and Pennsylvania. The country antiques, wood-burning fireplaces, and period touches throughout breathe life into these historic gems. Most have fully equipped kitchens, some have Jacuzzi tubs, and all have outdoor grills. Far more than just spending the night, staying at Settler's Crossing is like living in pioneer times, albeit much, much more luxuriously.

Local Flavors

Taste of the town—local
restaurants, cafés, bistros, etc.

As in many "tourist towns," eating establishments in Fredericksburg cater to their captive—and hungry—audience with little impetus to alter the menu or force a direct correlation between quality and price. You can get a burger anywhere, pay more than you'd like, and walk away full; but if you know where to look, there are

plenty of really special and memorable meals to be had in Fredericksburg. I've also included recommendations for treats, snacks, and samplings. Many restaurants are closed Monday, and some are open only for lunch; check Web sites before you go.

Housed in a little cottage on Adams Street, the **Sunset Grill** (830-997-5904; www.sunsetgrilltx.com) is a charmer that manages to be modern and cute at the same time. The dining room is casual, open, and bright, with orange walls and fun accents, and the

Texas Peaches

Gillespie County, which includes both Fredericksburg and Stonewall, grows 40 percent of Texas's peach crop annually, making it the largest peach-producing county in Texas. Though the crop is susceptible to variable weather conditions—a late frost or spring hail can wreak havoc—when the conditions are right, the peaches are perfect and sun-ripened to a golden juicy sweetness.

To find a farm stand or an orchard that allows you to pick your own peaches, this 35-mile route is suggested: From Fredericksburg head east along US 290; in approximately 13 miles turn left onto Gellerman Lane, the site of the largest concentration of peach trees in Texas; continue to FM 2721, where you turn west back toward Fredericksburg. Continue to FM 1631 and follow it the 7 miles back to Main Street. Allow 45 minutes for the drive. Check **www.texaspeaches.com** for orchards and ripening dates, which fall anywhere between early May and late July.

Hill Country peaches for sale at a roadside stand

shaded patio is adorable. The smoked salmon Benedict is a creamy, smoky, salty, fluffy wonder atop a toasted English muffin, sprinkled with capers and bits of red onion then covered with an herb-infused hollandaise—a menu standout. Panini, burgers, and enormous salads are on the menu for lunch. The Grill stays open for dinner on Friday and Saturday nights.

Gourmet burgers are on offer at **Hondo's** (830-997-1633; www.hondos onmain.com). Hondo, the "clown prince" of Luckenbach (see p. 182), was a local character with a capital "C." Though he passed away in 1976, his legend, humor, and free-spirited approach to life live on in this part of the Hill Country. The burgers here are tailored to your whims. Made in the form of a donut and grilled over a mesquite fire, you can customize yours with irreverent ingredients like goat cheese and poblano peppers. The backyard picnic tables and live music concerts make Hondo's a vibrant, informal place to kick back.

In a restored 1890s building in the middle of the action on Main Street, the **Fredericksburg Brewing Co.** (830-997-1646; www.yourbrewery.com) is known for its microbrews, which are brewed onsite and served on tap. Try the 4-ounce samples to determine your favorite. The beer and the sausage sampler eclipse the other offerings, and the biergarten is a great place to enjoy both.

Fredericksburg Herb Farm (830-997-8615; www.fredericksburgherb farm.com) is a cluster of buildings—a restaurant, B&B cottages, spa, and gift shop—surrounded by herb gardens and located just a short walk from Main Street. The 1890s-era stone house is home to the farm's restaurant and makes an atmospheric place to dine on fresh salads, quiches, chicken

salads, and more elaborate dinner entrées.

One mile south of Main Street, far from the crowds, **The Nest** (803-990-8383; www.thenestrestaurant.com) strikes a nice balance between relaxed and sophisticated. Housed in an old bungalow, the restaurant has homey wood floors and window trim, soothing wall color, and simple décor. The refined menu features items such as rack of lamb with a pecan pesto, quail stuffed with bacon, spinach, goat cheese, and sun-dried tomatoes, and a signature lightly grilled escargot appetizer. The Nest is a popular place for celebrating special occasions or a romantic night out.

With over 30 years of service and several cookbooks under its belt, the **Peach Tree Tea Room** (830-997-9527; www.peach-tree.com) is now run by the children of the couple who founded it. Savory quiches, soups, and tasty, dainty sandwiches such as ham and Swiss on raisin pecan bread or the fried green tomato BLT make the Peach Tree a terrific option for lunch. Several child-friendly items and a relaxed atmosphere make this an enjoyable rest stop for families. Peach Tree is located on Adams Street, just south of its intersection with Main, which cleaves the thoroughfare into East and West.

Sitting on a hilltop overlooking the scrubby countryside a few minute's drive outside of town, the **Hill Top Café** (830-997-8922; www.hilltopcafe .com) has the look and feel of a well-worn honky-tonk—creaky wooden floors and walls jammed with old signs, license plates, posters, and memorabilia to which there seems very little rhyme or reason. The same could be said of the menu, where *kefalotiri saganaki* (an appetizer of flaming Greek cheese), Cajun spiced frog legs,

Enjoy a memorable meal at the Hill Top Café

crusty, homemade sourdough bread that greets you at your table to the "Come back and see us again" sign that ushers you out the door, the Hill Top Café is a pure delight. The menu description of the fried oysters could be used to describe this entire enterprise—"cornmeal-breaded and fried with love." Then there's the live music. Bluesman, musician, and transplanted Rhode Islander, owner Johnny Nicholas hosts live blues, jazz, and boogie-woogie at his joint when he's not on the road performing with his band, Johnny Nicholas and the Texas All-Stars. See the Web site for details.

There are plenty of treats and snacks to be had along Main Street, and a good place to start sampling is Rustlin' Rob's (830-990-4750; www.rustlinrobs.com). Hankering for pickled quail eggs? Jalapeño peanut butter? Chowchow relish? Rob's rustled a huge variety of Texas-made sauce, salsas, jams, jellies, and preserves and put them up for sale in this condiment emporium.

A stone's throw away, the Clear River Pecan Company (830-997-8490; www.icecreamandfun.com) has ice cream, shakes, malts, coffee, and a

and pan-seared quail are all on offer. Though the atmosphere seems scattered, the Hill Top is very focused when it comes to service and hospitality. From the breadbasket of warm,

Texas Back Roads

Leaving Fredericksburg now, take the scenic route—east on US 290 for 3 miles, then south on Old San Antonio Road, aka "Old No 9," traveling for 10.5 miles and following signs to "Old Tunnel Wildlife Area"—to the **Alamo Springs Café** (830-990-8004; www.alamospringscafe.com). Known for its outstanding, old-fashioned burgers, Alamo Springs is the real deal. Try one of the enormous green chile cheeseburgers served with grilled onions and avocado, or order their most popular burger, a massive patty with cheddar cheese, grilled onions, and mushrooms on a jalapeño cheese bun. The café is located beside the **Old Tunnel Wildlife Area** (see page 175), whose caves, from March through October, are home to some three million bats that funnel into the sky and fan out over the Hill Country each night at dusk; an amazing spectacle.

ridiculous number of baked treats fresh from the oven; a great place for families to unwind over sugar.

Stroll over to the **Fredericksburg Pie Company** (830-990-6992; www .fredericksburgtexasshopping.com), where you can enjoy a slice of bourbon orange pecan, fresh peach, or any number of other flavors of pie and a cup of coffee on the delightful patio. They tend to sell out fast, so plan on pie for a morning snack.

The Great Outdoors
Outdoor adventures and activities

Though it is a commercial nursery, **Wildseed Farms** (800-848-0078; www.wildseedfarms.com) feels like an education center, botanical garden, or nature preserve, with its winding paths through fields exploding with color. This is a must-stop wildflowers photo-op. Wildseed Farms has seeds of both native and nonnative plants, workshops, tips for growing and identifying native plants, and a Butterfly Haus filled with butterflies. While there is a fee to stroll "The Meadows," the distant view is free, and you are welcome to meander to your heart's content through the rows and rows of plants for sale. A small café serves refreshments.

Nearby
Located at the western edge of the Hill Country, Fredericksburg is a great home base for exploring the surrounding area. From Fredericksburg, TX 16 heads north to **Enchanted Rock State Natural Area** or south to **Kerrville**; US 87 travels a particularly scenic stretch on its way south to **Comfort**, and a short trip east along US 290 takes in both **Stonewall** and **Johnson City**, deep in historic LBJ country, and the legendary **Luckenbach**. The **Wine Trail** swings past Fredericksburg, and wildflower lovers might enjoy driving the picturesque **Willow City Loop**—take US 16 north for 13 miles, turn right on FM 1323, follow it to Willow City, and turn left, staying on FM 1323, to begin the loop.

Culture
History, Heritage, and the Arts

The guardian of the county's history, the **Gillespie County Historical Society** (830-997-2835; www.pioneer museum.com) looks after 11 buildings spread out over three acres, including the **Vereins Kirche Museum**, a replica of Fredericksburg's first social building and home to a permanent historical display and a gallery with changing photography exhibits, and the homestead of Henry Kammlah. The Society has over 300,000 artifacts within its rich and diverse collection and offers a fascinating look at pioneer life in the mid-1800s.

Fort Martin Scott (830-997-9895; www.fortmartinscott.org) is an old U.S. Army frontier outpost, used between 1848 and 1853, though various groups, the Texas Rangers among them, have been cycling in and out ever since.

The state-run **National Museum of the Pacific War** (830-997-4379; www .pacificwarmuseum.org) encompasses 9 acres and includes the George Bush Gallery, Admiral Nimitz Museum, Plaza of Presidents, Veterans' Walk of Honor,

Japanese Garden of Peace, Pacific Combat Zone, and the Center for Pacific War Studies. The National Museum of the Pacific War leads visitors through both the chronology and the emotions of World War II in the Pacific, through restored artifacts such as a South Pacific PT boat, Avenger dive-bombers, and pieces of battleships, photographs, and personal effects. From the scary sounds of mortar fire to the distressing reports of casualties, the only respite seems to be the reverence of the commemorative Veterans' Walk of Honor or the calm of the Japanese Garden of Peace. Honoring Admiral Chester Nimitz, the war icon and native of Fredericksburg, the museum that bears his name is located in the old Nimitz Hotel, once his family's business. A must for military-history buffs.

FESTIVALS

Fredericksburg loves its festivals, and the city seems to be in a perpetual state of celebration. The biggest is **Oktoberfest** (830-997-4810; www.oktoberfestinfbg .com), a weekend extravaganza of German food, music, and beer held at the beginning of October. At the end of the month, a great way to sample area cuisine is the **Fredericksburg Food and Wine Festival** (830-997-8515; www.fbgfoodandwine fest.com). The first weekend in December, the **St. Nikolausmarkt** (830-997-8515; www.stnikolausmarkt.com), or traditional German Christmas market, ushers in the holiday season. The **Easter Fires Pageant**, held the Saturday evening before Easter, commemorates the Meusebach-Comanche Treaty. As the story goes, during the tense moments before the treaty was announced, a pioneer mother told her anxious children that the fires they saw in the hills—the fires belonging to Comanche families awaiting news—were those of the Easter Bunny boiling eggs

Texas wildflowers

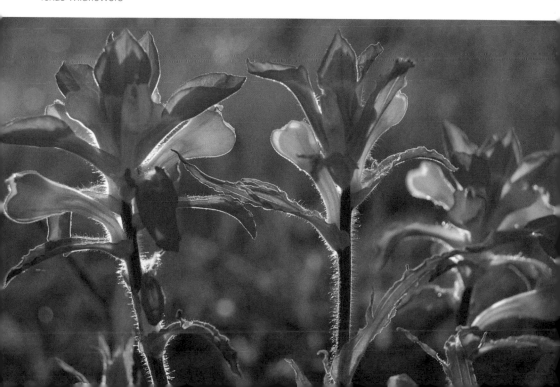

Texas State Parks

Texas' state parks preserve the natural icons of Texas, the sunsets that stretch for miles, the springtime fields of bluebonnets, the earnest roadrunners, and pokey armadillos. In the Hill Country, the limestone ravines, extensive caverns, wooded trails, and gurgling streams showcase the diversity of the region's plant life and wildlife. The Hill Country is home to the gray fox, white-tailed deer, armadillo, coyote, opossum, raccoon, bobcat, rock squirrel, and javelina, as well as rarer species, such as the golden-cheeked warbler, who is partial to nesting in the region's Ashe junipers,

Picnic at a state park

the Cagle's map turtle, the Guadalupe bass, the Texas salamander, and the Honey Creek Cave salamander.

Given that over 96 percent of the land in Texas is privately owned, the state park system really is a gift to the public. The parks of the Hill Country are a popular recreation destination, particularly for those making day trips from Austin and San Antonio for hiking, biking, climbing, birding, or fishing. Since the parks are so popular, many have capacity limits in an effort to reduce wear and tear on the environment, and it is not unusual for those parks to close because that number has been reached. Scheduling a visit for early morning, after 5 PM, or weekdays is a good way to beat the crowds.

Unfortunately, Texas' state parks, like many around the country, are experiencing serious financial troubles. Belts are so tight that many have scaled back hours, cut unnecessary services, and even closed amenities such as restrooms rather than repairing them. To avoid disappointment, consider calling your destination in advance of your visit. Despite cutbacks, the staff and rangers remain as helpful, informative, and energized as ever and more than happy to chat about the wonders of their respective parks; visit them in person or online at www.tpwd.state.tx.us. Help support America's natural heritage, and get your boots dirty in a Texas state park. Listed alphabetically:

Blanco State Park
(see "The Great Outdoors," under Blanco, page 154)

Enchanted Rock State Natural Area
(830-685-3636; www.tpwd.state.tx.us)

It is easy to imagine how Enchanted Rock might have gotten its name. Amid the scrubby woods of oak, cedar, and mesquite, and prairielike grasslands, the enormous, pink-granite dome gleams in the sun and emits mysterious creaking and

Enchanted Rock State Park

groaning sounds that have astounded human visitors for thousands of years. The Tonkawa Indians attributed the noises to ghosts, but scientists now say they are due to the expansion and contraction of the rock in the heat of the day and cool night air. The rock itself, covering 640 acres, is a batholith, an underground rock formation that has been partially exposed by erosion. The surrounding area is home to abundant wildlife and birds; a bird checklist is available at the office. Hiking, primitive camping, and rock climbing are all options, though campers will need reservations and climbers must check in at headquarters. A much-loved, natural Hill Country wonder, Enchanted Rock is on the National Register of Historic Places and tops many locals' lists of rural day-trip destinations and sights to show visitors. Due to the fragility of its environment, the park limits the number of visitors per day and must close when it reaches capacity. It is best to arrive early in the morning or after 5 PM; in both cases consider calling ahead.

Guadalupe River State Park
(830-438-2656; www.tpwd.state.tx.us)

Hugging an idyllic, 9-mile stretch of the river, Guadalupe River State Park is a favorite nature retreat for day-trippers from San Antonio, 30 miles to the south, and a popular place for camping, picnicking, and hiking. Depending on the time of year and rainfall, the river can be placid or powerful, making tubing, swimming, and fishing along the bald-cypress-lined river an adventure. This park is also a favorite of canoeists. The 5-mile equestrian trail (you'll need to bring your own horse!) is also open to mountain bikers. Nature enthusiasts may enjoy the adjacent Honey Creek State Natural Area (www.honeycreekfriends.org), which is open only for guided interpretive tours offered Saturday at 9 AM; call Guadalupe River State Park to confirm.

Hill Country State Natural Area
(830-796-4413; www.tpwd.state.tx.us)

This 5,300-acre park is minimally developed, making it a good choice for more experienced hikers, backpackers, and campers who enjoy primitive sites. The 40 miles of trails are terrific for horseback riding and mountain biking. The water in the park is not potable, so be sure to bring your own. From Bandera take TX 173 south, across the Medina River to CR 1077, and turn right. Follow the paved road for 10 miles, continuing along the unpaved road and following signs to the park.

(continued next page)

(continued from previous page)

Inks Lake State Park
(See "Highland Lakes," page 185)

Longhorn Cavern State Park
(830-598-2283; www.tpwd.state.tx.us)

A natural landmark, Longhorn Cavern is an amazing formation with a history to match. Years ago, a drop in underground water levels dissolved, bit by tiny bit, the solid limestone rock, slowly carving a subterranean streambed and cavern with soft, undulating curves. The Comanche used the cavern for shelter, and with the temperature inside a constant 68 degrees, it is easy to speculate why. Legends surround the cavern—for instance, there has been talk of Sam Bass's hidden treasure of $2 million in stolen bills—but the big draw is its beauty. Located on Park Road 4, approximately 6 miles west and 6 miles south of Burnet, off US 281.

Lost Maples State Natural Area
(830-966-3413; www.tpwd.state.tx.us)

Lost Maples State Natural Area covers more than 2,000 acres of craggy limestone canyons with the clear-running Sabinal River, grassy plateaus, and one very dramatic and lovely stand of unusual Uvalde bigtooth maples, whose fall color is by far the brightest in the area. During the last two weeks of October and the first two weeks of November, visitors descend on the park to catch a glimpse of the glowing red and

Goin' fishin'

yellow leaves. The bigtooth maple can stand 50 feet tall, is drought tolerant, prefers the local limestone and igneous soil, and has a fragile root system that is easily damaged by foot traffic—visitors are urged to remain on the 11 miles of marked trails. It is possible to drive 1 mile into the park to a scenic viewing location, a particularly helpful option for those with limited mobility. Lost Maples is home to many birds, including the rare green kingfisher and the endangered golden-cheeked warbler, making the park a boon for birders.

Lyndon B. Johnson State Park and Historic Site
(830-644-2252; www.tpwd.state.tx.us)

Dedicated to President Lyndon B. Johnson, the state park and historic site are located across from the LBJ Ranch. The park offers fishing, swimming, and picnicking, and, in spring, its many, many acres are dotted with wildflowers. Visitors have a chance to see the buffalo, longhorn cattle, wild turkey, and white-tailed deer that roam in grassy enclosures, and the visitors center contains exhibits of memorabilia from President Johnson's time in office (see "LBJ's Texas," above). The Sauer-Beckmann Living History Farm, just east of the visitors center, brings to life daily existence on a Texas farm in the early 1900s.

Old Tunnel Wildlife Management Area
(866-978-2287; www.tpwd.state.tx.us)

The Old Tunnel Wildlife Management Area occupies a snug 16 acres, but up to 3 million Mexican free-tailed bats (*Tadarida brasiliensis*) and 3,000 cave myotis bats (*Myotis velifer*) call this old and abandoned railroad tunnel home from April to October. As the story goes, when the railroad moved out in 1942, the bats moved in and have been here ever since. They emerge from their tunnel each night in a spectacular vortex of flapping wings, heading toward either the Guadalupe or Pedernales River in search of food—moths and other insects—and return to the tunnel sometime after midnight. Bat viewing is possible from either the upper viewing areas, which are open daily and free of charge, or from the lower viewing area, which is part of a guided tour.

Pedernales Falls State Park
(830-868-7304; www.tpwd.state.tx.us)

The Pedernales River runs through this 5,000-acre park, at one point gently tumbling down a series of stepped layers of limestone known as the Pedernales Falls, the park's main attraction. Depending on the time of year and amount of rainfall, the current can be brisk, slight, or even nonexistent. Those unfamiliar with the Hill Country's rivers and streams should always be on alert for any change in water level, which may indicate imminent, and quite possibly immediate, flooding, even in pleasant weather. The park features opportunities for camping, picnicking, swimming, and tubing. Additionally, there are close to 20 miles of hiking and mountain-biking trails. For birders, this park has an enclosed watching station, which is wheelchair accessible, with feeders providing lots of close-ups of the area's many birds.

LBJ's Texas

Johnson City and nearby Stonewall are each home to significant sites from the life of President Lyndon Baines Johnson. There is no entrance fee for the parks, though donations are accepted, and there is a charge for the 90-minute bus tour of the LBJ Ranch.

In Johnson City, the **National Park Service Visitors Center** (830-868-7128; www.nps.gov/lyjo) is located in the former Pedernales Hospital. It displays exhibits, photographs, and videos pertaining to President Johnson's life and times. Behind the center, visitors can take a free guided tour of **Johnson's boyhood home**, which has been restored to the look and feel of the 1920s. To the west, a short, 10-minute walk away, the Johnson Settlement includes original buildings built by President Johnson's ancestor James Polk Johnson. The barn, windmill, water tank, and cooler house help to illustrate the pioneer ranching life of the 1800s.

President Lyndon Baines Johnson

Located on US 290 14 miles west of Johnson City, near Stonewall, is the **LBJ State Park and Historic Site Visitors Center** (830-644-2252; www.tpwd.state .tx.us). LBJ spent so much time at his beloved ranch during his administration that it became known as the Texas White House. These days it remains a working ranch, with an operating Head Start preschool started during Johnson's administration. It is the final resting place of the president, who was buried here, in the family's cemetery, on January 25, 1973.

for Easter. To this day, Easter fires are lit Easter eve, the story is retold, and peace cherished. Throughout the spring and summer, festivals of peaches, lavender, wildflowers, and wines abound; details online at www.fredericksburgtexas.com.

JOHNSON CITY

Johnson City was established in 1876 and named for James Polk Johnson, an ancestor of the town's most famous native son, President Lyndon Baines Johnson. A rural ranching center and county seat, Johnson City did not have modern utilities as late as the 1930s. When President Franklin D. Roosevelt established the Rural Electrification Administration in 1935, the 28-year-old Lyndon Johnson, by then a congressman, lobbied hard for services in the sparsely populated Hill Country, succeeding in 1938.

Located at the intersection of US 281 and US 290, Johnson City makes a convenient stopover and is the destination of LBJ devotees who come to visit his childhood home in town and the family's ranch in nearby Stonewall. Johnson City is also the site of the **Blanco County Fair and Rodeo** (www.bcfra.org), held at the end of August and showcasing livestock, arts and crafts, food, and country music.

Pick Your Spot

Best places to stay in Johnson City

Though reminiscent of a Charleston-style plantation home, the wide porches and large windows of the **Rose Hill Manor** (877-767-3445; www.rose-hill .com) in Stonewall seem well suited to the Hill Country. Each of the four rooms in the main house are thoughtfully decorated with a restrained use of floral prints and appointed with queen-size beds, sun porches, sitting areas, or access to the veranda. The cozy cottages have king-size beds, simple, white bead-board walls, vaulted ceilings, warm wood floors, and small front porches for lounging. A full gourmet breakfast is served each morning and is included in the price. Austin's, the manor's on-site restaurant, is a treat (see below).

Local Flavors

Taste of the town—local restaurants, cafés, bistros, etc.

Austin's (877-767-3445, www.rose-hill .com) tops the list for fine dining in the Johnson City/Stonewall area. Large windows filled with views of the Hill Country, crisp table linens, candles, and flowers all contribute to the ambience at the Rose Hill Manor's lovely on-site restaurant. The fundamentally French menu in the large dining room is a five-course prix fixe that changes with the seasons, while the small dining room features à la carte dining, with soup, salad, desserts. The wine list is impressive.

Alternatively, Johnson City itself has some folksy restaurants to stop in for a laid-back meal. Across from the courthouse, the **Pecan Street Brewing Company** (830-868-2500; www.pecan streetbrewing.com) is a new business in an old building that has won over diners with very reasonably priced, freshly brewed beers, wood-fired pizzas, and juicy burgers. Pecan Street also serves up breakfast, live music, and Texas wines and has a pleasant patio out back for enjoying it all.

The tables at the **Hill Country Cupboard** (830-868-4625; www.hill countrycupboard.com) are covered with disposable checkered tablecloths, and iced tea is served in battered plastic tumblers. Then again, there's no need for niceties when your specialty is chicken-fried steaks the size of dinner plates. The **290 Diner** (830-868-2424) is a cheerful roadside stop for fried okra and pecan pie. The black-and-white checkered floor and lunch counter suit this place perfectly.

Nearby
Leaving Johnson City and heading east on RR 2766, you can stop in for a glass of wine at **Texas Hills Vineyard** (830-868-2321; www.texashillsvineyard.com) before continuing on to **Pedernales Falls State Park**.

Culture
History and Heritage

LBJ National Historical Park is in Johnson City, and the LBJ State Park and Historic Site is in nearby Stonewall; taken together, they offer insight into both LBJ, the man who was president, and LBJ, the little boy who grew up in rural Texas, an upbringing that affected and informed his domestic policies. See "LBJ's Texas," below.

KERRVILLE

Established in the early 1850s, Kerrville has always depended on water for its success and prosperity. In 1857 a German miller and millwright duo built a large gristmill and sawmill here that transformed the town into a regional economic center and supplier of lumber and other goods to growing San Antonio, 62 miles to the southeast.

Water is still important here, with the clean, cool Guadalupe River running right through town and the surrounding parks. A quiet county seat, Kerrville is the largest town in the area and perhaps best known these days for its highly acclaimed music marathon, the Kerrville Folk Festival (see page 181).

Pick Your Spot
Best places to stay in Kerville

It is essential to book a room in advance, particularly during festivals. Reservations may be made directly or through the following reservation services (the reservation services in Fredericksburg book rooms in Kerrville as well): Main Street Reservations Service (888-559-8555; www.travel mainstreet.com) and Gastehaus Schmidt (866-427-8374; www.fbg lodging.com). If you are looking for the charm of a B&B, you may want to stay closer to Fredericksburg, 25 miles north on TX 16. Kerrville does, however, have several conference centers that are happy to rent rooms to individuals, families, and groups.

Over 40 years old, the Inn of the Hills Resort and Conference Center (830-895-5000; www.innofthehills.com) has stood up to hundreds of family reunions, business conferences, and the stampede of children's feet racing through the courtyard to the tree-shaded, Olympic-size pool. While the rooms can feel somewhat dated, they are all clean and serviceable, with native-stone walls and ironwork details; ask for one of the pleasant poolside rooms on the ground floor. Annemarie's Alpine Lodge, the on-site restaurant, is known for its buffets, especially Sunday brunch, with its prime rib and abundant desserts. The Inn Pub features drinks and country and western music for dancing.

With its western décor, ranch-themed carpets, and memorabilia-filled lobby, the Y.O. Ranch Resort and Conference Center (877-967-3767; www.yoresort.com) is definitely a little bit o' Texas. Spacious rooms, two-room suites with bunk beds, a children's playground, swimming pool, and tennis, basketball, and volleyball courts, coupled with fairly reasonable rates and a convenient location near town, have made this resort a family favorite for years. Of course, this has also meant

The pace slows down in the Hill Country.

years of gentle wear and tear, but while it could use some updating or a fresh coat of paint, the Y.O. Ranch currently has a comfortable, well-worn feel that is right at home in the Hill Country. The weekday lunch buffet at the Branding Iron, their on-site restaurant, is very popular with locals.

The Presbyterian-affiliated **Mo Ranch Conference Center** (800-460-4401; www.moranch.com), located near the town of Hunt, west of Kerrville, is known for hosting conferences, youth groups, and Elderhostels, but there is also plenty of room for individuals and families who would like to come to enjoy swimming, horseback riding, a ropes course, and other recreational activities. Accommodations range from simply furnished two-bedroom apartments to tent camping sites, with hotel rooms and cabins in between. Since Mo Ranch is in a remote, rural area, all guests are required to purchase the modestly priced meal plan served in the communal dining hall.

Local Flavors

Taste of the town—local restaurants, cafés, bistros, etc.

Though there aren't a lot of options, dining in Kerrville ranges from gourmet to grab-and-go, so you're sure to find something to suit your tastes.

Rails Café at The Depot (830-257-3877; www.railscafe.com) is known for its elegant dining room, lovely patio, and delicious food. Diners single out the salads, oso buco, and the shrimp Creole for praise.

For fine Mexican dining in Kerrville, folks head to **Francisco's** (830-257-2995; www.franciscos-restaurant .com), at the corner of Earl Garrett and Water Street, where the tortilla soup and *chile rellenos* are tops.

Nearby, fish tacos, outstanding antelope sliders with goat cheese, and an extensive selection of beer and wine, and a slightly upscale but still casual atmosphere, make **Grape Juice** (830-792-9463; www.grapejuiceon line.com) popular with foodies.

If a burger is what you're after, stop in at **Classics Burgers and More** (830-257-8866; www.classicsburgers .net) for an enormous patty, massive onion rings, and a side of country charm.

Not surprisingly, the menu at **Cowboy Steak House** (830-896-5688; www.cowboysteakhouse.com) on Main Street is all meat. Stick with a porterhouse or try some quail. Sample shish kebab sirloin chunks or branch out into buffalo steak. Choose between rack of lamb, chicken breast, and whole catfish. While any entrée is served with soup or a salad, vegetables are available only "on request."

Also on Main Street, **Hill Country Café** (830-257-6665; www.hill-country -cafe.com) has been around forever, serving eggs, toast, bacon, and hot coffee to Kerrville's early risers. Cash only.

The Lakehouse (830-895-3188; www.hillcountrycookin.com) is known for its all-you-can-eat fried catfish filets and bite-size shrimp served with pinto beans, coleslaw, french fries, and hush puppies. A comfortable, no-nonsense place right on the water.

The Great Outdoors
Outdoor adventures and activities

The 500-acre **Kerrville-Schreiner State Park** (830-257-7300; www .kerrville.org), on the banks of the Guadalupe River three miles southeast of Kerrville, offers picnicking, boating, and camping. There is tent camping along the water, two dozen air-conditioned cabins, and one large cabin that sleeps six. This stretch of the river is known for its fishing, and swimming is allowed, though there aren't lifeguards on duty.

Another natural area to explore is the **Riverside Nature Center** (830-257-4837; www.riversidenaturecenter.org), which began to take shape in 1992, when a parcel of land was purchased and its native plants and habitat were restored through great community effort and volunteerism. The center opened in 1999, and its trails, which meander past native trees, wildflowers, birds, and butterflies, are as educational as they are relaxing.

Culture
History, Heritage, and the Arts

A dozen galleries and museums in Kerrville have organized the **Second Saturday Art Trail** (www.artinthehills .com), hosting afternoon receptions and special events in their respective establishments on the second Saturday of every month.

Schreiner Mansion (830-896-8633; www.mansion.schreiner.edu), formerly the Hill Country Museum, is housed in Captain Charles Schreiner's home, a massive native-stone structure built between 1879 and 1896. A native Frenchman, Schreiner moved to San Antonio with his family in 1852 and joined the Texas Rangers in 1854 at the age of 16. Schreiner fought in the Civil War, opened a mercantile establishment, excelled in banking, ranching, and marketing wool and mohair, and, in 1880, purchased the Y.O. Ranch. As Schreiner's wealth grew, so

Medina

Midway between Bandera and Kerrville, along a picturesque stretch of TX 16, is Medina, a blink-and-you'll-miss-it gem of a town. Spend the night at Koyote Ranch, slurp an apple cider slushy at Love Creek Orchards, and savor a little bit of Texas that's off the beaten path.

Love Creek Orchards (830-589-2202; www.lovecreekorchards.com) If you aren't hungry when you arrive, the smell of fresh hot apple pie wafting through Love Creek Orchards will have you salivating for a snack in no time. The Patio Café serves big, juicy burgers and sandwiches, with a side of chips and apples, daily for lunch, and the country store sells all things apple, from ciders to jams and ice cream.

Koyote Ranch (800-225-0991; www.koyoteranch.com) Koyote Ranch is a collection of new cabins, campsites, and RV sites hugging the lovely green hillside outside Medina. With heated and air-conditioned bathrooms in the campground, a pool, and a camp store complete with a reasonably priced grill and deli, the Koyote Ranch is "roughing it" with family-friendly amenities.

did his philanthropic interests, and he established the Schreiner Institute, now Schreiner University, in 1917. This museum, with its creaky hardwood floors, period furnishings, and quirky details, such as the trapdoor leading to a tunnel the captain used to safeguard money, tells the story of his bygone era and his lasting effect on Kerrville.

The **Kerr Arts and Cultural Center** (830-895-2911; www.kacckerrville.com) is right at home in Kerrville's historic, former post office, exhibiting works from photography to quilting, basketry to ceramics, created by the center's 600 member artists.

In a limestone building designed by Texan architect O'Neil Ford, the **Museum of Western Art** (830-896-2553; www.americanwesternart.org) pays homage to the West and its inhabitants. The artwork depicts western life from a wide range of perspectives, with images of the hardworking cowboy, Native Americans, and pioneer women figuring prominently. The interior of the museum is a juxtaposition of elements—mesquite wood floors and Saltillo tiles, crisp-white display walls, and bronze statues—with as much rough-hewn gracefulness as the artwork adorning it.

FESTIVALS

The nationally acclaimed **Kerrville Folk Festival** (830-257-3600; www.kerrville folkfestival.com) is held on an outdoor stage at the Quiet Valley Ranch RV Park and Campgrounds (www.qvranch.com) in the peaceful Hill Country nine miles south of Kerrville on TX 16. When the festival began in 1972, it was centered on folk music, but it has grown to include acoustic rock, bluegrass, blues, country, and jazz. Many major-label artists played "Kerrville" on their way up, and some frequently return. The event takes place in May, starting the Thursday before Memorial Day, and lasts for 18 days.

Kerrville celebrates Easter weekend with an event that includes lots and lots of food and exercise, the **Annual Kerrville Easter Festival and Chili Classic** (www.kerrvilleeasterfest.com). With a 5K Easter Run, egg hunts, children's games, washer pitching (akin to the game of horseshoes), armadillo races, and copious amounts of steaming hot chili, this one's fun. At the same time, the Easter Hill Country Bike Tour draws cyclists from throughout the region to the back roads of the Hill Country.

In May, on Memorial Day weekend, the **Texas State Arts and Crafts Fair** (803-896-5711; www.tacef.org) is a family-friendly good time with close to 200 artists, music, and activities for children.

In September, the **Kerrville Wine and Music Festival** (www.kerrville-music .com) is four days of mellow singer-songwriter music and regional wine tasting. Organized by the folks at the Kerrville Folk Festival, the Wine and Music Festival is held over the Labor Day weekend and is a very popular Hill Country event, drawing crowds from near and far.

At the end of September, the Texas Heritage Music Foundation hosts the **Texas Heritage Living History Weekend** (830-792-1945; www.texasheritage music.org), a three-day event devoted entirely to Texas music and heritage. An impressive and eclectic lineup of talent includes gospel choirs, storytellers, trick ropers, *vaqueros* (cowboys), square dancers, and cloggers, all performing on the Schreiner University campus.

The **Kerr County Fair** (830-257-6833; www.kerrcountyfair.com) in October features a parade, carnival, 4H livestock exhibits, chili and BBQ cook-offs, dancing, and music.

Kerr County Market Days (www.kerrmarketdays.org) are held at the Kerr County Courthouse Square on the second and fourth Saturday of each month, April through December, except August.

LUCKENBACH

If you really want to slow down, grind to a halt in Luckenbach, where the only movement is tapping feet and guitar picking in the shade of surrounding oak trees. A tiny cluster of rustic wooden buildings, including the multipurpose General Store, make up this little community, which is worth a trip for the music and dancing alone.

Immortalized in Waylon Jennings' song "Luckenbach, Texas (Back to the Basics of Love)," little Luckenbach came into being in the 1840s and 1850s when several German-speaking families decided to settle along the banks of Grape Creek. The population fluctuated from 150 in 1896 to 492 in 1902, but by the 1960s it had leveled off to 25. In 1971, John Russell (Hondo) Crouch purchased the settlement, declared himself mayor, and set its spirit free. Live music on holidays brings out the locals, visitors, and Harley riders, who queue up for pulled-pork sandwiches and beer. Offbeat and good-natured events, such as the annual Hug-In held in February, capture the character of the hamlet beautifully. As the town slogan goes, "Everybody is somebody in Luckenbach." And if you're lucky enough to go, you will be too.

Open for business since 1849, the **General Store** (830-997-3224; www.lucken bachtexas.com) is old and creaky, with a sloping front porch, a bar in the back, and spaces in between the floorboards that let in the draft. Folks here just love it to death. With live music every night at 7 and plenty of Hondo-style cowboy hats for sale, what's not to love? The store's sleek Web site has all the details.

Pick Your Spot
Best places to stay in Luckenbach

There aren't many options for lodging in Luckenbach, but fortunately there is the **Full Moon Inn** (830-997-2205; www.fullmooninn.com). A log cabin from the 1800s, an old smokehouse, and a replicated Sunday house form a little compound of accommodations on 12 grassy acres with a creek. Soft sheets, Jacuzzi tubs, and sweet potato pancakes more than make up for the lack of television. While the mailing address for the Full Moon Inn is Fredericksburg, it is a half mile from Luckenbach.

MARBLE FALLS
Marble Falls, so named for the marble outcroppings over which the nearby Colorado River flows, was founded in 1887. Located just north of town on RM 1431, Granite Mountain was once a huge dome of pink and red granite; it was quarried in the 1880s to construct the Texas Capitol in Austin. These days, there is not much granite to see; a plaque at the picnic area across the road tells the story. Located on US 281 between Johnson City and Burnet, and within striking distance of many of the Highland Lakes, Marble Falls is a good place to stop for a bite to eat.

Sleepover
The Hill Country is filled with off-beat places to stay. The really adventurous may enjoy perusing the offerings at **www.backroads texas.net** for some truly out-of-the-ordinary places to spend the night.

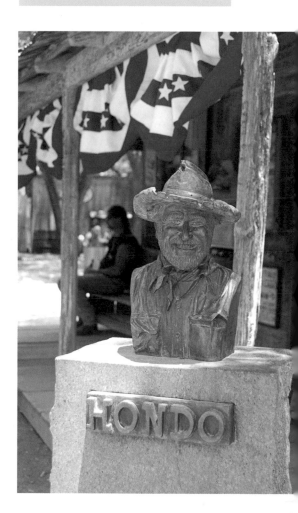

Statue of John Russell "Hondo" Crouch, former "Mayor" of Luckenbach

Local Flavors

Taste of the town—local restaurants, cafés, bistros, etc.

The **Bluebonnet Café** (830-693-2344; www.bluebonnetcafe.net) is not much to look at. In fact, you just might miss its red and white sign when rounding the curve over the bridge in Marble Falls. One thing you're sure to notice is the line of people snaking out the front door, particularly on weekends. Constantly crowded, this very casual diner has pot roasts, chicken-fried steaks, fried okra, catfish, an all-day breakfast menu, and all kinds of pie.

In the mood for a pint? Swing by the **Double Horn Brewery** (830-693-5165; www.doublehornbrewing .com) and wash down overstuffed sandwiches, sliders, shrimp and grits, and appetizers—try the fried avocado with lump crab—with a brew. The spacious dining room and patio out back are both light and bright.

Stop by **Noon Spoon** (830-798-2347; www.noonspooncafe.com) for lunch. The colorful café has healthy salads, sandwiches, wraps, hot baked potatoes, breakfast tacos, casseroles, and quesadillas galore.

Another option is **Brothers Bakery** (830-798-8278; www.brothersbakery .com), where the tuna salad with walnuts, apples, and olives is particularly popular. Plenty of pastries, cookies, and treats go well with a midday cup of coffee.

Nearby

From Marble Falls, you can easily visit the Highland Lakes, Spicewood Vineyards (see "Hill Country Vineyards," above), and Sweet Berry Farm (830-798-1462; www.sweetberryfarm.com), with its mazes, hayrides, picnic tables, and U-pick fruits and vegetables—strawberries and blackberries in the spring, tomatoes in the summer, and pumpkins in the fall.

Chocolate cream pie and coffee at the Bluebonnet Café

Highland Lakes

The Colorado River passes through the northern part of the Hill Country, picking up the spring-fed Pedernales, Llano, San Saba, and Concho Rivers as tributaries before flowing through the city of Austin. The river then continues over the flat, alluvial land of the Coastal Plain and into the Gulf of Mexico. Throughout the early 1800s, the Colorado was prone to impassable logjams and periodic flooding that threatened riverside settlements. The need for irrigation, a reliable water source, and flood control prompted the Lower Colorado River Authority (LCRA) to construct six dams along the river between 1935 and 1951, creating a chain of six lakes known as the Highland Lakes. The Highland Lakes and their 25 waterside parks are favorite spots for boating, fishing, camping, and ecotourism. The lakes and their shorelines also provide habitat for rare, endangered, and migratory birds, including the American bald eagle, and support a large variety of wildlife.

Area Web sites—www.highlandlakes.com, www.lakesandhills.com, www.lcra .org, and www.texasoutside.com—provide details of the region's lodging, dining, and recreation.

LAKE BUCHANAN

Lake Buchanan, some 31 miles long, is the largest, oldest, and northernmost of the Highland Lakes; it is located approximately 75 miles north of Austin. The eastern shoreline is rocky, with granite cliffs, waterfalls, and deep cold water, while the western shore has beaches for swimming. The majestic American bald eagle nests in the area surrounding the lake during the winter and early spring. The closest large towns are Burnet to the east and Llano to the west.

BURNET

Designated as the Bluebonnet Capital of Texas, Burnet stages the **Bluebonnet Festival** (512-756-4297; www.burnetchamber.org) the second weekend in April, complete with a parade, carnival, food, and music.

Austin Steam Train (512-477-8468; www.austinsteamtrain.org) The *Hill Country Flyer* travels south from downtown Burnet and loops back again. While the train does not have air conditioning, it makes up for it with plenty of vintage details such as wood window moldings, upholstered seating, and an old-time concession stand.

Canyon of the Eagles Lodge and Nature Park (512-334-2070; www.canyon oftheeagles.com) This lodge, complete with fairly basic accommodations, cabins, campground, restaurant, and tiny swimming pool, is located within the confines of an LCRA-owned, 940-acre public park, most of which is a nature preserve. The park includes 14 miles of hiking trails (maps available at the main lodge), an educational nature center, and boat rentals.

Vanishing Texas River Cruise (512-756-6986; www.vtrc.com) The boat leaves from the Canyon of the Eagles Lodge and Nature Park for ecological cruises on Lake Buchanan; vineyard tours and wildflower and dinner cruises are also offered.

Eagle Eye Observatory (800-977-0081; www.austinastro.org; Austin Astronomical Society) This observatory houses a 16-inch Ealing Educator Telescope and hosts monthly stargazing parties; see Web site for details.

LLANO

Cooper's Old Time Pit Barbeque (325-247-5713; www.coopersbbq.com) Pick your meat at the pit, watch the pit master submerge it in sauce, and proceed inside to pick out your sides.

TOW

Fall Creek Vineyards (325-379-5361; www.fcv.com; see "Hill Country Vineyards," above) Situated at the northwest end of the lake, Fall Creek Vineyards makes a good destination for wine lovers.

INKS LAKE

Inks Lake State Park (512-793-2223; www.tpwd.state.tx.us) Formerly ranchland, Inks Lake State Park is now a recreational facility on the eastern shores of Inks Lake, whose water levels remain constant throughout the year, regardless of drought, making it a reliable spot for swimming (unsupervised beach), fishing, and boating. Tent camping and primitive backpack camping are available. Brand-new limited-use cabins are equipped with two bunk beds, air conditioning, electricity, an outdoor grill, and a water spigot. Two of the cabins are handicapped accessible. Canoes and paddleboats are also available for rent, as are golf clubs and carts for the waterfront nine-hole golf course. Nearby **Longhorn Cavern State Park** (see "Texas State Parks," above) is a geological wonder.

LAKE LBJ

The shoreline of Lake LBJ is very developed, with large homes along the resort town of Horseshoe Bay and particularly Applehead Island. A popular spot for boating, the lake can get crowded on weekends. Nearby, Longhorn Cavern State Park makes an easy side trip. The closest large town is Marble Falls, to the east. Part of the **Texas Wine Trail** winds through the region, with **Lost Creek Vineyard** near Sunrise Beach on the western shore of Lake LBJ and **Spicewood Vineyards** just a short drive south along TX 71. **Lake LBJ Resort, Marina, and Country Club** (325-388-9393; www.lakelbjfun.com) rents condos and watercraft year-round.

LAKE MARBLE FALLS

The smallest of the Highland Lakes, this narrow, almost riverlike lake is surrounded by mostly steep, rocky, and privately owned land, though there are three modest city parks on the north shore of the lake just west of US 281. In August, the **Marble Falls LakeFest** (www.marblefallslakefest.com) brings ear-splitting speedboat drag racing to the lake. The nearby town of Marble Falls (see page 183) offers several tasty restaurants, all of which are local favorites.

LAKE TRAVIS

A party lake, Lake Travis is often swarming with motorized watercraft on weekends. Numerous parks allow day-trippers to get a little closer to nature on the outskirts of Austin, and a variety of eateries make this Highland Lake a sophisticated stopover for drinks or a meal.

Parks

Hippie Hollow (www.hippiehollow.com) A favorite spot along the rocky shores of Lake Travis for folks who like to swim and sunbathe in the buff. From MoPac (Loop 1), Capital of Texas Highway (Loop 360), or I-35, take 2222 west to Ranch TX 620 and follow signs.

Boat Rentals
Daybreak Boat Rentals (512-266-2176; www.daybreakboatrentals.com)

Just for Fun (512-266-9710; www.jff.net)

Dining
Hudson's on the Bend (see "Local Flavors" in Austin section) For wild game, try this place.

The Oasis (512-266-2442; www.oasis-austin.com) With multiple levels of decks jutting over Lake Travis, each dotted with dozens of colorful umbrellas, the Oasis has a very casual, come-as-you-are atmosphere; just the sort of place to relax and unwind over drinks. Splendid views of Lake Travis and the stunning Central Texas sunset.

LAKE AUSTIN

Located within the city limits, Lake Austin is an aquatic playground of parks, boats, cruises, plenty of casual, family-friendly spots to grab food and drinks, and lots of live music.

Parks
Emma Long Metropolitan Park (512-346-1831; www.austinparks.org) Biking, camping, hiking, and swimming.

Boat Rental
Sun & Fun Watercraft Rentals (512-306-1820; www.sunfunrental.com) Rents Jet Skis and pontoon and ski boats.

Cruises
Lake Austin Riverboats (512-345-5220; www.austinriverboats.com) Enjoy a leisurely cruise aboard an authentic stern-wheel riverboat.

Austin Duck Adventures (512-477-5274; www.austinducks.com) Drive around Austin in an amphibious British Alvis Stalwart before splashing into Lake Austin.

Lodging
Lake Austin Spa (see "Pick Your Spot" in Austin section)

Dining
County Line BBQ (512-346-3664; www.countyline.com) The place to go for great BBQ with a great view.

Hula Hut (512-476-4852; www.hulahut.com) A favorite spot for drinks, Hula Hut specializes in Mexico-meets-Polynesia cuisine with guacamole salads served beside pupu platters, seating overlooking the water, and a fun, breezy vibe. Owned by the creators of the local Tex-Mex chain restaurant Chuy's (www.chuys.com) and the Shady Grove (www.theshadygrove.com) in Austin.

Mozart's Coffee Roasters (512-477-2900; www.mozartscoffee.com) On the banks of Lake Austin a few minutes' drive from downtown Austin, Mozart's can do things with coffee, chocolate, and cheesecake that defy restraint and define indulgence. Stellar views of Lake Austin, outdoor seating on a spacious deck, and nightly live jazz, folk, or classical guitar music add romance to the euphoria of caffeine and sugar.

Ski Shores Waterfront Café (512-349-7511; www.skishoresaustin.com) Super-casual place for a burger right on the water. Laughing children, folks in flip-flops, live music, and weekend movie nights.

WIMBERLEY

Along the banks of Cypress Creek, just 30 minutes south of Austin or 15 minutes west of San Marcos along RR 12, Wimberley is a small but thriving town of artists and other folks who just like living "not in Austin." Its creek lined with bald cypress and pecan trees, the town is beautifully scenic. The dramatic Devil's Backbone (see "Attractions, Parks, and Recreation," below) is visible from certain lookout points.

Founded in 1856, when a Mr. Winters built a small gristmill along the creek, the tiny settlement was first known as Winters Creek. The Cude family then bought the mill, and the community became known as Cude's Mill. In 1874 Pleasant Wimberley took over the mill, and the town's moniker changed again, this time to Wimberley's Mill. In 1880, on a petition for a post office, the town was referred to as Wimberleyville. The name stuck and was shortened over time to simply Wimberley. The mill continued operating, as a lumber mill, gristmill, flour mill, molasses mill, and cotton gin, before being razed in 1934. The community that had built up around the mill remained, and starting in the 1930s Wimberley became a tourist destination. Market Days, held the first Saturday of each month from April through December, are a big draw. Wimberley has a culture, community, and charm all its own and is enjoyable as a day trip or as an overnight retreat.

Pick Your Spot

Best places to stay in Wimberley

With deluxe cottages, a cooking school, an art gallery, and a restaurant, pool, and spa here, once you arrive at **Blair House Inn** (512-847-1111; www.blair houseinn.com) you'll have no reason to leave. The themed rooms revolve around Texas and the Southwest, with three archangels thrown in. The Fort Worth Room, for example, has a rich, leather sofa and chair, tan walls, a dark wood sleigh bed, crimson details, and a few requisite stars on the walls, just enough to capture the feel but not overly drawn out. Stunning views round out the luxurious offerings.

Creekhaven Inn (512-847-9344; www.creekhaveninn.com) may be relatively new, but it shares the banks of Cypress Creek with several towering cypress trees that are as old as anybody's guess. The 13 rooms are as unique and colorful as the wildflowers they're named for.

Between Wimberley and Blanco, the **Red Corral Ranch** (830-833-4801; www.redcorralranch.com) is a large facility that frequently hosts weddings, corporate functions, reunions, and spiritual retreats but also rents several freestanding guesthouses to individuals and small groups. Each guesthouse has a full kitchen, grill, and hot tub, and a continental breakfast is included in the price. What makes Red Corral Ranch really stand out are its grounds: over a thousand acres of hike-and-bike trails, along with a walking labyrinth, a cool, crystal-clear, aquifer-fed swimming pool, an organic garden, pecan groves, stands of wildflowers, dozens of white peacocks, and multitudes of deer, butterflies, and birds.

Go Texan

As part of a marketing campaign of the Texas Department of Agriculture, when you travel in Texas you may see the GO TEXAN sticker or stamp on agricultural products such as food, wine, and beef that indicates the item was grown or processed in Texas. Nonagricultural products—art and jewelry, for example—are also sometimes designated. The Department of Agriculture provides education and encourages various practices such as gardening with native plants. For a list of statewide produce stands and farmers' markets, organized by county, or even recipes using state-grown produce, visit www.picktexas.com and support Texas businesses. Check www.gotexan.org for more information.

Big local flavor

Local Flavors

Taste of the town—local restaurants, cafés, bistros, etc.

The **Leaning Pear** (512-847-7327; www.leaningpear.com) serves gourmet food in a cute-as-a-button café, winning over Wimberley with whimsy. Perky salads, savory quiches, luscious soups, a BLT with brie, and roasted poblano pimento cheese sandwiches are just some of the many reasons diners line up for a seat in the tiny dining room.

Enjoy a slice and a craft-brew at the **Wimberley Brewing Company** (512-847-3299; www.brewsters pizza.com). While pizza can be ubiquitous, the pies here are exceptional, as is the attached deck with its Hill Country views.

Cypress Creek Café (512-847-0030; www.cypresscreekcafe.com) has been serving up homemade breakfasts, lunches, and dinners for over 25 years now. The lightly breaded Home Style Steak is "griddle fried" and covered with a ladleful of cream gravy and seems much lighter than its cousin, the deep-fried chicken-fried steak. The chicken scampi strikes a delicious balance, with grilled chicken and sautéed mushrooms served over penne with a lemon garlic sauce. Live music almost every night; check the Web site for details.

The Great Outdoors

Outdoor adventures and activities

Natural attractions in Wimberley include **Blue Hole** (www.friendsof bluehole.org), a renowned natural swimming hole where folks come to splash and swing among the cypress trees, just a short walk from the center of town. Stunning scenery is visible from **Devil's Backbone**, a steep scenic ridge that offers stunning views; drive out RR 12 to RR 32 and turn west. **Bella Vista Ranch** (512-847-6514; www.bvranch.com) opened a *frantoio,* or olive pressing facility, in 2001, and it offers samples of the oils fresh off the press as well as wines made from grapes and berries grown on the ranch.

RECREATION

A tremendous online resource for all outdoor recreation in Texas is **Texas Outside**, www.texasoutside.com.

Hill Country vista

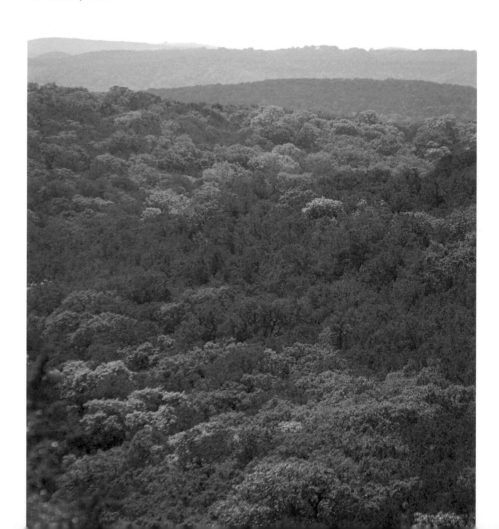

Bicycling

Bicycling, both road and mountain biking, is big in Central Texas, especially in Austin and the Hill Country. Rentals are available through Hill Country Bicycle Works (830-990-2609, www.hillcountrybicycle.com), which has shops in both Kerrville and Fredericksburg.

Helpful Web sites include:

Cycle Texas (www.cycletexas.com)

Hill Country Bicycle Touring Club (www.hcbtc.org)

Texas State Park System (www.tpwd.state.tx.us/exptexas/bike)

Bird Watching

The Hill Country is a great spot to catch a glimpse of rare, migratory, and native birds. Online, Texas Parks and Wildlife, www.tpwd.state.tx.us, and the Travis County Audubon Society, www.travisaudubon.org, both offer a wealth of information. See "Suggested References" in the Information chapter for a selection of bird-watching guides.

Boating, Canoeing, and Kayaking

Boat rentals are available at the Highland Lakes and Kerrville-Schreiner State Park in Kerrville.

Camping

The state parks dotting the Hill Country offer a variety of camping opportunities. There is a state park with camping on Inks Lake in the Highland Lakes and another in Blanco (see "Texas State Parks," p. 172). Kerrville's city park has camping. A terrific online source for all camping in the region—private or public, tent or RV—is www.texasoutside.com.

Climbing

Cypress Valley Canopy Tours (512-264-8880; www.cypressvalleycanopytours.com) Tour participants use steel zip lines to travel between treetop platforms among old-growth cypresses. In the Hill Country 30 minutes west of Austin.

Mountain Madness Rock Climbing School (512-590-2988; www.mtmadness .com; P.O. Box 162643, Austin, TX 78716) Weekend classes held at Enchanted Rock State Natural Area near Fredericksburg.

Fishing

There is plenty of fishing in the Highland Lakes and state parks, and you don't need a license to fish from shore in a Texas State Park. See www.tpwd.state.tx.us for details. Other online resources include www.texasoutside.com and www.tx fishing.com.

Golf

Lady Bird Johnson Municipal Golf Course (830-997-4010; www.golffredericks burg.com)

Scott Schreiner Municipal Golf Course (830-257-4982; www.golfkerrville .com)

Country music on a hot afternoon

Swimming

Swimming is available at the beaches of the Highland Lakes and several of the state parks (see separate listings).

Tours

The Bluebonnet Trail, Texas Lavender Trail, and **Texas Wine Trail** are self-guided. The **Austin Steam Train** (512-477-8468; www.austinsteamtrain.org) runs vintage trains through the Hill Country, and boat cruises are available on the Highland Lakes. (See separate listings on all the above.) **Texpert Tours** (512-383-8989; www.texperttours.com) offers a variety of tours throughout Austin and the Hill Country.

Tubing

Probably the best spot to tube in the Hill Country is Blanco State Park (see "The Great Outdoors" under Blanco).

Culture
History, Heritage, and the Arts

An enclave of artists, Wimberley has some galleries and cultural events of particular note and a full calendar of festivals; see www.wimberley.org for details. The **Crawfish Festival,** usually the last Saturday in April, has live music and an enormous catch of crawfish boiled up for partygoers. If hundreds and hundreds of crawfish aren't enough to get you in the mood, perhaps a variety of gumbo, étouffée, red beans and rice, andouille

sausage, key lime pie, or bread pudding eaten elbow to elbow might just do the
trick. The **Wimberley Winter Jazz Festival** brings together jazz musicians from
Texas and beyond to play a series of intimate concerts in February.

The **EmilyAnn Theatre** (512-847-6969; www.emilyann.org) is an outdoor
community theater that stages, among other productions, a summerlong Shakespeare under the Stars, performed entirely by children and young adults no older
than high school seniors (the only accredited high school Shakespearean theater in
the United States). The theater also hosts a number of family-friendly events, such
as a holiday tree lighting in December and a Butterfly Festival in April.

Opened by Tim de Jong in 1992, the **Wimberley Glass Works** (512-393-3316;
www.wgw.com) rose quickly to become one of the region's foremost art glass studios and galleries. While the gallery space here is filled with exquisite handblown
glass in every imaginable shape, size, and color, the best part of the Wimberley
Glass Works is the live demonstrations, where you can see artists coaxing vases,
pitchers, stemware, and art out of molten glass. After many years in Wimberley,
the Glass Works has a new space on RR 12 halfway between Wimberley and San
Marcos, and a new San Marcos address.

4

Nearby and In Between

EN ROUTE

INTERSTATE 35, the highway connecting Austin and San Antonio, also passes **Georgetown, New Braunfels,** and **San Marcos**, which are great places to pull in for a meal, a day, or even a weekend. Thirty miles north of Austin, historic **Georgetown** (see below) is a remarkably well-preserved town with a restored courthouse at its center, antique shops surroundings its square, and a lovely hike and bike trail. Thirty miles south of Austin, **San Marcos** (see p. 207) has become known for its outlet malls, though nature enthusiasts will enjoy a trip to the educational Aquarena Center for a ride down the river on a glass bottom boat. Another 20 miles south, **New Braunfels** (see p. 199) has a reputation for some of the best river tubing in the area and as home to lovely historic **Gruene** (see p. 199).

GEORGETOWN

Straddling I-35, Georgetown is located at the spot where the fertile plains of East Texas start to give way to the jagged wooded ravines and sloping hills of the Hill Country. A pleasant side trip from Austin, Georgetown is home to Southwestern University. Chartered in 1875, Southwestern is often cited at the state's oldest university. Southwestern's relationship with Georgetown is one of quiet intermingling; the university's concerts, gallery shows, and theatrical productions are offered throughout the school year and are open to the public. Details at www.southwestern.edu.

Georgetown has won awards for its well-preserved, historic downtown, which comprises dozens of detail-rich buildings and homes dating to the 1880s gathered around a traditional Texas square with a courthouse in its center. The seat of Williamson County, Georgetown has become a popular commuter town for families and, with the construction of age-restricted developments, a home for retirees

LEFT: The Best BBQ in Texas

'Cue

If you're coming to Texas, chances are you're expecting to sample some drip-down-your-chin juicy BBQ. Before you settle in with a dozen paper napkins and a pack of saltines, you might like to know the provenance of the tradition of which you are about to partake. Though the earliest details are somewhat murky, we know that folks around the world have been cooking outdoors since the dawn of time. At some point, these chefs began to dig pits to cook in, concentrating heat, smoke, and flavor and rendering even tough, stringy, and sinewy slabs of meat edible, moist, and tender. From clambakes to pig roasts, each culture has its version. The origins of the name—barbecue—are even more elusive, but theories abound. It may derive from *barbacoa*, the Spanish version of the name that the Taino Indians of the Caribbean gave to the process they had perfected of slow-cooking and smoking large pieces of meat over a pit fire.

A packed dining room at Smitty's in Lockhart

In the United States, the style and flavor of BBQ depend on the region. In the Southeast, folks love to drown their pork BBQ in a sweet tomato sauce with a vinegary twang, while the Southwest favors its meat dry-rubbed without any sauce at all. Chicago BBQ is heavy on both the sauce and the pepper. Generally speaking, the farther north you go, the greater the chance that if you order BBQ, you'll get chicken. In Texas, BBQ has always meant beef above all. Typically, the meat is dry-rubbed, smoked, and sauced with various signature concoctions that run the gamut from sweet and smoky to hot and spicy.

Some of the best BBQ anywhere is at **Franklin BBQ** (see p. 48) in Austin, **Cooper's** (see p. 186) in Llano, and **Luis Mueller Barbecue** (512-352-6206; www .louiemuellerbarbecue.com) farther afield in Taylor. However, heading east of Austin and following the smell of the pits will take you on a self-guided tasting tour of come great, old-school 'cue. Starting in Lockhart at **Kreuz Market** (512-398-2361; www .kreuzmarket.com; pronounced "krites"), you will be served a huge hunk of hot-from-the-pit beef, pork, or sausage wrapped in butcher paper, a meal you will likely remember for years to come. No sauce and no utensils come with your order—the custom for over 100 years—you get just meat, some saltines, a huge pickle, and half an onion, and off you go to one of the communal tables to dig in. Many customers come for the brisket alone, but the prime rib and clod (shoulder) have garnered raves; and although it is very un-Texan, the pork chop is fabulous. When Kreuz moved from more modest digs down the street to this newer, larger space in 1999, it updated its menu by adding German potato salad, sauerkraut, and beans. Other than that, happily, the owners haven't changed a thing. **Black's BBQ** (512-398-2712; www.blacks bbq.com) and **Smitty's Market** (512-398-9344; www.smittysmarket.com) both rank high on locals' lists of regional favorites, and are open on Sunday, when Kreuz is closed. In Central Texas, BBQ is often served with a side of sausage—a smoky beef bratwurst—and the region's gold standard is Elgin sausage, made in Elgin, TX. **Meyer's Elgin Smokehouse** (512-281-3331; www.meyerselginsausage.com) and **Southside Market** (512-281-4650; www.southsidemarket.com) are legendary.

BBQ with all the fixin's at Luling City Market in Luling

who come for the area's livability, climate, and access to Austin. Rapid growth has Georgetown focused on maintaining the small-town atmosphere that makes it such an enjoyable destination.

Stop in and say howdy at the friendly **Visitor Center** (800-436-8696; www .visitgeorgetown.com), poke around the square's antique and gift shops, and stay for a bite to eat.

Local Flavors

Taste of the town – local restaurants, cafés, bistros, etc.

Lunch with the ladies at **Laurie's** (512-863-5875; www.lauriescafe.com), where daily quiches, crunchy broccoli salad, ultra fresh salads with homemade dressings, and piping hot yeast rolls take top billing. Homespun and just as sweet as can be, Laurie's is the sort of place where you can slow down, sip your iced tea, and enjoy the chatter of this beloved neighborhood restaurant.

A few blocks away, the **Monument Café** (512-930-9586; www.themonu mentcafe.com), opened in 1995, has become an institution; trying to get a seat in its '40s-style dining room or lunch counter at meal time can take some patience. Fried whole catfish, the Kobe steaks, and the fried chicken with cream gravy are all served with generous side portions of comfort foods, many organic and/or locally sourced. Monument's signature chocolate pie is the real thing, from its thick, nutty

crust made of toasted pecans, through its silky, rich, chocolate mousse filling, straight to the luscious, homemade whipped cream slathered on top.

Just off the square, **Wildfire** (512-869-3473; www.wildfiretexas.com) is Georgetown's "date night" restaurant. The oak-fired grill serves as the inspiration for an inventive menu featuring southwestern fare. A casual yet sophisticated ambience pairs nicely with expertly prepared dishes such as ostrich medallions drizzled with a cilantro-citrus demi-glace and agave honey-glazed carrots, oak-grilled Jamaican jerk pork loin with habanero apple chutney, or *pepita*-encrusted American bison strip loin.

You'll find family-friendly fare at **Dos Salsas** (512-930-2343; www.dos salsas.com), where tacos, enchiladas, tostadas, and tamales come stuffed with chicken, beef, brisket, pork, or *carne guisada* (slow-cooked beef tips with gravy) and are paired with rice, beans, or guacamole salad. This family-run restaurant on Main Street is a local favorite and, consequently, frequently packed.

Attractions

Things to do and see

Theater buffs throughout the region frequent the **Georgetown Palace Theatre** (512-869-7469; www.the georgetownpalace.org). Built in 1925, the Palace was originally a silent movie house. "Talkies" arrived in 1929, and the building was given its present art deco facade in 1936. A respite from the hard times during the Great Depression, World War II, and droughts in the 1950s, the Palace was the town's cultural and creative center. In 1989, the building was put up for sale; three hundred concerned citizens

Browse the shops in Georgetown.

bonded together to purchase, improve, and convert the Palace from a cinema to a theater. A true community endeavor, the now-thriving Palace stages spirited shows all year long, offering up both enjoyable theater and a slice of small-town Texas.

Georgetown's historic small-town ambience makes a scenic backdrop for a variety of festivals and special events. In April, Georgetown, the "Red Poppy Capital of Texas," hosts the weekend-long **Red Poppy Festival** (www.redpoppyfestival .com). The **Georgetown Symphony Society** (www.georgetowntexassymphony.org) produces live classical music performances throughout the year; and **Market Days** (www.visitgeorgetown.org) are held from 10 until 5 on the second Saturday of each month between March and December.

Stop by **Inner Space Cavern** (512-931-2283; www.myinnerspacecavern.com), located directly below busy I-35; it was discovered in 1963 during drilling to determine the stability of the ground prior to highway construction. As the holes were bored, the bit being used abruptly dropped dozens of feet, indicating the presence of a cavity beneath 40 feet of solid limestone. An adventurous highway worker rode a drill bit underground to take the first peek. Today, Inner Space Cavern is one of the more accessible caves in the region, with a unique cable car, paved trails, and a year-round temperature of 72 degrees.

NEW BRAUNFELS AND GRUENE

New Braunfels, located right off I-35 approximately 45 miles south of Austin and 30 miles north of San Antonio, was established under the auspices of the *Verein zum Schutze deutscher Einwanderer* in Texas, the "Society for the Protection of German Immigrants in Texas," or, simply, the Adelsverein.

The Rivers

People come from far and wide to spend the afternoon just floating down the rivers in New Braunfels, an activity that can be wonderfully relaxing or invigorating. The gentle little Comal River, the shortest river in the world, begins at Comal Springs in Lanada Park (see below) and travels 2.5 miles to meet the swifter and choppier Guadalupe River in downtown New Braunfels.

The Spanish discovered Comal Springs in 1691, stumbling upon the Native Americans who were living here. Early written references describe the springs and their almost unimaginable amounts of pure cool water surrounded by lovely groves; even today the springs gush 8 million gallons of water per hour, water that is both consistently clear and a refreshing 72 degrees.

The Comal is favored by families, while the Guadalupe has been known for its revelry, an image the city is working to shake. Local authorities are in no-nonsense mode after the public and politicians put pressure on them to keep the river clean and safe. While alcohol is legal on the rivers in certain areas, there are restrictions, and authorities issue stiff fines for infractions.

Smack in the middle of town, just north of the Main Plaza, **Lanada Park** (www .nbpard.org) is a terrific place for recreation. Fun for the whole family, the park has miniature golf and a miniature train, as well as the gentle 1.6-mile Panther Canyon Nature Trail (trail map available in the Parks Department Office). Adjacent **Prince Solms Park** (830-608-2165; www.nbpard.org) is home to the Chute, a section of the Comal River channeled by concrete that provides a smooth, swift ride for tubers. Admission, parking, and tube rental are $5 apiece. Fishing is another popular pastime in area parks; anglers enjoy the Guadalupe River for its rainbow and brown trout, though largemouth, smallmouth, striped, and Guadalupe bass, as well as sunfish, also swim the river.

TUBE RENTAL

There are dozens of tube rental places up and down the rivers, and all tend to follow the same general rules, routines, and pricing. Each outfit allows guests to park their car at the rental location, to which a free shuttle service downstream will provide a lift back. Generally, rental fees run $10–15, and life jackets are free. Consider paying a few dollars extra for the tube with a bottom in order to avoid scraping yours. The

As immigration to Texas picked up in the early 1800s, word of the region's potential reached a group of 21 enterprising noblemen near Mainz, Germany, who started making plans for a mass immigration and sent two men to investigate the possibilities. In May 1842 Count Joseph Boos-Waldeck and Count Victor August of Leiningen-Westerburg-Alt-Leiningen arrived and approached Sam Houston, who offered them acreage in the hostile frontier west of Austin, which they politely declined.

In 1845, after much discussion and many failed attempts, the first wagon train of German immigrants staggered into Central Texas. The group founded New Braunfels, named for Prince Carl of Solms-Braunfels, and immediately began

Cypress Trees along the Guadalupe River

Web sites below post handy checklists of what to bring and expect, and many have coupons you can print and bring with you for discounts. Try **Texas Tubes** (830-626-9900; www.texastubes.com), **Gruene River Company** (830-625-2800; www.too bing.com), or **Rockin 'R' River Rides** (830-629-9999; www.rockinr.com).

NEARBY

For more water recreation, **Canyon Lake** (830-964-2223; www.canyonlakechamber .com), located 20 miles north of New Braunfels, has eight public parks around its 80 miles of shoreline. These seasonal parks, managed by the Army Corps of Engineers, offer plenty of opportunities for fishing, swimming, camping, boating, and picnicking. Thirty-seven miles west of New Braunfels, Guadalupe River State Park (see "Texas State Parks," above) is a nice natural retreat with lots of swimming, tubing, and hiking trails.

readying the parcel of land on the banks of the Comal River to receive more Germans, who would number between 300 and 400 by the following summer. Soon, the operation was handed over to John I. Meusebach, who, confident he could deal diplomatically with the Native Americans in the Hill Country to the west, went on to phase two of *Adelsverein* and founded Fredericksburg in 1846.

New Braunfels quickly established itself as a commercial and manufacturing center in the region, feeding, clothing, and fixing the wagons of pioneers headed to the frontier. These days, visitors make the trip to New Braunfels for several reasons. One is Schlitterbahn (see below), the slippery, soaking wet, family magnet of a water park that draws visitors from near and far. Another is the Guadalupe and

Comal Rivers, whose lazy courses are perfect for that beloved Central Texas pastime of tubing, floating slowly with the current on large inflatable inner tubes for hours and hours on end. And then there is Gruene.

In the 1850s, the tiny settlement of Gruene (pronounced "green") was founded by German farmers who built a thriving economy based on cotton growing and processing. By the 1870s a busy cotton gin was up and running, as were a mercantile store and dance hall. When the railroad passed

Kick up your heels on the creaky wooden dance floor in Gruene Hall.

through in the 1880s, commercial development grew and the town prospered. When the boll weevil blight of the 1920s decimated the cotton crops, however, and the Great Depression of the 1930s hit, many residents abandoned the town. In the 1970s interest in preserving the town grew, and it was placed on the National Register of Historic Places. These days, the restored town is a favorite of visitors who come for the restaurants and the music at the historic Gruene Hall (see below). Located just 3 miles north of downtown New Braunfels, Gruene is considered a historic district within that city's limits.

Pick Your Spot

Best places to stay in and around New Braunfels and Gruene

In warm weather, water enthusiasts are drawn to New Braunfels like flies to honey. The city is an easy day trip from San Antonio or Austin, but if you plan to spend the night, it is necessary to book a room or campsite in advance.

There are several bed and breakfasts to choose from. Located beside Gruene Hall, the **Gruene Mansion Inn B&B** (830-629-2641; www.gruene mansioninn.com) is within easy walking distance to anything in town, including the river. The converted stables, barns, corncrib, and carriage house are now home to 30 individu-

ally decorated rooms, each with its own porch for lounging.

A few minute's drive outside of town, the **Gruene Homestead Inn** (830-606-0216; www.gruenehome steadinn.com) is a collection of seven historic homes, dating from the 1850s to 1900s, was moved to this location, renovated, and readied to receive guests on its 8-acre spread.

West of New Braunfels, you'll find the **Keubler Waldrip Haus and Danville Schoolhouse B&B** (830-625-8300; www.kueblerwaldrip.com), set on 43 rural acres teeming with deer. Three buildings, two dating from the mid-1800s, house the 11 rooms of this B&B, which is a particularly family-friendly place, and the size and configuration of the rooms is conducive to groups.

The region is also known for its

camping, and opportunities are ample. Strap the bikes on the car, pack s'more fixings, slide on your flip-flops, and bring the family for that damp-swimsuit, dirty-feet, sticky-face, stay-up-too-late-playing-cards kind of vacation that memories are made of. Campsites offer tube and raft rentals and fishing advice is free. No pets, loud music, excessive drinking, or rowdy behavior allowed.

Camp Huaco Springs (830-625-5411; www.camphuacosprings.com) operates the first-come, first-served campsite and owns **Rockin 'R' River Rides** (830-629-9999; www.rockinr .com), which rents tubes at several locations in the area. **KL Ranch Camp** (830-625-3038; www.kl-ranchcamp .net), on the Guadalupe River, has tent and RV camping, and **Mountain Breeze Camp** (830-964-2484; www .mountainbreezecamp.com) offers tent camping near the river, tiny cabins lined up in a row in a sunny field, each with air conditioning and a bed, and some RV sites.

Huisache Grill and Wine Bar (830-620-9001; www.huisache.com) started out in a rundown building in New Braunfels, but thanks to a renovation its wood floors and a soaring ceiling have grown to seem chic. The menu includes reworked southern staples like an angus beef chicken-fried steak or pecan-encrusted pork chops served with a Jack Daniel's butter sauce. The Hot and Crunchy Rainbow Trout with a sesame almond breading and jalapeño tartar sauce is decidedly different, while the hot Cheezy burger tastes familiar and homey.

Speaking of homey, **Naegelin's Bakery** (877-788-2895; www.naegelins .com) has been baking German strudels and cookies such as *springele*, *pfefernuesse*, and *lebkuchen* since 1868 and stakes claim to being the oldest bakery in Texas. With apricot *kolaches*, bear claws, and ten different kinds of bread pulled fresh from the oven, you really could follow your nose to Naegelin's.

After you've spent a day tubing,

Naegelin's Bakery in New Braunfels

seafood sure hits the spot, and the **Clear Springs Café** (830-629-3775; www.clearspringscafe.com) is a local favorite. The pan-seared tilapia, served with a Dijon peppercorn crawfish

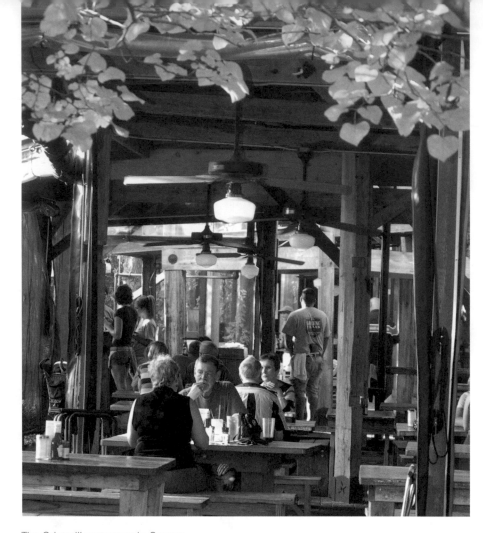

The Gristmill restaurant in Gruene

sauce, is popular, as are the blackened catfish filets topped with crawfish étouffée; both are served with a scoop of garlic mashed potatoes and steamed vegetables. While this is the original eatery, located in a building that dates back to 1869, the Clear Springs Café also operates restaurants in several locations in Texas, including Greune, where you'll find the **Gruene River Grill** (830-624-2300; www.grueneriver grill.com). The offerings here are similar to its sister restaurant—a few with a kick, such as the spicy southwestern

meat loaf or the chipotle chicken Diablo in a spicy cream sauce. The patios and porches overlooking the river are a fantastic spot for a drink or dessert.

Located in the shell of an old cotton-gin mill, the **Gristmill River Restaurant and Bar** (830-625-0684; www.gristmillrestaurant.com) is situated behind Gruene Hall in historic Gruene. Seating is at well-worn wooden tables inside the rough-hewn mill, in the shady river grove, or on the decks overlooking the river. The atmosphere at the Gristmill is fantastic, as is the menu. There are chicken-fried steaks, Polish Wedding Sausage with BBQ sauce, meal-sized salads topped with grilled meats, and whatever fish is the catch of the day, served blackened or grilled. You can kick up the flavor of any sandwich or burger order with the addition of one of the Gristmill's homemade sauces, Spicy Queso, Garlicky Hot Sauce, Tomatillo Verde, or Gringo Pico de Gallo. The Gristmill can get crowded, so consider stopping in early.

Don't be fooled by **Dry Comal** Creek Vineyards' (830-885-4076; www.drycomalcreek.com) whimsical labels, laid-back operation, and fanciful tasting room—they are serious about their wine. In a secluded valley west of New Braunfels, Dry Comal Creek Vineyards have coaxed native grapes into very dry, dark red wines, such as the 2004 Black Spanish, which has been declared the Texas Grand Star Winner at the Lone Star International Competition. For wine tasting in Gruene, stop in the **Grapevine** (830-606-0093; www.grapevineingruene.com).

Attractions
Things to do and see

HISTORY AND HERITAGE

The Gruene Historic District (www.gruenetexas.com) is easily identifiable by its gray water tower, which is visible for miles. The town motto is "gently resisting change," and the pace of life flows along as slowly as the nearby river.

Packed with shops and restaurants, Gruene is perhaps best known as home of **Gruene Hall** (830-606-9525; www.gruenehall.com), the oldest dance hall in Texas, with a reputation for fantastic music from the likes of Willie Nelson, Lyle Lovett, and George Strait. Folks come to kick up their heels and throw back a cool one, and the place is packed most weekends.

Stop in the **Museum of Texas Handmade Furniture** (830-629-6504; www.nbheritagevillage.com) for a fascinating look at history through craft, and the museum displays fine examples of Texas Biedermeier furniture, 1845–80. Located in New Braunfels Heritage Village, which is open by appointment only for area schoolchildren.

Tables in Gruene Hall, the oldest dance hall in Texas

Families looking to meet some new friends or pass a rainy day will appreciate the **McKenna Children's Museum** (830-620-0939; www.mckennakids.org), a bright, cheerful, and educational museum in New Braunfels that appeals most to elementary school-aged children.

FESTIVALS

In April, the **New Braunfels Wein and Saengerfest** (830-221-4350; www.wein andsaengerfest.com) celebrates area music and wine making with dancing, food, and a "Grape Stomp." The tasty **Gruene Music and Wine Fest** (www.gruenemusicandwinefest.org) ushers in October, and the cooler weather of November brings the **Wurstfest** (830-625-9167; www.wurstfest.com), New Braunfels's annual 10-day sausage festival, toward the start of the month. Between February and November, the Gospel Brunch in **Gruene Hall** (www.gruenehall.com) elevates the second Sunday of the month, while the **Old Gruene Market Days** (830-832-1721; www.gruenemarketdays.com) occupy the third weekend of the month February through November.

Statue of Texas Ranger Jack C. Hays in front of the courthouse in San Marcos

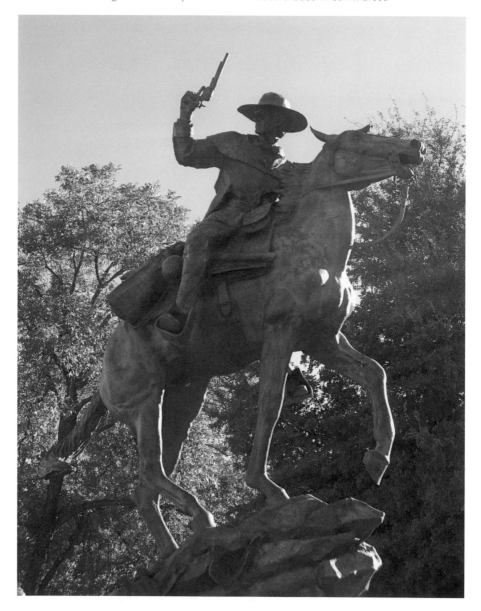

San Marcos is located on I-35 at the eastern edge of the Hill Country, 30 miles south of Austin and 49 miles north of San Antonio, making it an easy day trip from either city. Home to a state university, two huge outlet shopping areas, and plenty of recreation, San Marcos makes an agreeable side trip.

Established in 1846, San Marcos has always been a crossroads. The site of several failed missions in the 1700s, it was an important stopping point for travelers on the Old San Antonio Road, the route from northern Mexico to Nacogdoches in East Texas, used by Native Americans and the Spanish crisscrossing Texas. It was on the Chisholm Trail, used for the cattle drives between 1864 and 1884. Southwest Texas State Normal School, later Southwest Texas State University, and now Texas State University–San Marcos, was chartered in 1899. The San Marcos Baptist Academy followed in 1907, establishing the city as an education center and diversifying its economy.

With lovely natural resources, San Marcos has long been a regional recreation destination. Aquarena Springs flows at a rate of 150 million gallons of crystal-clear water a day, feeding the San Marcos River, which runs through the city. By the 1960s a resort had grown up around Aquarena Springs, Wonder World was opened as an attraction, and the tourist industry became a reliable and growing source of income. At the same time, population growth, increasing water demands, and the constant threat of drought have been a cause for concern for the spring's future. Both the San Marcos River Foundation (www.sanmarcosriver.org) and Aquarena Center (see below) work to educate the public about the importance of their river, a fragile ecosystem that is home to several endangered species.

These days, San Marcos has the comfortable, lived-in feel of a college town, with an old-fashioned town square lined with casual eateries and shops, and is rapidly becoming a residence for commuters to Austin. Just minutes from Wimberley, San Marcos is also a good jumping-off point into the Hill Country.

Outlet Malls

Popular attractions in San Marcos are the **Prime Outlets** (512-396-2200; www.primeoutlets.com) and **Tanger Outlets** (512-396-7446; www.tangeroutlet.com), which straddle I-35 at exit 200, approximately 30 minutes south of Austin and 45 minutes north of San Antonio. This is a mecca for discount shoppers, and things can get hectic here on the weekends.

Local Flavors

Taste of the town—local restaurants, cafés, bistros, etc.

Café on the Square (512-369-9999) is a well-worn spot that locals and students visit for a simple breakfast, brunch or lunch, and pre-read copies of the newspaper. Stop in for a fruit or sausage kolache at **Dos Gatos** (512-392-1444; www.dosgatoskolaches.com), a breakfast taco at **Lolita's** (512-392-3441), or a sandwich at **Alvin Ord's Sandwich Shop** (512-353-8042). Enjoy a fantastically fresh and flavorful meal at the charming **Cool Mint Café** (512-396-2665; www.coolmintcafe.com), or duck into the **Root Cellar Café** (512-

392-5158; www.rootcellarcafe.com), where wood beams and exposed rock walls add ambiance to match the casual lunch menu and slightly more upscale dinner specials. Enjoy the lovely patio and extensive menu of steaks, pastas, poultry, and seafood at **Palmer's Restaurant Bar and Courtyard** (512-353-3500; www.palmerstexas.com), or grab a burgers and a beer at the **Tap Room** (512-392-9824; www.taproom sanmarcos.com).

The Great Outdoors
Outdoor adventures and activities

The spring-fed San Marcos River flows through town, joining the Blanco River and merging with the Guadalupe River farther along in South Texas before spilling into the Gulf of Mexico. The river guarantees water recreation in even the driest summer months; generally speaking, there is just enough current to keep tubing and boating interesting, but not enough to make it dangerous. The newly reopened Rio Vista Dam in the **San Marcos City Park** is a good place to get your feet wet; when cracks were discovered recently in the hundred-year-old, low-water dam containing the San Marcos River, the city of San Marcos opted for a full-scale redesign of its urban park. Included in the project were provisions for saving wildlife, environmental enhancements to favor the endangered Texas wild rice, and the creation of three artificial rapids to provide for better water flow and more public recreation. The result is a great place for picnicking and swimming, with a brand-new family-friendly river chute for tubing at Rio Vista Dam. A charitable project of the local Lions Club, **Tube San Marcos** (512-396-5466; www.tubesanmarcos.com) rents tubes. The more adventurous can rent canoes and kayaks at **Austin Canoe and Kayak** (512-396-2386; www.austin kayak.com), located across from the Tanger Outlet Mall (see below).

In 1994, Texas State University–San Marcos acquired the dilapidated Aquarena Springs Resort and re-created it as a nonprofit nature center whose focus is education, conservation, and preservation of the spring. **Aquarena Center** (512-245-7540; www.aquarena.txstate.edu) runs a relaxing glass-bottom boat ride that offers underwater views of the Balcones Fault, the springs, and aquatic life. Additionally, you can stroll through the surrounding wetlands on the Floating Wetlands Boardwalk, or watch the 2 PM fish-feeding at the modest aquarium, which is home to several San Marcos salamanders, fountain darters, and Texas blind salamanders, all federally protected species. Ecotourists, the naturally curious, and children will find Aquarena to be especially fascinating and informative.

Wonder World Park (www.wonderworldpark.com; 512-392-3760) gives visitors a rare view of the geological effects of earthquakes, one of which formed the Balcones Fault and the Balcones Fault Line Cave, the most-visited cave in Texas and Wonder World's main attraction. The cave is small, slippery, and wet, and since it was formed by an earthquake and not from the effects of millions of years of dripping water, it lacks the typical cave formations found in other area caves. The short tour concludes with a ride up the elevator to the top of the 110-foot Tejas Observation tower for a view of the land aboveground. A train ride takes visitors through a petting zoo, where children can feed deer and other tame animals. The antigravity room is fun, and the gift shop is filled with rock candy and other amusements. Wonder World is well suited to families with elementary-age children.

Attractions

Things to do and see

MUSEUMS

It may be a little hard to locate, but the **Wittliff Gallery of Southwestern and Mexican Photography** (512-245-2313; www.thewittliffcollections.txstate.edu) curates provocative, insightful, and educational exhibits that appeal to both art aficionados and history buffs.

FESTIVALS

San Marcos festivals make a good day trip from either Austin or San Antonio. In May, the city of San Marcos celebrates the **Texas Natural/Western Swing Festival** (www.ci.san-marcos.tx.us) with a weekend of Texas history, traditions, and music in Courthouse Square, featuring a "Texas Grown" farmers' market. Also in May, the **Viva Cinco de Mayo** and **Menudo Cook-Off** are held together and add up to great fun. In October, the San Marcos River Fall Fest (512-353-1103) fills San Marcos Plaza with music, games, food, arts and crafts, and kiddie rides. December brings the Sights and Sounds of Christmas (512-393-5900; www.sights-n-sounds .org), a festival of lights, food, and music along San Marcos Plaza and San Marcos City Park. Details of city events can be found on the San Marcos Convention and Visitor Bureau Web site, www.toursanmarcos.com.

5

Information

ESSENTIAL DETAILS

TRAVELING THE AREA COVERED IN THIS BOOK means crossing several counties, traversing varied terrain, and moving in and out of area codes. The information in this chapter covers the practicalities pertinent to daily life as well as the sorts of details you might need in an emergency:

EMERGENCY NUMBERS

In an emergency, dial 911 and tell the operator your location and the nature of your emergency and your call will be directed to the appropriate responder.

Poison Control is 800-222-1222; www.poison.org.

For further assistance, see "Hospitals," page 214.

AREA CODES

Austin 512

San Antonio
Bexar County, including
  downtown 210
Comal County 830

The Hill Country
Bandera 830
Blanco 830
Boerne 830, 210
Comfort 830
Fredericksburg 830
Johnson City 830
Kerrville 830
Marble Falls 830
Stonewall 830
Wimberley 512

Nearby and In Between
Georgetown 512

New Braunfels/Gruene 830
San Marcos 512

ZIP CODES

Austin . . . 73344, 73301, 78701–78799
San Antonio 78201–78299

The Hill Country
Bandera 78003
Blanco 78606
Boerne 78006, 78015
Comfort 78013
Fredericksburg 78624
Johnson City 78636
Kerrville 78028–78029
Stonewall 78671
Wimberley 78676

Nearby and In Between
Georgetown 78626–78628
New Braunfels/Gruene . 78130–78135
San Marcos 78666, 78667

BANKS AND MONEY

A good many national banks, or banks that participate in national networks, are represented in Austin and San Antonio. However, depending on the bank, you could incur several dollars in fees per ATM withdrawal. Alternatively, many national stores, such as Target or Walmart, grocery stores, and the post office will allow you "cash back" if you use your debit card to make a purchase. Though there is frequently a maximum withdrawal of $100, there is generally no additional fee. In the Hill Country, ATM machines are fewer and farther between, so plan accordingly, and be sure to check in advance that a shop or restaurant accepts credit cards.

CLIMATE AND WEATHER REPORTS

The weather in Austin, San Antonio, and the Hill Country is generally favorable, with about 300 sunny days a year, warm nights, and gentle breezes. Mid-July to mid-September is the hottest time of year, with temperatures easily reaching the high 90s. Austin and San Antonio can become stiflingly humid, the Hill Country somewhat less so; the farther west you travel, the more arid it becomes. Winters tend to be cool but not often freezing, with snow an aberration. The region gets most of its rainfall in the spring, when steady showers soak the ground and fill lakes and streams.

When it gets hot in Texas, it gets really, really hot. When it gets humid in Texas, it gets really, really humid. In fact, the best way to describe the summertime in San Antonio, in particular, is tropical. Since dehydration and heatstroke are not uncommon conditions, it's important to be aware and prepared. Sunglasses, sunscreen, a light cotton long-sleeved shirt, a wide-brimmed hat, an umbrella, or even a small spray bottle filled with water for misting can help provide protection and relief. Staying hydrated is essential; steering clear of sodas and alcoholic beverages in favor of water, sports drinks, and juice is considered wise.

Storms

Arriving sometimes without warning, summertime thunderstorms can bring torrential rain and flash floods. When flash-flood warnings are issued, it is best to exercise caution and avoid creeks, drainage ditches, and low-water road crossings, as signs in these areas will indicate. Tornadoes frequently accompany thunderstorms, so it is best to listen to or watch the news for any words of caution. A tornado or severe thunderstorm watch serves as an alert that conditions are favorable for either event, while a tornado or severe thunderstorm warning means that either event has been detected on radar and danger may be imminent. In this case, it is best to seek cover in a substantial building, away from windows. In cooler weather ice storms can occur, and since Central Texas does not maintain a large fleet of sand or salt trucks, the roads can become treacherously slick and hazardous. Texas drivers are inexperienced with slick or icy roads, and during storms accidents tend to be frequent.

GROCERY STORES/DRUGSTORES

HEB is a grocery-store chain based in San Antonio with many locations throughout Austin, San Antonio, and the Hill Country. HEB also owns Central Market.

Austin

HEB (512-459-6513; www.heb.com) There are many HEBs in Austin, but this one is open 24 hours a day with a 24-hour pharmacy (512-450 8300).

San Antonio

HEB (210-829-7373; www.heb.com) The store is open until 1 AM and the pharmacy is open Monday through Friday 9–9, Saturday 9–8, and Sunday 10–5. Pharmacy phone is 210-829-1705.

HANDICAPPED SERVICES

A good site for information and links about handicapped services worldwide is www.access-able.com. In Austin and San Antonio, Wheelchair Getaways (800-723-6028; www.wheelchairgetaways.com) rents accessible vans. In San Antonio, the Riverwalk will present some challenges for anyone with restricted mobility; see p. 89 for a list of elevators and visit www.thesanantonioriverwalk.com for maps detailing access points, ramps, and walkways.

Austin
University Medical Brackenridge Hospital (512-324-7000; www.seton.net)
Dell Children's Medical Center (512-324-000; www.dellchildrens.net)
Seton Medical Center Austin (512-324-1000; www.seton.net)
Seton Shoal Creek (512-324-2000; www.seton.net) Emergency psychiatric care
St. David's Medical Center (512-476-7111; www.stdavidsmedicalcenter.com)

Bandera
Closest facility is in Kerrville.

Blanco
Closest facility is in Fredericksburg.

Boerne
Closest facility is in San Antonio.

Burnet
Seton Highland Lakes Hospital (512-715-3000; www.seton.net)

Comfort
Closest facility is in Kerrville.

Fredericksburg
Hill Country Memorial Hospital (830-997-4353; www.hillcountrymemorial.org)

Georgetown
St. David's Georgetown Hospital (512-943-3000; www.georgetownhealthcare.org)

Johnson City
Closest facilities are in Fredericksburg or Marble Falls.

Kerrville
Peterson Regional Medical Center (830-896-4200; www.petersonrmc.com)

Marble Falls
Marble Falls Minor Emergency Center (830-798-1122; www.mfmec.org)
Seton Highland Lakes Hospital (512-715-3000; www.seton.net)

New Braunfels/Gruene
McKenna Memorial Hospital (830-606-2180; www.mckenna.org)

San Antonio
Baptist Medical Center (210-297-7000; www.baptisthealthsystem.com)

Nix Medical Center (210-271-1800; www.nixhealth.com)

Christus Santa Rosa Health Care (210-704-2361; www.christussantarosa.org)

San Marcos
Central Texas Medical Center (512-353-8979; www.ctmc.org)

Stonewall
Closest facility is in Fredericksburg.

Wimberley
Central Texas Medical Center (512-353-8979; www.ctmc.org)

LATE-NIGHT FOOD, FUEL, AND GROCERIES

When it comes to food, the pickings late at night are slim, but beggars really can't be choosers in this case. If you find yourself fighting the midnight munchies or starving from a missed mealtime, head to I-35 for your pick of **IHOP**, **Denny's**, or any other—national chain. If you are looking for more local flavor, consider some of the options below.

Austin
Catering to students' insomnia and club-goers late-night tendencies, there are a few spots to eat all day and night in Austin. Try **24 Diner**, **Kerbey Lane Café**, or **Magnolia Café** (see individual listings under "Local Flavors" in the Austin chapter).

San Antonio
Mi Tierra serves Mexican food and **Lulu's** has breakfast treats 24/7 (see individual listings under "Local Flavors" in the San Antonio chapter).

LICENSES

Hunting and fishing, popular recreational activities in Texas, require state-issued licenses, which are available at numerous locations, including some grocery and sports stores, online through the Texas Parks and Wildlife Department's Web site, www.tpwd.state.tx.us, or by phone at 800-895-4248. However, fishing from shore or pier within a Texas State Park does not require a license; check at the park's headquarters for details. For a full overview of state hunting and fishing regulations, go to www.tpwd.state.tx.us/regulations. Texas game wardens are especially strict, and any violation of state hunting and fishing regulations will be taken very seriously.

MEDIA

Magazines and Newspapers
Both Austin and San Antonio have dailies as well as free weekly papers, all of which are likely to include information regarding events in the towns nearby and in between and in the Hill Country.

Austin

Austin American-Statesman (www.statesman.com) The Austin daily. The *Statesman's* Entertainment, Calendar, and Life sections and archived reviews can also be viewed online at www.austin360.com.

Austin Chronicle (www.austinchronicle.com) Excellent free weekly guide to entertainment, with politics and news thrown in. Published on Thursdays.

San Antonio

San Antonio Express-News (www.mysanantonio.com) The San Antonio daily news; in print or online.

San Antonio Current (www.sacurrent.com) News, culture, free. Published on Thursdays.

Hill Country

Many of these tiny papers are regional, serving the city mentioned and, oftentimes, the entire county.

Bandera Bulletin, www.banderabulletin.com

Blanco County News, www.blancocountynews.com

Boerne Star, www.boernestar.com

Burnet Bulletin, www.burnetbulletin.com

Comfort News, www.comfortnews.com

Fredericksburg Standard, www.fredericksburgstandard.com

Herald-Zeitung (New Braunfels/Gruene), www.heraldzeitung.com

Johnson City Record Courier, www.jcrecordcourier.com

Junction Eagle, www.junctioneagle.com

Kerrville Times, www.dailytimes.com

San Marcos Daily Record, www.sanmarcosrecord.com

Williamson County Sun (Georgetown), www.wilcosun.com

Wimberley View/Hill Country Sun, www.hillcountrysun.com

Radio Stations

Austin

KBPA 103.5 "BOB" FM. Their tagline, "Bob plays anything," says it all.

KMFA 89.5 FM. Outstanding classical since 1967.

KUT 90.5 AM. National Public Radio and outstanding music.

KVET 98.1 FM. Country music and Longhorns sports.

San Antonio

KLEY 94.1 FM. Tejano music.

KPAC 88.3 FM. National Public Radio and classical music.

KROM 92.2 FM. Mexican pop.

KRTU 91.7 FM. Trinity University station.

KSTX 89.1 FM. National Public Radio.

KTXI 90.1 FM. National Public Radio.

PESTS

For whatever reason, pests love Texas and tend to thrive in its temperate climate despite efforts to control them. The truth is that many serve an important ecological function and most are harmless, but there are a few pests that should have you watching where you sit, step, or stand.

Fire Ants

The biggest pests in Central Texas are the fire ants, for which you will frequently see warning signs posted. Fire ants tend to make mounds in sunny, open fields and parks, by the side of the road, and at the base of trees and other objects, such as picnic tables. When their nest is disturbed, they swarm and deliver many simultaneous stings, which are similar to bee stings in look and feel. Usually no medical intervention is required, but as with bees, a small percentage of the population may have a severe allergic reaction, in which case emergency medical care is essential. The only prevention is avoidance, so watch where you sit and stand, and be especially aware of small children.

Snakes

Snakes are common in Texas, but of the 72 native species and subspecies, only 15 pose any threat to humans. In Central Texas, snakes keep to themselves and do not tend to initiate interactions. Since both poisonous and nonpoisonous snakes bite, if you have the unfortunate experience of being bitten, a precautionary trip to the emergency room would be wise.

Spiders

Of the 900 species of spiders present in Texas, only two groups pose any threat to humans, the recluse and widow spiders. In many cases, if you are bitten by one of these, you may not notice until the appearance of a suspicious wound coupled with fever, chills, nausea, pain, vomiting, or weakness, among other symptoms. In all cases, swab the wound with alcohol, relieve swelling and pain with ice, and call your doctor or, depending on the severity, visit the emergency room.

RELIGIOUS SERVICES

Texas is known for its religious enthusiasm, and there are plenty of places of worship in Central Texas. The *Austin American-Statesman*, the *San Antonio Express-News*, and the newspapers in the larger towns of the Hill Country list upcoming services in their Saturday editions. Alternatively, check the yellow pages of the phone book. While many religious organizations in the region identify themselves as Christian, they are widely varied in focus, practice, and beliefs. You will find the most religious diversity in Austin and San Antonio, where Jewish, Islamic, and other religious communities are active.

SHOPPING

Austin
The Arboretum at Great Hills (512-338-4437; www.simon.com)

Barton Creek Square (512-327-7040; www.simon.com)

The Highland Mall (512-454-9656; www.highlandmall.com)

San Antonio
Alamo Quarry Market (210-824-8885; www.quarrymarket.com)

Crossroads of San Antonio (210-735-9137)

Ingram Park Mall (210-864-9570; www.ingramparkmall.com)

North Star Mall (210-340-6627; www.northstarmall.com)

River Center Mall (210-225-0000; www.shoprivercenter.com)

The Shops at La Cantera (210-582-6255; www.theshopsatlacantera.com)

San Marcos
Premium Outlets (512-396-2200; www.premiumoutlets.com)

Tanger Outlets (512-396-7446; www.tangeroutlet.com)

TOURIST INFORMATION

Local visitors centers and convention bureaus are great sources of information, maps, advice, and even coupons for discounts on tours and admission fees.

Austin
Austin Convention & Visitors Bureau (800-926-ACVB; www.austintexas.org; 301 Congress Ave., Suite 200, Austin, TX 78701)

Austin Visitors Center (866-GO-AUSTIN; www.austintexas.org; 209 E. Sixth St., Austin, TX 78701) Open Mon.–Fri. 9–5, Sat.–Sun. 9–6.

San Antonio
San Antonio Convention and Visitors Bureau (210-207-6700 or 800-447-3372; www.sanantoniocvb.com; 203 S. St. Mary's St., 2nd floor, San Antonio, TX 78205)

San Antonio Chamber of Commerce (210-229-2100; www.sanantonio.com; 602 E. Commerce St., San Antonio, TX 78205)

Stop in a friendly Visitor Center

Bandera
Bandera Convention and Visitors Bureau (830-796-3045 or 800-364-3833; www.banderacowboycapital.com; P.O. Box 171, Bandera, TX 78003)

Blanco
Blanco Chamber of Commerce (830-833-5101; www.blancochamber.com; 312 Pecan St., Blanco, TX 78606)

Boerne
The Boerne Convention and Visitors Bureau (830-249-7277 or 888-842-8080; www.visitboerne.org; 1407 S. Main St., Boerne, TX 78006)

Greater Boerne Chamber of Commerce (830-249-8000 or 888-842-8080; www.boerne.org; 126 Rosewood Ave., Boerne, TX 78006)

Burnet
Burnet Chamber of Commerce (512-756-4297; www.burnetchamber.org; 229 S. Pierce St., Burnet, TX 78611)

Comfort
www.shopcomfort.com. Information available in Fredericksburg and Kerrville.

Fredericksburg
Fredericksburg Chamber of Commerce and Visitors Bureau (830-997-6523 or 1-888-997-3600; www.fredericksburg-texas.com; 302 E. Austin St., Fredericksburg, TX 78624)

Johnson City
Johnson City Tourism Bureau (830-868-7684; www.lbjcountry.com) Located inside the Texas Hill Country Visitors Center (830-868-5700; www.hillcountry info.com; 803 US 281 South, Johnson City, TX 78636)

Kerrville
Kerrville Convention and Visitors Bureau (830-792-3535 or 800-221-7958; www.kerrvilletexascvb.com; 2108 Sidney Baker St., Kerrville, TX 78028) Open Mon.–Fri. 8:30–5, Sat. 9–3, Sun. 10–3.

Kerrville Area Chamber of Commerce (830-896-1155; www.kerrvilletx.com; 1700 Sidney Baker St., Suite 100, Kerrville, TX 78028)

Marble Falls
Marble Falls/Lake LBJ Visitors Center (830-693-4449 or 800-759-8178; www .marblefalls.org; 801 US 281, Marble Falls, TX 78654) Open Mon.–Fri. 8–5.

Stonewall
Stonewall Chamber of Commerce (830-644-2735; www.stonewalltexas.com; 115 St. Francis St., Stonewall, TX 78671)

Wimberley

Wimberley Chamber of Commerce and Visitors Center (www.visitwimberley.org; P.O. Box 12, Wimberley, TX 78676)

Nearby and In Between

Georgetown

Georgetown Visitor Information Center (512-436-8696; www.visitgeorgetown .org; 101 W. Seventh St., Georgetown, TX 78626)

New Braunfels

New Braunfels Chamber of Commerce (800-572-2626; www.nbjumpin.com; P.O. Box 311417, New Braunfels, TX 78131). Gruene (830-629-5077; www.gruene texas.com)

San Marcos

San Marcos Convention and Visitors Bureau (512-393-5900 or 888-200-5620; www.toursanmarcos.com; 202 N. C. M. Allen Pkwy., San Marcos, TX 78667)

Tourist Information Center (512-393-5930; 617 I-35 North, San Marcos, TX 78666)

Suggested Bibliography

WHETHER YOU LIKE TO READ up on your destination before you go or find that your curiosity is piqued by the trip, below are books recommended to enrich your experience, arranged here alphabetically by author.

Ajilvsgi, Geyata. *Wildflowers of Texas.* Fredericksburg, TX: Shearer Publishing, 2003.

Alsop, Fred J. III. *Birds of Texas.* New York: DK Publishing, 2002.

Awbrey, Betty Dooley. *Why Stop? Texas Roadside Markers: A Guide to Texas Historical Roadside Markers.* Lanham, MD: Taylor Trade Publishing, 2005.

Barkley, Roy, ed. *The Handbook of Texas Music.* Austin, TX: Texas State Historical Association, 2003.

Bryant, Helen. *Fixin' to Be Texan.* Plano, TX: Republic of Texas, 1998.

Bull, David. *The Driskill Hotel: Stories of Austin's Legendary Hotel/A Cookbook for Special Occasions.* Austin, TX: The Driskill Hotel. Packed with tidbits of juicy local lore and history.

Caro, Robert. *The Path to Power (The Years of Lyndon Johnson, Volume 1).* New York: Vintage Books, 1981.

———. *Means of Ascent (The Years of Lyndon Johnson, Volume 2).* New York: Vintage Books, 1990.

———. *Master of the Senate: The Years of Lyndon Johnson.* New York: Knopf, 2002.

Cerf, Bennett and Van H. Cartmell, eds. *The Best Short Stories of O. Henry.* New York: Modern Library, 1994. Though O. Henry's muse was New York City, he spent part of his formative years in Austin.

Cornell, Kari A. *Our Texas.* Osceola, WI: Voyageur Press, 2004. Coffee-table book.

Dallek, Robert. *Lyndon B. Johnson: Portrait of a President.* New York: Oxford University Press, 2004.

Fisher, Lewis F. *Saving San Antonio: The Precarious Preservation of a Heritage.* Lubbock, TX: Texas Tech University Press, 1996.

———. *The Spanish Missions of San Antonio.* San Antonio, TX: Maverick Publishing, 1998.

Ford, Norman D. *25 Bicycle Tours in the Texas Hill Country and West Texas.* Woodstock, VT: Countryman Press, 1995.

Friedman, Kinky. *Kinky Friedman's Guide to Texas Etiquette: Or How to Get to Heaven or Hell without Going Through Dallas–Fort Worth.* New York: HarperCollins, 2001. Kinky is a Texas original whose personality, politics, and antics are threaded through the contemporary social history of Central Texas.

Gilliland, Tom, and Miguel Ravago and Virginia B. Wood. *Fonda San Miguel: Thirty Years of Food and Art.* Frederickburg, TX: Shearer Publishing, 2005. A feast for the eyes as well as the palate.

Goodwin, Doris Kearns. *Lyndon Johnson and the American Dream.* New York: St. Martin's, 1991.

Ivins, Molly. *Molly Ivins Can't Say That, Can She?* New York: Vintage, 1992. Witty commentary on Texas politics.

Loughmiller, Campbell, and Lynn Loughmiller and Damon Waitt. *Texas Wildflowers: A Field Guide,* revised edition. Austin, TX: University of Texas Press, 2006. Updated version of a 1984 classic.

Meinzer, Wyman, and John Graves (introduction). *Texas Sky.* Austin, TX: University of Texas Press, 1998. Photographs of the awesome Texas sky.

Michener, James A. *Texas.* New York; Fawcett, 1987. Packed with drama and stereotypes, Michener's book paints a bold picture of the state.

Moran, Mark, and Mark Sceurman, Wesley Treat, and Heather Shades. *Weird Texas.* New York: Sterling, 2005.

Peterson, Roger Tory. *Field Guide to the Birds of Texas.* Boston: Houghton Mifflin, 1998. Written by an expert.

Rather, Rebecca, and Alison Oresman. *The Pastry Queen: Royally Good Recipes from the Texas Hill Country's Rather Sweet Bakery & Café.* Berkeley, CA: Ten Speed Press, 2004.

Reid, Jan, and Scott Newton. *The Improbable Rise of Redneck Rock: New Edition* (Jack and Doris Smothers Series in Texas History, Life, and Culture). Austin, TX: University of Texas Press, 2004.

Richards, David. *Once Upon a Time in Texas: A Liberal in the Lone Star State.* Austin, TX: University of Texas Press, 2002.

Rucker, Sid, and Clifford E. Shackelford, Madge M. Lindsay, C. Mark Klym, Shirley Rucker, and Clemente Guzman III. *Hummingbirds of Texas.* College Station, TX: Texas A&M Press, 2006.

Rybczyk, Mark Louis. *San Antonio Uncovered.* Plano, TX: Republic of Texas, 2000. A good look at the history of San Antonio.

Taylor, Tom, and Johnny Malloy. *60 Hikes within 60 miles: San Antonio and Austin.* Birmingham, AL: Menasha Ridge Press, 2004.

Tekiela, Stan. *Birds of Texas Field Guide.* Cambridge, MN: Adventure Publications, 2004.

Thompson, Karen R., and Kathy R. Howell. *Austin (Scenes of America).* Mount Pleasant, SC: Arcadia Publishing, 2006.

Tveten, John L. *The Birds of Texas.* Fredericksburg, TX: Shearer Publishing, 1993. Miraculous photos.

Walsh, Robb. *Legends of Texas Barbecue Cookbook: Recipes and Recollections from the Pit Bosses.* San Francisco: Chronicle Books, 2002.

Woods, Randall. *LBJ: Architect of American Ambition.* New York: Free Press, 2006.

Index